LEARNING THE LITERACY PRACTICES OF GRADUATE SCHOOL

Insiders' Reflections on Academic Enculturation

LEARNING THE LITERACY PRACTICES OF GRADUATE SCHOOL
Insiders' Reflections on Academic Enculturation

CHRISTINE PEARSON CASANAVE
XIAOMING LI

Editors

ANN ARBOR

THE UNIVERSITY OF MICHIGAN PRESS

CONTENTS

Part 3: Situated Learning

ACKNOWLEDGMENTS

We are grateful to many people who contributed to this four-year project. First, we thank the authors, for their patience with us and responsiveness to our requests (many) for revisions. Each draft got better and better, just as the writing research tells us. We are sure that we all wish we could provide our own students with such opportunities, but most of us have only a semester or two with them, not four years. We are also thankful to friends, colleagues, and relatives—our own and those of the authors—who directly and indirectly participated in this project through feedback, conversations, and support. Chris offers special thanks to her doctoral students at Temple University's Japan Campus for taking her back to a world she thought she had left behind forever, and for helping her realize what an exciting, challenging, and worthwhile endeavor the graduate school experience can be. Hang in there, guys and gals— *gambatte.* Xiaoming's special thanks go to Don Murray and Bob Connors, who, though having passed away, continue to inspire her. They, together with other professors and fellow graduate students at the University of New Hampshire, made an otherwise arduous journey enlightening and richly rewarding. Finally, we thank Kelly Sippell, the reviewers, and the editors and designers at University of Michigan Press for their expert support and for once again taking a chance with something a little bit different from the conventional academic book.

Dedication

We would like to dedicate this book to graduate students from around the world who choose to pursue their studies in English-dominant universities, at great personal and financial cost, and for whom the book was first conceived.

FOREWORD

JOHN M. SWALES

When I arrived at the University of Michigan in the mid-1980s, I found in the Department of Linguistics much the same kind of doctoral education I had encountered in England except for the first two years of required coursework. The more senior students worked largely in isolation on their own research projects, with occasional meetings with their main advisors. As in the British university from which I had come, this was essentially a "sink or swim" environment, where the students were expected, presumably as part of their "training" to be academics, to struggle largely unaided with their topics, as well as often having to scour the university to secure funding for next year's tuition and living expenses.

As the excellent introduction to this volume makes clear, over the subsequent two decades leading up to today, much has been changing in the ways graduate education in the United States is perceived, structured, and orchestrated. From my own departmental perspective, I could note the following. Much more stable funding packages are available for students admitted to the doctoral program. The old comprehensive exams—and very much exams they were—have been replaced by qualifying research papers designed to approximate to the reality of the writing-for-publication process. The department has instigated various kinds of research group meetings, whereby groups of students and faculty can discuss readings and comment on drafts of papers and dry-runs of conference talks. Various units on campus—such as the Graduate School, the Center for Learning and Teaching, and the English Language Institute—provide numerous courses, workshops, panels, and discussion groups specifically designed for more advanced graduate students, both native speakers of English as well as those that have English as an additional language. Study groups of all sorts spring up. In effect, various kinds of formal and informal systems have come into being so that younger scholars are better supported and nurtured, with the hope that personal anxieties, individual frustrations, and interpersonal conflicts are reduced to manageable levels.

The growth of the socio-academic networks I have just alluded to is, I believe, being actively encouraged across the research universities of North America. One positive outcome of all this is that the United States produces more than 40,000 PhDs each calendar year. On the other hand, attrition rates have remained stubbornly high. The editors, Casanave and Li, report in their introduction that around half of the admitted doctoral students fail to complete their degrees, attrition being particularly severe in the first year of graduate school. They either fail or drop out, or, as the graduate chairs usually put it, "they are counseled out." The reasons for this are of course many and complex (money, personal, or family problems, shifts of interest, non-academic job offers), but a considerable proportion of those who do not win through to their degrees depart because of difficulties they experience within their chosen disciplinary cultures. It is this group that this volume is primarily designed to support and encourage, especially if they find themselves in areas where qualitative research is acceptable. As the editors say, they hope this book will act as a "'textual mentor,' so to speak, in the sense that experienced researchers and graduate students in the midst of their studies communicate in direct and accessible ways with readers who are joining them" (p. 2).

The sixteen chapters that follow the introduction offer a rich series of case histories into the vicissitudes of the graduate student experience. The first five are about lessons learnt—often the hard way—such as Fujioka's account of her struggles to change her approach and her advisor. The next half-dozen have the general title of "Mentors and Mentees" and are co-authored by erstwhile students and their advisors. And it is significant here I believe that three chapter titles contain the word *negotiate*—a sure sign (as Prior (1998) has brilliantly shown) that in the end there is little strictly or inexorably top-down in the professor-doctoral candidate relationship. Further, these chapters in the middle section are also valuable for those of us who advise graduate students, because here we can learn much as to how we are perceived. Weiser, in particular comments ruefully on this—a feeling I can share as it once happened to me! The contributions in Part 3 are a mix of single- and multiple-authored studies and explore somewhat further how personal, inter-personal, and academic experiences come together to underscore how learning and especially learning to write are situated and embodied in local contexts.

Despite the complexities of the stories told in this volume, they are welcomely "biased toward success." In the end, the students win through, collect their degrees, and in many cases go on to take up tenure-track positions. The mentors emerge as sympathetic, willing to negotiate, and conscious of how reflecting on the two sides of the story has given them further insights into what it means to mentor junior scholars. The socio-rhetorical and intellectual journeys reflected upon in this book are told in a refreshingly open style with occasional confessional episodes to add further insight into the mindsets of the moment and with just sufficient attention to theory to provide a framework for viewing the unfolding interactions.

I believe therefore that many will concur with me and the editors that this volume will do much to help graduate students, and especially those concerned about their academic writing, to overcome their frustrations and uncertainties. After all, a problem shared is a problem half-solved.

REFERENCE

Prior, P. A. (1998). *Writing disciplinarity: A sociohistoric account of literate activity in the academy.* Mahwah, NJ: Lawrence Erlbaum.

INTRODUCTION

XIAOMING LI AND CHRISTINE PEARSON CASANAVE

Overview

This book was first conceived during a coffee break at a conference in New York City in 2003. As often happens in a community that centers around texts, we were two strangers who first learned about the other through reading each other's works. We then met in person by chance at the conference when the nametag rang a bell, and we started to talk about cooperating on projects of shared interest. It was a casual, free-wheeling conversation. While sipping coffee, with no particular prompt from Chris, Xiaoming mentioned the recent suicide of a friend's daughter at an American university and deplored the heavy price many international students often paid for trying to succeed in English-dominant institutions of higher learning. Chris sympathized, commiserated, but recalled the difficulties that she, too, a white, middle-class female and native speaker of English, encountered in graduate school. We survived, we agreed, not because we were smarter, but lucky to be at the right place, studying with the right professors, and finding, haphazardly, the coping strategies that worked for us.

What has already happened to students who have experienced great difficulty cannot be undone. But is there anything we can do to convince those who are just beginning to acclimate to life in graduate school and those who are contemplating the prospect of entering graduate school that they are not alone? There and then, we decided to first plan a conference panel and then to co-edit a book on doing graduate school. Our panel on "learning to do graduate school" at the 2004 Conference on College Composition and Communication marked the official start of this adventure. As is the case for the notion of learning how to "do" gradu-

1

ate school, our conceptualization of literacy practices in this book's title is intended to connote more than an interest in how graduate students learn the textual features and conventions that characterize academic reading and writing. With the term *literacy practices* we include as well the tacit expectations and unwritten rules of participation, the interpersonal relationships between advisors and advisees and among peers, and the impact of enculturation and interaction on student and faculty identity. In short, this collection brings to light the textual, social, and political dimensions of graduate study that tend not to be talked about, still less written about for publication. Rare exceptions are an edited collection on the dissertation experience in the field of composition and rhetoric (Welch, Latterell, Moore, & Carter-Tod, 2002) and some portions of Gesa Kirsch's (1993) earlier book on "women writing the academy." We add our voices to this important endeavor and expand the disciplinary horizon to include second and foreign language-related fields.

We intend the book to be, mainly, a practical and inspirational resource book for graduate students, a "textual mentor," so to speak, in the sense that experienced researchers and graduate students in the midst of their studies communicate in direct and accessible ways with readers who are joining them. However, the rich descriptions of the lives of graduate students and faculty from various linguistic and cultural backgrounds and the tracing of their intellectual and social trajectories should be a resource as well to scholars of academic and disciplinary socialization. Faculty members and advisors/supervisors who are teaching classes that concern introduction to graduate study and who themselves mentor graduate students will also benefit from reading this collection, as we have from assembling and editing it.

Little did we know at the time we began this project that we were to join others in a "flurry of attention" paid to graduate education (Golde & Dore, 2004, p. 19). Concomitant to official reports that focused on the structural changes in response to changes in the job market, some scholars interested in the social dimension of graduate study examined the high attrition of graduate students, which is, to paraphrase the opening line of one study, the best kept non-secret (Lovitts, 2001, p. 1). It is reported that "the overall rate of doctoral student attrition in the United States has consistently been estimated to be around 50 percent" since at least the early '60s (p. 2). In a smaller sample of nine departments, the rate was found to be higher in social sciences and humanities disciplines than in natural sciences, and much higher in the urban than in the rural university (p. 12). The study by Golde (1998) finds that attrition during the first year of graduate school "accounts for nearly a third of all doc-toral student attrition" (p. 55). The figure, we believe, is probably even higher for the so-called marginal groups: non-native speakers of English, the 1.5 generation of immigrant students, minority students, and other non-traditional students. Many reasons account for this attrition, as Golde (1998) explained, most having to do with students' expectations not being met and with poor integration into departments, especially in the humanities and social sciences.

The result, however, should not surprise anyone who knows the challenges one faces in graduate school. Golde (1998) characterizes what students experience at graduate school as "an unusual double socialization"—that is, the direct socialization into the role of graduate students and the preparatory socialization into a profession. Gradu-ate students, according to Golde, need to accomplish four distinct but interrelated tasks: intellectual mastery, learning about the realities of life as a graduate student, learning about the profession, and integrating oneself into the department (p. 56). These challenges are difficult for all graduate students, but they are particularly daunting for non-native and non-mainstream speakers of English as they have to cope with triple socialization, the third being the immediate socialization into a language and culture that their mainstream peers have been immersed in for a life time. In all cases, learning to become a member of a graduate school academic community requires that students become familiar with new cultural, literacy, and sociopolitical practices while under the pressure of time, financial hardship, and possibly unclear authority relationships with faculty members. No single chapter in this collection addresses all four challenges, but each addresses at least one, and more important, all detail how the authors met the challenge and survived.

The contributors to this collection, current and former graduate stu-dents (now faculty), come from diverse English-dominant graduate pro-grams in North America, Hong Kong, Japan, Australia, and the United Kingdom. They generously share their personal experiences; ruminate over lessons learned in hindsight; explore the hidden structures, expecta-tions, and opportunities they stumbled on but often missed at the time; and offer some sort of a "cognitive map" (Lovitts, p. 44) for navigating the social, political, and literacy practices of graduate school. Besides a diversity of approaches and the use of personal narrative, another distinguishing feature of this collection is the pairing of advisor-advisee co-authors in some of the chapters, which provides multiple perspectives and voices on particular aspects of the graduate school adventure.

These unconventional features of writing result directly from our desire to reach the primary audience of novice graduate students in engaging ways, but also from a deliberate and collective effort to experiment with new forms as a way to break the monopoly of the citation-heavy, emotionally barren, formulaic, impersonal, and often slumberous prose, which is the standard bearer of academic writing. We were all in new territory with the endeavor. As it turned out, some chapters are more formal while others more conversational, but all are eminently accessible. Some authors were also more adventurous and imaginative than others, but with each revision, all eventually found the form that fit the content and the personae of the authors. The result, we feel, is high quality and sometimes unconventional writing throughout the collection.

Theoretical Underpinnings

Intended as an inspirational resource book, most chapters in this collection tread lightly on theory, but they all proceed from a set of concepts and constructs that can be grounded in certain theories. Here, we will discuss briefly some major theoretical frameworks that underlie this project: *communities of practice* and the related concepts of legitimate peripheral participation and situated learning; *genre studies;* and *identity.* We do not provide a thorough literature review of work in these areas. Rather, our discussion serves to link the chapters to some larger issues.

First, *community of practice.* Lave and Wenger's notion of "community of practice" (Lave & Wenger 1991; Wenger, 1998) is one of the central concepts of this collection. What is the significance of viewing the academic community as one of practice, parallel to communities discussed by them, such as insurance claim processors or midwives? As Lave and Wenger explain, the significance of their coinage lies in "shifting the analytic focus from the individual as learner to learning as participation in the social world, and from the concept of cognitive process to the more-encompassing view of social practice" (1991, p. 43).

This sociocultural perspective (cf. Vygotsky's work, Lantolf's adaptation to second language development, and Engeström's adaptation of Leont'ev's Activity Theory) highlights the situated nature of learning and the importance of learners' access to the experts in real time and in contexts not limited to formal school settings. The co-participation, legitimate but peripheral, of new members with more expert members is thus central to "the fundamental process of learning" (Barton & Tusting, 2005, p. 2). As shown in this collection, Lave and Wenger's theory provides a way for some of the advisors and their advisees to perceive and structure their relationships as less unidirectional and more participatory. This is most evident in the co-authored chapters in the section "Mentors and Mentees," but also in the chapters that mention study groups, joint projects, and other small, spontaneous, and creative co-participation. The point is that the authors depict learning to do graduate school as learning to participate in local communities of practice as legitimate if peripheral members. All learning is taken to be situated in local contexts.

Lave and Wenger's constructs are not without critics. Actually much of the criticism has been directed at the notion of "communities of practice" itself. Some find it frustratingly "slippery and elusive," and others question whether the non-hierarchical, conflict-free, homogeneous, relatively static, open and welcoming space to all, as often implied in Wenger's work in particular, is a realistic portrayal of any workplace, including the academy (cf. several chapters in Barton and Tusting; Haneda, 2006; Kanno, 1999). The chapters in this collection complicate this simplistic reading by challenging the unidirectional assumptions of learning behind an apprenticeship-style model, and by documenting the complex interactional nature of participation in academic literacy practices.

Second, *genre studies*. Unlike traditional genre study, where genre is portrayed as "fixed and immutable" "textual regularities in form and content," the later generation of genre studies sees genre as "typified rhetorical actions based in recurrent situations" (Miller, 1984, p.159). From this perspective, genre has a distinct social and rhetorical orientation from the beginning (Bazerman, 1994). Since the mid-1980s, the field of genre studies has produced an impressive array of works and grown into a brand of inquiry that encompasses a range of theoretical affiliations and practices. Two approaches pertain to our project in that they deal with academic contexts. Swales's work (1990) uncovers the *sui generis* features and constituents of academic and research papers. The influence of his investigations can be seen in many of the dissertation-related discussions in the collection. The other approach is represented by the "social-cognitive theory of genre," which views genre "as a form of situated cognition embedded in disciplinary activities" (Berkenkotter & Huckin, 1995, p. 3). The object of such studies is, thus, the interplay between the social contexts and the actual genre users; the research examines both the written products and the processes of learners' socialization into different academic disciplines. A number of contributors to this collection have published significant works with comparable theoretical orientations (Casanave, 1995, 2002; Paltridge, 2002; Prior, 1998).

Notably, in the works of some authors who frame their studies with community-of-practice or genre theory, the analytical lens is often focused on the experiences of non-native speakers of English in academic disciplines where English is the medium of instruction and writing. This focus highlights the experiences of second language (L2) writers that typify and dramatize the challenges of socialization that novice participants undergo to become members of a new discipline. The chapters in this collection by authors from linguistic and cultural backgrounds outside the English-speaking countries can be read in the same way. However, the perspectives of mainstream authors reveal that the challenges are not unique to L2 speakers.

Third, *identity*. Identity, an underlying theme of all chapters, is a converging point of various theories of socialization, some already mentioned. Literacy theorists and educators (Ivanič, 1998; Lave & Wenger; Wenger; Gee, 2001; Norton, 1997, 2000) have argued, quite persuasively, that to become a member of a community of any kind entails a change in one's identity. For as one accepts and internalizes a set of values and practices, semiotic or material, one's "internal plane of consciousness" (Leont'ev 1981a, p. 57, cited in Prior, p. 21) is invariably modified or reshaped in the process.

The transformation, however, is not a one-way assimilation through which the dominant social, cultural, and historical forces impose their values and practices on hapless individuals. A number of chapters in this collection show that participants, while socialized into academic disciplines, are also active agents of change. They transform the communities by critically and consciously resisting and changing the existing ways of doing things, and, more often, by simply being who they are, by bringing their ways of living and coping into the mix.

It should be apparent from this brief discussion that the theories and analytical constructs this project employs—situated learning in communities of practice, genre studies, and identity—though different, overlap a great deal. Each stresses certain aspects of disciplinary learning, but they converge and complement each other at places. The social orientation of these theories, after all, befits our time's heightened awareness of the interconnection and mutual impact between what we do locally and what happens globally. It is, however, the social (and necessarily political) aspects of learning to participate in graduate school literacy practices that tend to remain tacit, given academe's more overt interest in cognitive and intellectual processes. Our collection aims to raise awareness of some of academe's more social, yet tacit, participatory activities that contribute to the ongoing learning of both students and faculty.

Content and Organization of the Collection[1]

The chapter themes in this book overlap in many ways, making our section divisions somewhat arbitrary. We therefore urge readers to select chapters that interest them—there is no beginning-to-end progression. We urge readers as well to connect issues and themes from different sections rather than be overly influenced by our choices of how to group the essays. All the chapters deal in one way or another with identity and with learning to participate in particular kinds of academic literacy practices, and many address mentor-mentee relationships and other kinds of guidance and support.

In Part 1, Learning to Participate, the authors discuss some of the tacit rules and practices they struggled to figure out at various stages in their doctoral study. Christine Pearson Casanave and John Hedgcock, both middle-class mainstream educators, reflect on the challenges they faced in learning how to read and write in graduate-level work in the absence of explicit instructions on how to do so, demonstrating that it is not only non-native speakers of English who face these challenges. Xiaoming Li discusses her journey from mainland China to a doctoral program in the United States, where she had to learn the unfamiliar practice of participating in written academic conversations that have an "argumentative edge." Mayumi Fujioka learned that graduate school means not only learning to participate in academic literacy and research practices, but also learning to negotiate relationships with powerful people—dissertation advisors and committee members. In the last paper in this section, Tracey Costley narrates her discoveries about the hidden assumptions behind labels such as "first generation student" (U.S.) and "nontraditional student" (U.K.) and how she gradually learned to participate successfully in academic literacy practices in ways that defy the labels.

---

[1] In keeping with our desire to maintain the voices and identities of the contributors, the spelling conventions in the chapters alternate between American and British style, according to the preferences of the authors.

In Part 2, Mentors and Mentees, paired graduate student–faculty authors offer valuable insights, from the perspectives of the mentor and the one mentored, of their shared journeys in doctoral work. Steve Simpson and his advisor, Paul Kei Matsuda, reveal how the mentor-mentee relationship can be viewed as one involving participation in a field's many professional activities, in which the mentee gradually takes on more responsibilities. Yongyan Li and her advisor, John Flowerdew, describe how Yongyan found her way into a very different kind of dissertation, a qualitative case study, from the original quantitative one she had planned. Alan Hirvela and his advisee from Korea, Youngjoo Yi, discuss their negotiations on the results chapter of Youngjoo's dissertation, revealing that the advisor-advisee relationship can be complex, balanced, and collegial. Rui Cheng and her advisor, Wei Zhu, with backgrounds in China, similarly discuss their long and difficult negotiations on Rui's literature review chapter. In all four of these chapters, we find guidance, interaction, and a refreshing balance of negotiating strategies and decision-making. In the chapter by Yanbin Lu and her advisor, Gayle Nelson, we see a reflective look on the part of both authors at the changes they underwent as they engaged in an academic literacy practice that was completely new to Yanbin and relatively new to Gayle, that of "online posting," as they wrote the chapter for this book. Finally, Lu Liu brings a variety of her mentors on board (Irwin Weiser, Tony Silva, Janet Alsup, Cynthia Selfe, and Gail Hawisher) to comment from each of their perspectives on Lu's development from a graduate student to a budding professional academic.

In Part 3, Situated Learning, we placed essays that view learners, both faculty and graduate students, as concrete living people, entangled in human relationships that are situated in specific local environments and historical moments. To no one's surprise, not all this embodied learning takes place within the institution or concerns learning to write a doctoral dissertation. Natsuko Kuwahara takes us through the challenges she faced in her first year of a doctoral program. She provides examples of resources and survival strategies, especially for international students, that can be actively sought both within and outside the institution itself. She stresses the need for connections with others. Marcia Buell and So Jin Park, Marcia's peer in another discipline (anthropology), describe the mutual assistance they provided each other in their graduate work, weaving in their connections as mothers of young children. Their stories unravel the stereotypical dichotomies of researcher-researched and of native- and non-native speaker. Jun Ohashi, Hiroko Ohashi, and Brian

Paltridge reveal the many ways, both in the institution and at home, that a doctoral student (Jun) can receive support as he goes through the high-pressure experience of trying to finish his dissertation after having taken on a tenure-track position. Participatory and embodied learning not only stemmed from the positive psychological support he received but also included the difficult and emotional political lessons that come from negotiating department politics. Paul Prior and Young-Kyung Min write from their respective positions as an established faculty member and a graduate student in the throes of redefining her identity and reshaping the path of her life. Each reflects on the practices, trials, and joys that emerge in the interstices between the formal, official surfaces of literate work in academic worlds and the everyday events and emotions that happen under, beyond, and around that work. Finally, Hanako Okada, a doctoral student in Japan, tells a moving story of her battle with chronic illness and the joys that graduate work has brought to a life that would otherwise be unbearably bleak. Her life as a graduate student, researcher, and teacher can never be separated from her bodily experiences, and her coping strategies, theorizing, and reflecting should inspire all readers.

Onward

And now, as you begin this journey, which for us was four years in the making, we hope that you will document your own adventures in graduate school, whether you are student or faculty, and share them with others. Much of what is hidden and tacit in the graduate school adventure does not need to be experienced in silence. The more we can bring untold stories to life, the less alone we will all feel on the difficult and life-changing journey that is graduate school.

REFERENCES

Barton, D., & Tusting, K. (Eds.). (2005). *Beyond communities of practice: Language power, and social context.* New York: Cambridge University Press.

Bazerman, C. (1994). Systems of genres and the enactment of social intentions. In A. Freedman & P. Medway (Eds.), *Genre and the new rhetoric* (pp. 79–101). London: Taylor & Francis.

Berkenkotter, C., & Huckin, T. (1995). *Genre knowledge in disciplinary communication: Cognition/culture/power.* Hillsdale, NJ: Lawrence Erlbaum.

Casanave, C. P. (1995). Local interactions: Constructing contexts for composing in a graduate sociology program. In G. Braine & D. Belcher (Eds.), *Academic writing in a second language: Essays on research and pedagogy* (pp. 83–110). Norwood, NJ: Ablex.

————. (2002). *Writing Games: Multicultural case studies of academic literacy practices in higher education*. Mahwah, NJ: Lawrence Erlbaum.

Engeström, Y. (1999). Activity theory and individual and social transformation. In Y. Engeström, R. Miethinen, & R.-L. Punamäki (Eds.), *Perspectives on activity theory* (pp. 19–38). Cambridge, UK: Cambridge University Press.

Gee, J. P. (2001). Identity as an analytic lens for research in education. *Review of Research in Education, 25*, 99–125.

Golde, C. M. (1998). Beginning graduate school: Explaining first-year doctoral attrition. *New Directions for Higher Education, 101*, 55–64.

Golde, C. M., & Dore, T. M. (2004). The survey of doctoral education and career preparation: The importance of disciplinary contexts. In D. H. Wulff, A. E. Austin, & Associates (Eds.), *Path to the professoriate: Strategies for enriching the preparation of future faculty* (pp. 19–45). San Francisco: Jossey-Bass.

Haneda, M. (2006). Classrooms as communities of practice: A reevaluation. *TESOL Quarterly 40*, 807–817.

Ivanič, R. (1998). *Writing and identity: The discoursal construction of identity in academic writing*. Philadelphia: John Benjamins.

Kanno, Y. (1999). The use of the community-of-practice perspective in language minority research. *TESOL Quarterly, 33*, 126–131.

Kirsch, G. (1993). *Women writing the academy: Audience, authority, and transformation*. Carbondale: Southern Illinois University Press.

Lantolf, J. P., & Thorne, S. L. (2006). *Sociocultural theory and the genesis of second language development*. Oxford, UK: Oxford University Press.

Lave, J., & Wenger, E. (1991). *Situated learning: Legitimate peripheral participation*. Cambridge, UK: Cambridge University Press.

Lovitts, B. E. (2001). *Leaving the ivory tower: The causes and consequences of departure from doctoral study*. Lanham, MD: Rowman & Littlefield.

Miller, C. (1984). Genre as social action. *Quarterly Journal of Speech, 70*, 151–167.

Norton, B. (1997). Language, identity, and the ownership of English. *TESOL Quarterly, 31*, 409–429.

Norton, B. (2000). *Identity and language learning: Gender, ethnicity and educational change*. London: Longman.

Paltridge, B. (2002). Academic literacies and changing university communities. *Revista Canaria de Estudios Ingleses, 44*, 15–28.

Prior, P. A. (1998). *Writing/disciplinarity: A sociohistoric account of literate activity in the academy*. Mahwah, NJ: Lawrence Erlbaum.

Swales, J. M. (1990). *Genre analysis: English in academic and research settings.* Cambridge, UK: Cambridge University Press.

Vygotsky, L. S. (1978). *Mind in society: The development of higher psychological processes* (M. Cole, V. John-Steiner, S. Scribner, & E. Souberman, Eds.). Cambridge, MA: Harvard University Press.

Welch, N., Latterell, C. G., Moore, C., & Carter-Tod, S. (Eds.). (2002). *The dissertation & the discipline: Reinventing composition studies.* Portsmouth, NH: Boynton/ Cook Heinemann.

Wenger, E. (1998). *Communities of practice: Learning, meaning, and identity.* New York: Cambridge University Press.

PART 1

Learning to Participate

Chapter 1

Learning Participatory Practices in Graduate School: Some Perspective-Taking by a Mainstream Educator

CHRISTINE PEARSON CASANAVE

Introduction

Learning to "do" graduate school does not come naturally to most people. Even students who enter graduate school prepared to read and write a great deal (especially in the social sciences) may stumble at the depth and breadth of sociopolitical and interpersonal engagement required to move from the periphery of a community toward fuller membership (Lave & Wenger, 1991; Prior, 1998). In addition to finding that the many socially and politically grounded literacy-related activities are unfamiliar, U.S. mainstream students may also find that the relatively brief and superficial writing tasks they did as undergraduates (Foster, 2004) did not prepare them for the more extended research-based literacy activities in graduate school. Moreover, the more mature students, mainstream and non-mainstream alike, who come to graduate school with already well-established professional identities need to relearn what it means to be a student (Hirvela & Belcher, 2001). The result is that many students, native and non-native English speakers alike, may feel like fish out of water until they learn to play the serious academic literacy games in their local environments (Casanave, 2002).

This is not to say that mainstream or "center" (Canagarajah, 2002) graduate students will not enjoy some advantages. A primary advantage of course is that they are not struggling to read and write in a second language, except to the extent that we can refer to disciplinary jargon and ways of using language as a kind of second language. A second advantage might be that they will probably not be surprised to find that their main activities in graduate school involve interactions with print and electronic text rather than with in-depth oral discourse, as is the case in some periphery communities (Canagarajah). Nevertheless, I am not the only mainstream[1] educator and former graduate student who wondered what the expectations were when I began graduate school, and who longed for more transparency in the journey from my status as novice to that of marginally participating member.

The classic case study of the acculturation of a mainstream graduate student is that of Berkenkotter, Huckin, and Ackerman's (1988, 1991) "Nate," who turned out to be Ackerman himself, a white male American. According to the authors, Nate struggled mightily with his writing in his Ph.D. program in composition and rhetoric, finding himself confused about and resistant to shifting his persona from that of teacher (who could write and think well) to researcher (who did not know how to write and think according to disciplinary expectations). Certain features of his writing, however, such as decreased use of first person pronouns and increased sentence length and complexity, shifted over time and suggested to the authors that Nate was gradually learning to become a participating member of his disciplinary community. In a postscript to this study, Ackerman (1995) expands the interpretation of his experiences from the mainly text-based inferences of the earlier analyses to a more sociopolitical interpretation of what he went through. Reflecting on his entire experience, he was able to point out the dangers of the "interpretive leap from textual analysis to intellectual identity" (Ackerman, p. 145), particularly when the analysis consisted of just a few of the many papers he wrote. A more accurate interpretation would link his writing in part to sociopolitical survival strategies: "exercises in getting by" (p. 148) as he learned how to write for particular professors, each of whom demanded that he craft somewhat different intellectual identities even within the same program. He points out that the more uniform interpretation of a developing intellectual identity in the earlier accounts says more about the genre of the research report than it does about him as a developing scholar (p. 150). For my purposes in this chapter, it is

---

[1] Labels are always risky, but I don't know how to get around them. I use *mainstream* here to refer to myself as a middle class European-American whose L1 is English, recognizing full well that sometimes greater diversity can be found within this label than across cultural and linguistic boundaries.

sufficient to note that Nate was pushed, pulled, and stretched in his Ph.D. program in multiple ways, under the influence of many people. He was not socialized into a coherent intellectual community where genre conventions and thinking styles uniformly represented a discipline. He learned strategies for surviving in a hybrid intellectual environment that differed from the less formal more teacherly world he came from. What surprises some people in multicultural studies is that Nate, as a white native English–speaking male, faced the challenges he did. He was the prototypical mainstream student against whom minorities and second language speakers are often compared. The dichotomy suggests that mainstream students don't have literacy socialization problems in school and non-mainstream students do.

Like Nate, as a white middle class doctoral student, perhaps I too was not supposed to have had problems with the literacy practices in my doctoral program, but I (and others?) did. We found not all but many practices strange or at the very least unfamiliar. In this chapter, I first discuss literacy-related activities in graduate school as a form of participatory practice. I follow with examples of some of the challenges I faced learning to participate in the communities and cultures of my graduate school, and speculate about the extent to which the challenges are similar to or different from those faced by international and non-native English–speaking students. I conclude by returning to the theme of participatory practice as a way to expand a view of graduate-level academic literacy that encompasses mainstream and minority, and native- and nonnative–English speakers alike.

Literacy Activities as Participatory Practice

When I refer to graduate-level academic literacy experiences as a form of participatory practice, I am drawing on Lave's (1993, 1996, 1997; Lave & Wenger) and Wenger's (1998) notion of learning as a person's evolving ability to participate in the defining and conventional practices of special-ized communities, and on activity- and sociohistorical-oriented theories of literacy activities (Engeström, 1993, 1999; Prior, 1998; Russell, 1995, 1997). In literacy studies, this work shifts our focus as researchers and educators exclusively from written texts (how they are produced; their rhetorical and linguistic characteristics) to literacy-related issues such as extra-textual influences on writing (personal histories and exigencies), social and political forces and alignments, material and spatial resources, and (from Lave and Wenger) the shifting patterns of participation in academic communities that signal novices' moves toward fuller membership as they interact with more experienced members and expand their repertoires of practices. Although it is true that many of these changing patterns of participation involve interaction with texts in the graduate school context, it is not the texts themselves that I am concerned with in this chapter, but the participatory practices that surround and are embedded in textual practices. Citation practices, for example, are usually considered textual conventions, which they are, but they are also deeply social (they connect authors to other authors) and political (they reveal an author's perception of status, prestige, and alliances within disciplinary communities). A second example is research reports, often studied draft by draft in composition research for textual features. Less often investigated are processes of learning to do research itself, and the many collaborative and social interactions that go into a final report, as Prior (1998) and others have shown (e.g., Blakeslee, 1997; Flowerdew, 2000). In short, looking at academic literacy as participatory practice involves looking at what people do, particularly in relationship to other community members, not just at what they write. The activities students become involved in and the alliances they forge while pursuing graduate degrees immerse students in a variety of practices within disciplinary communities heretofore unknown to them even if they are familiar with disciplinary subject matter.

My point is that most students, whatever the nationality, ethnic group, or social class, experience graduate school for the first time when they enter a program in their first year. Graduate school, especially at the doctoral level, is unlike previous schooling in many ways, and one does not need to be a stereotypical outsider to find the cultural and intellectual adjustment to graduate level literacy practices challenging. Situated between novice and expert, graduate students discover that they are moving into a world populated by people in competing camps, where people are driven by motives for intellectual prestige as well as knowledge construction, and where it matters who they align themselves with and how they go about forging these alliances. Distinguishing the academic community from other kinds of communities we all belong to is the fact that certain kinds of texts lie at the heart of what it means to participate in the community's sociopolitical activities and that texts come to be linked to members' identities.

Participating in Multiple Advanced-Level Disciplinary Communities of Practice

Because I was in a school of education in the U.S., one that encouraged students to take a great deal of coursework in relevant social science disciplines such as anthropology, sociology, linguistics, and psychology, my classmates and I faced a situation similar to that of the undergraduate student described by Lucille McCarthy (1987): To some extent, we were strangers in strange lands. We dabbled in each area, taking just one or two graduate courses in each, without ever developing expertise in any beyond our evolving areas of concentration. Moreover, each of these disciplinary communities already had a cohesive core of graduate students and faculty who were working together and who knew each other well. As an outsider to those communities, I did not know how to relate to them at their levels, including not knowing clearly what their research goals and methods were, who the key players and readings were, or what the core concepts and language consisted of. One or two terms did not allow enough time for me to develop the familiarity they had. I sensed an undercurrent in some of those classes that "education students" couldn't keep up with the insiders, and that we would be tolerated but not included. I recall sitting in a sociology class, an advanced linguistics class, and a small seminar in psychology (with a well-known professor) and feeling like a silent, intimidated observer. I did not fight this feeling, because I was in fact an outsider, there for a brief stay only. Within the school of education, however, multiple "programs" also existed, and within them subprograms. As part of the normal state of affairs in social sciences, the education faculty themselves differed in knowledge, commitment to various research methods, goals for research, and acknowledged cliques of heroes and opponents. This diversity made for exciting intellectual exchanges among faculty and between faculty and students, but caused some of us to wonder whether we would ever find a disciplinary "home."

Participating in Conversations

The term *conversation* is now commonly used to describe the activity of participating in the oral and written textual practices of specialized communities. Some time ago, Berkenkotter, Huckin, and Ackerman (1988) described "Nate's" initiation into his disciplinary community (described earlier) as one of learning the "conventions and conversations" of that community, by which they meant written, genre-specific conventions in Nate's writings and readings. I wish to expand that earlier focus on written discourse conventions to include the oral interactions that graduate students have in classes, seminars, meetings with advisors, and consultations with classmates and colleagues, even though many of these oral interactions emerge from written texts. I also wish specifically to include the "conversations" that writers have with readers: Graduate students need to learn that when they read, they are being "spoken to" by real people and need therefore to respond thoughtfully and critically rather than just absorb information from so-called experts. They also need to learn that when they write for professors or for publication, they are communicating with readers who have various levels of knowledge and prestige and therefore need to situate themselves appropriately, in politically sensitive ways, within these already established communities (Hyland, 2000). Learning to participate in a field's conversations thus involves not only learning specialized ways of using language, but also learning something about who the key players in the conversation are and what the relations are among experienced members and others at various stages of expertise. In this section, I discuss some of the linguistic challenges that I faced as a mainstream graduate student, and ways I tried to disguise my ignorance.

Learning the Lingo

The specialized language of any field reflects the field's main concepts and abstractions, research methods, and ways of interpreting events and, by extension, ways of constructing knowledge. In classes outside the school of education—those one-shot introductions to the social sciences that feed into educational knowledge—I did not have enough time in most cases to learn specialized ways of using language well enough to be able to participate deeply in conversations of any kind. Even within the school of education, I had numerous experiences of trying to read academic educational literature in English and not understanding what I was reading. In classes and seminars and in my writing, I therefore had to use avoidance strategies to get by. Like many others, I was often afraid to confess my lack of understanding to teachers or more advanced graduate students. What was the problem?

First, meanings of common words used in specialized ways were not necessarily transparent.

theory
text
discourse
X "shapes" Y
joint construction of meaning
parallel processing
distributed learning
learning vs. acquisition
subject position vs. identity
variable (as noun)
correlation
significant

In some ways, this kind of language may have been more difficult for first language speakers than for second language speakers, given the persistent connections we made of individual common words with their everyday connotations.

Second, new terminology was used by professors and in published literature as if everyone knew what the terms meant:

hermeneutic
phenomenology
schemata
instantiation
reflexivity
intersubjectivity

In classes my first year, I don't recall anyone publicly confessing ignorance to a professor or asking for explanations, except me, once. I tended not to be very intimidated by my professors, perhaps because I felt quite distant from them, and because seeing them up close made me realize that they had flaws and imperfections and that they did not know everything. And some of them were not much older than I. So in one class my first year, I was the only student to raise my hand to ask a famous professor what a term meant. However, when I did not understand his explanation, I did not pursue the matter. After that class, another student approached me (white middle class) to thank me for asking the question. Discovering in my first year that I was not alone in not understanding some of the lingo felt quite liberating.

However, perhaps because of my boldness in asking a question about a key word that I had presumed everyone else knew, this professor thought I was ready for public interaction with him. He later tried to engage me in one-on-one discussion in front of the entire class as a way to pull ideas out of me and help me develop literate thinking. I had seen him do this with others. I flushed, went blank, and he never called on me again.

Third, I found some readings nearly impossible to comprehend. In particular, I suspected that common educational phenomena and experiences (what I think were common experiences) were described in ways that were designed to obfuscate and to elevate the personae of the authors. From a more recent example, but displaying my point:

> Analysis of the sequence of activity across the morning showed that the teacher initiated community with an event (a period of concerted activity) in which students were afforded an opportunity to begin establishing their positions at a table group and to begin shaping local identities within this developing collective. . . . (Putney, Green, Dixon, Durán, & Yeager, 2000, p. 106)

After some years of immersion in this kind of discourse, I still find it frustrating but it no longer seems extraordinary. Professors and advanced graduate students have lost their sense of the strangeness of this way of communicating. What I don't know is the extent to which others come to understand this kind of language, or choose to cover up their ignorance through silence or through avoidance (i.e., not reading certain materials).

During my early graduate school years, I wondered if other students who remained silent understood everything, or if they too were hesitant to parade their ignorance in public. I tried to figure out who was contributing to open class discussion and who was not, and inevitably just a handful of students participated. Contrary to the stereotype that was widespread about middle class American students' ease at critical thinking and active class participation, the vast majority of these students, and the majority of international students as well, sat silently through their classes, partly because the language was simply not accessible or embodied yet.

Covering Up Ignorance

I believe that many of my graduate school peers were as insecure as I, and we thus sought ways to cover up our ignorance when we had trouble understanding particularly dense readings. A turning point came when suddenly we could begin using a term or concept with understanding instead of silence or pretense (see the case of Richard in Casanave, 1990). Confessions about this lack of understanding could be made to a trusted classmate, and in my case it paid off to find someone (another middle class white woman) who suffered this particular affliction. It helped that we both had a sense of humor and could laugh at ourselves (with some pain) for not understanding our native language. I didn't belong to a study group of any kind, let alone one that contained more experienced graduate students, so my occasional meetings with this classmate were all I had. Even though it was a bit like the blind leading the blind, I learned that I was not alone in trying to pretend that I knew what was going on. I was also not alone in finding it impossible to read everything in a course packet thoroughly, with the result that I often felt I knew very little about everything, even if readings were comprehensible.

Then, in small seminar classes in which I could not easily escape participating, I developed a strategy that prevented my broader ignorance from being discovered—reading abstracts and (if present) methods sections thoroughly and then identifying one or two points in a reading that I would volunteer to ask a substantive question about or to critique before I was called on. I learned that finding flaws in research was an expected activity, and that most flaws could be located in methods sections. This worked as a strategy to cover up a larger sense of incompetence I had, but prevented me from learning more quickly how to interpret what I was reading and how to apply what I was supposedly learning to my own projects.

I don't think I am unique in having been a mainstream graduate student who found it challenging to learn to participate in the scholarly conversations of the academy, who felt silenced in certain classes, and who developed strategies to cover up ignorance. Dichotomous characterizations of the linguistic and text-related challenges facing mainstream and non-mainstream students can go too far if they suggest that mainstream students working in their first languages fit right in from the beginning. Some may, but I and many of my classmates did not.

Learning to Participate in a Field's Sociopolitical Networks

With many years of hindsight and having become a professor myself, I now view the lives and work of my graduate school professors in ways that I did not when I was under their tutelage. Their job, as I saw it then, was to select readings, devise and deliver a course plan, involve some students in busy-work aspects of their own (the professors') research projects, and guide students through the doctoral hurdles. I did not ask some of the questions I now consider basic to understanding graduate school socialization: What networks of colleagues do my professors belong to, both on and off campus? Who are their heroes and opponents? For whom are they heroes or opponents? To what extent do they know the members of their network personally as opposed to knowing them via published texts or electronic communication? What can the citation practices in their own writing tell us about these alliances? According to what vision of themselves are they, and have they been, shaping their public identities as scholars? What were their own trajectories of participation like, and how did their own identities as authoritative participants in their communities evolve? What kinds of competition and collaboration exist for them in the power-infused academic world? How do all these factors influence the ways they introduce students to networks of participatory practice within their subfields? In this section, I ponder two of these questions, one on citation practices and the other on professor-student relationships in classes and on projects.

Citation Practices

In the social sciences, successful writing in graduate school and later in professional life depends partly on how writers situate their work within existing bodies of work. In writing classes, students learn the formal conventions of citing others—how to do within-text citations, what style to use for these citations or for footnotes, the proper form for a reference list or bibliography (including the differences between the two). These formalities are relatively easy to teach and to learn. In my case, I copied a style from the main journal in the field of TESOL for most of my graduate school papers. Books are also now available that introduce graduate students to the formalities of scholarly citation practices (e.g., Swales & Feak, 1994, 2000).

However, when I was a doctoral student, the rationale for citation practices was not made explicit, so I was not sure who to cite, when to cite, and importantly, which authors to cite together or not to cite at all. Looking at published readings for traces of an author's decision-making processes was no help here: Published writing ordinarily covers up all traces of how a paper was written (Casanave & Vandrick, 2003; Geisler, 1994). In a paper I had to write on reading, for example, I looked for sources, any sources, on reading, and tended to present them as A said this, B said that. I was not able to see or sense who the competing camps were in the contested field of reading research. It was never suggested to me that when scholars read articles and books, they often turn first to reference lists to get a sense of the networks authors situate themselves within. Neither was I made aware of the various subtle ways that a writer can refer to the work of others to signal approval, allegiance, qualified approval, disapproval, or outright dismissal and thus contribute to the construction of knowledge (Hyland, 1999, 2000). Such techniques are not merely textual, but sociopolitical in that they help define a writer's identity and location in relation to others within power-sensitive academic fields. However, even if my classmates and I had been made aware of the sociopolitical side of citation practices, we could not easily have used this awareness to our advantage. There was no time. Until a critical foundation of knowledge builds in a student's repertoire of readings and professional associations, there is no way to use this knowledge skillfully. Mainstream and non-mainstream graduate students alike face this challenge together, and it is in fact an area in which second language speakers can excel (see Matsuda, 2003).

Faculty-Student Relationships

A number of scholars in language education have written about faculty-student interactions in graduate school, particularly in areas of research, writing, and dissertation preparation (e.g., Belcher, 1994; Belcher & Hirvela, 2005; Prior, 1994, 1998). These interactions happen in classes, particularly in small seminars, in counseling and advising sessions, and in research group meetings. If my experience was in any way typical, they range from tight, "hand-holding" apprenticeships to little mentoring of any kind. A faculty member with a large number of advisees working on her own research projects as co-researchers and co-authors would be able to induct students rather quickly into a specific academic community of practice and acquaint them explicitly with the key players, research methods, goals, and values of the community. A faculty member who spent little time on campus and who used graduate students as assistants on her own single-authored publications, on the other hand, might not conceptualize the faculty-student relationship as one of apprenticeship into her own community of practice, but as one of guidance into students' own areas of interest. I had experiences with both kinds of faculty members.

In the first case, I had a very difficult time in an educational sociology class trying to figure out what my role was both in the class and in relation to the jargon, research methods, goals, and values. The faculty member was well known for having tightly controlled relationships with her multicultural graduate student advisees, for co-authoring with them, and for getting them through their Ph.D. dissertations relatively quickly by having them work on her large ongoing projects. I felt at loose ends early in my program, and was seeking an advisor. However, after my first course with this faculty member, I found myself chafing. Everyone else seemed to use language, concepts, and research methods that I didn't understand or believe in, such as the need to turn human qualities into numbers ("variables") so that they could be examined statistically. The style of the many readings we had to do, mostly correlational studies, struck me sometimes as parodies of themselves in their denseness and pomposity, and, additionally, I was not able to critically evaluate the research methods except to reach the point where I could say that not everything in sociology should be turned into a number. Moreover, the professor relied a great deal on group work, and I didn't know how to participate effectively in a group that consisted of people who already knew each other and the professor well and who spoke insider jargon, nor did I know how to contribute to a group report for a final term paper. I ended out writing almost nothing, that job being left to a competent Korean student who was one of the professor's advisees.

In the other case, I found that I was able to wrestle with ideas and research methods more suitable to my personality and beliefs with an advisor who was less controlling and who put up with my resistant stances to much of what I was reading about theory and research. She rarely published with students, nor did she encourage me or others working with her to publish and become involved professionally before we graduated. Do the dissertation first, then begin your professional life, was the message (one that I disagreed with at the time and continue to find misguided). I was pretty much on my own to pick and choose from different sources and from other faculty members' areas of expertise, which led both to greater freedom and to greater fragmentation of acculturation than I would have had with the former professor. Indeed I felt much less specialized when I ended my doctoral program than when I began. But I also felt opened, broadened, and enriched. The real struggle came at dissertation time, when I was on my own, with few models and no supporting research cohort that was working on similar issues. I did manage to get lengthy feedback from my advisor and others on my committee on different parts of the dissertation, and finally was able to put it all together, by dint of tenacity rather than expertise or intelligence. But many times in the dissertation years (yes, years) I wondered if I might have been better off under the thumb of a "do-it-my-way" advisor, but never regretted my choice.[2] And it was my choice. In understanding that I had this choice, that I was allowed to flail and flounder, I may have had an advantage over non-mainstream or second language students who did not perceive choices in their graduate education. International students on a strict timeline and funded by home governments may in fact not have had these choices, or may not have known that at most U.S. universities it is possible to change advisors if one is miserable with the one assigned. But even with a successful dissertation experience, I and the students I knew had only begun to learn the participatory literacy practices of their fields, however clearly or vaguely those fields were defined. In this respect, my international and non-mainstream colleagues and I shared the challenges that were awaiting us after graduation.

Final Thoughts

Without wishing to underestimate the very real differences between mainstream graduate students and their international or minority counterparts, I wish to highlight here some of the challenges that face all of them in their journey from the peripheries toward the centers of their fields. Students who may feel isolated and out of place in this journey are not alone. The exceptions—the students who really do seem to have everything figured out from the beginning—do not prove the rule. Many

---

[2] For more dissertation stories, see the edited collection by Welch, Latterell, Moore, and Carter-Tod (2002) on student and faculty dissertation experiences in the field of composition and rhetoric.

of us in the mainstream hide our feelings of insecurity, incompetence, and displacement through silence and pretense, occasional or persistent.

In a nutshell, the challenge is not just one of becoming proficient in the English language or learning strategies for efficient reading and the conventions for writing research papers. These things can be taught in preparatory classes. It is one of learning what it means to participate fully, not superficially, in an academic community of practice.[3] Patterns of and possibilities for participation cannot be taught in preparatory classes because they are locally contingent, including the specifics of reading and writing (e.g., Casanave, 1995; and, more broadly, the specifics of adaptation to social and cultural life in graduate school—Myles and Cheng [2003]). But awareness of them not only could be taught, but discussed and reflected upon throughout a graduate student's journey. It is with this hope in mind that I conclude this chapter.

Incomplete Acculturation

I finished my Ph.D., including a long qualitative dissertation, without showing much outward evidence that I had struggled, or that I had felt out of place in graduate study. In fact, I took enormous pleasure in the life of a graduate student in spite of the insecurities and frustrations. But from the 15-year perspective I now have, I see that even my final opus, the dissertation, was a pretense at recognizing and situating myself comfortably within a community of practice. I had no choice. I simply had not participated for enough years within any coherent communities to feel that I really knew something of their literatures, their issues, their key players. Mainstream or minority, first or second language speaker, most of us end our graduate study still residing on the distant periphery of our future communities of practice. Recognizing this fact at the time could help students develop a vision of their futures as academics (assuming this is what many Ph.D. graduates intend to become) that fundamentally includes a life of further study. As is often preached at graduation ceremonies, completing a degree represents a beginning not an end.

---

3 See Prior's (1998) discussion of passing, procedural, and deep participation in graduate education, pp. 100–103; Prior's case study of two non-native students in an M.A. program revealed that it is not one's non-nativeness that can inhibit a student's academic acculturation, but the depth of his or her participation (Prior, 1998, Ch. 4).

Continuing to Learn to Participate

As an academic interested in continuing to read, write, and publish, and who now knows some of the people personally in my subfield (which I guess I would call second language writing and language teacher education), I rarely struggle the way I used to in trying to situate my work, my voice, within an active community of second language educators. The tables are now turned. I teach and advise graduate students, and try to help them find their way into a community of practice—to recognize who is who, to build a body of background knowledge, to meet people in person whenever possible. I talk with them about the issues I have discussed in this paper, and I share with them my efforts at reading and writing, both of which continue to be difficult for me even though I am more confident in my "community membership." At the same time, I find it impossible to keep up with the explosion of knowledge in language education. To be honest, because I cannot find time even to read the journals I receive at home let alone to peruse the growing body of Internet and other print sources, and because at any one conference I can attend only a handful of sessions relative to what is available, I wonder if I have any idea as to what is going on. Is knowledge really growing? Or are more scholars simply juggling what we already know? Whatever the reality, I seem less confident at making assertions now than ever before. My written work tends to be full of more and more questions. I suppose in the coming years this frustration could lead either to dropping out altogether or to continued efforts at figuring out how to participate. The journey doesn't have to end.

Speaking Openly

Finally, I am finding that the worst mistake to make, from graduate school on, has been to cover up insecurity with pretense or silence. In graduate school, I hesitated to confess my ignorance to anyone but a close friend. What if I had spoken more openly with professors? (I did not have the language or the awareness at that time to speak about academic literacy as a form of participatory practice, but if I had?) My ignorance would not have gone away, but my sense of incompetence might have. I might have learned that I was on a normal trajectory of participation, one that would last a lifetime. What if conference presenters and authors of scholarly articles spoke and wrote with less pomposity and certainty, with more openness about their own (hidden) insecurities, and more about what they don't, rather than do, know? And if some speakers and writers really do believe they know everything there is to know in their communities of practice, how can we find the courage to speak out and refute this arrogance in ways that will not damage us politically? (Or is this a case where silence really is the best solution?) Whatever the answers are to such questions, it seems clear that open discussion and reflection on participatory practices in academic communities of practice can only serve to bring people together: mainstream students, non-mainstream and second language students, and their faculty. Open and ongoing reflection among these variously located newcomers and old-timers in an academic community of practice can make the hard work of learning to participate more transparent, and thus more tolerable, less stressful, and more driven by a vision of a professional life after graduation.

CHRISTINE PEARSON CASANAVE, TEMPLE UNIVERSITY, JAPAN CAMPUS
I never imagined myself in a Ph.D. program, let alone at Stanford University, until I actually got my acceptance letter. I was the first in my family to do this. In spite of difficulties, these were perhaps the best 6 and 1/2 years of my life. As an older student in my 40s, I relished the chance to study as part of my "job." I persisted because I knew that after graduating I wanted to work at the university level and that the Ph.D. would help me reach this goal. Which it did. My greatest joy now comes from inspiring other struggling doctoral students to forge ahead.

REFERENCES

Ackerman, J. (1995). Postscript: The assimilation and tactics of Nate. In C. Berkenkotter & T. N. Huckin, *Genre knowledge in disciplinary communities: Cognition/culture/power* (pp. 145–150). Hillsdale, NJ: Lawrence Erlbaum.

Belcher, D. (1994). The apprenticeship approach to advanced academic literacy: Graduate students and their mentors. *English for Specific Purposes, 13*, 23–34.

Belcher, D., & Hirvela, A. (2005). Writing the qualitative dissertation: What motivates and sustains commitment to a fuzzy genre? *Journal of English for Academic Purposes, 4*, 187–205.

Berkenkotter, C., Huckin, T. N., & Ackerman, J. (1988). Conventions, conversations, and the writer: Case study of a student in a rhetoric Ph.D. program. *Research in the Teaching of English, 22*, 9–45.

————. (1991). Social context and socially constructed texts: The initiation of a graduate student into a writing research community. In C. Bazerman & J. Paradis (Eds.), *Textual dynamics of the professions* (pp. 191–215). Madison: University of Wisconsin Press.

Blakeslee, A. M. (1997), Activity, context, interaction, and authority: Learning to write scientific papers in situ. *Journal of Business and Technical Communication, 11*(2), 125–169.

Canagarajah, A. S. (2002). *A geopolitics of academic writing.* Pittsburgh, PA: University of Pittsburgh Press.

Casanave, C. P. (1990). *The role of writing in socializing graduate students into an academic discipline in the social sciences.* Unpublished doctoral dissertation, Stanford University.

————. (1995). Local interactions: Constructing contexts for composing in a graduate sociology program. In G. Braine & D. Belcher (Eds.), *Academic writing in a second language: Essays on research and pedagogy* (pp. 83–110). Norwood, NJ: Ablex.

————. (2002). *Writing games: Multicultural case studies of academic literacy practices in higher education.* Mahwah, NJ: Lawrence Erlbaum.

Casanave, C. P., & Vandrick, S. (Eds.) (2003). *Writing for scholarly publication: Behind the scenes in language education.* Mahwah, NJ: Lawrence Erlbaum.

Engeström, Y. (1993). Developmental studies of work as a testbench of activity theory: The case of primary care medical practice. In S. Chaiklin & J. Lave (Eds.), *Understanding practice: Perspectives on activity and context* (pp. 64–103). Cambridge, UK: Cambridge University Press.

————. (1999). Activity theory and individual and social transformation. In Y. Engeström, R. Miettinen, & R.-L. Punamäki (Eds.), *Perspectives on activity theory* (pp. 19–38). Cambridge, UK: Cambridge University Press.

Flowerdew, J. (2000). Discourse community, legitimate peripheral participation, and the nonnative-English-speaking scholar. *TESOL Quarterly, 34*(1), 127–150.

Foster, D. (2004). Temporal patterns in student authorship: A cross-national perspective. *Research in the Teaching of English, 38*(3), 262–303.

Geisler, C. (1994). *Academic literacy and the nature of expertise: Reading, writing, and knowing in academic philosophy.* Hillsdale, NJ: Lawrence Erlbaum.

Hirvela, A., & Belcher, D. (2001). Coming back to voice: The multiple voices and identities of mature multilingual writers. *Journal of Second Language Writing, 10*(1–2), 83–106.

Hyland, K. (1999). Academic attribution: Citation and the construction of disciplinary knowledge. *Applied Linguistics, 20*(3), 341–367.

————. (2000). *Disciplinary discourses: Social interactions in academic writing.* London: Longman.

Lave, J. (1993). The practice of learning. In S. Chaiklin & J. Lave (Eds.), *Understanding practice: Perspectives on activity and context* (pp. 3–32). Cambridge, UK: Cambridge University Press.

————. (1996). Teaching, as learning, in practice. *Mind, Culture, and Activity, 3*, 149–164.

————. (1997). The culture of acquisition and the practice of understanding. In D. Kirshner & J. A. Whitson (Eds.), *Situated cognition: Social, semiotic, and psychological perspectives* (pp. 17–35). Mahwah, NJ: Lawrence Erlbaum.

Lave, J., & Wenger, E. (1991). *Situated learning: Legitimate peripheral participation.* Cambridge, UK: Cambridge University Press.

Matsuda, P. K. (2003). Coming to voice: Publishing as a graduate student. In C. P. Casanave & S. Vandrick (Eds.), *Writing for scholarly publication: Behind the scenes in language education* (pp. 39–51). Mahwah, NJ: Lawrence Erlbaum.

McCarthy, L. P. (1987). A stranger in strange lands: A college student writing across the curriculum. *Research in the Teaching of English, 21,* 233–265.

Myles, J., & Cheng, L. (2003). The social and cultural life of non-native English speaking international graduate students at a Canadian university. *Journal of English for Academic Purposes, 2*(3), 247–283.

Prior, P. (1994). Response, revision, disciplinarity: A microhistory of a dissertation prospectus in sociology. *Written Communication, 11,* 483–533.

————. (1998). *Writing/disciplinarity: A sociohistoric account of literate activity in the academy.* Mahwah, NJ: Lawrence Erlbaum.

Putney, L. G., Green, J., Dixon, C., Durán, R., & Yeager, B. (2000). Consequential progressions: Exploring collective-individual development in a bilingual classroom. In C. D. Lee & P. Smagorinsky (Eds.), *Vygotskian perspectives on literacy research: Constructing meaning through collaborative inquiry* (pp. 86–126). Cambridge, UK: Cambridge University Press.

Russell, D. R. (1995). Activity theory and its implications for writing instruction. In J. Petraglia (Ed.), *Reconceiving writing, rethinking writing instruction* (pp. 51–77). Mahwah, NJ: Lawrence Erlbaum.

————. (1997). Writing and genre in higher education and workplaces: A review of studies that use cultural-historical activity theory. *Mind, culture, and activity, 4,* 224–237.

Swales, J. M., & Feak, C. B. (1994). *Academic writing for graduate students: A course for nonnative speakers of English.* Ann Arbor: University of Michigan Press.

————. (2000). *English in today's research world: A writing guide.* Ann Arbor: University of Michigan Press.

Welch, N., Latterell, C. G., Moore, C., & Carter-Tod, S. (Eds.). (2002). *The dissertation & the discipline: Reinventing composition studies.* Portsmouth, NH: Boynton/Cook Heinemann.

Wenger, E. (1998). *Communities of practice: Learning, meaning, and identity.* Cambridge, UK: Cambridge University Press.

Chapter 2

Lessons I Must Have Missed: Implicit Literacy Practices in Graduate Education

JOHN S. HEDGCOCK

I am seated at my desk with a tall stack of manila folders at my side. Each folder contains a little piece of my history as an academic writer. Not surprisingly, I now find many of these relics to be downright embarrassing. Some papers are naïve and overly ambitious; a few reflect a degree of risk-taking; all show an understandable lack of polish. As I compare my fuzzy memories of generating these products to the papers themselves, I find myself asking, "Who wrote these things?" and "Did I ever know what I was doing—or did I at least *think* I knew?" The first question has an easy answer. Much as I would like to disavow any connection to some of this material, it is unmistakably mine. The second question, however, merits further reflection and retrospection, as I honestly do not recall learning to write for an academic audience, nor do I have any recollection of being *taught* to write (at least not explicitly) after leaving high school.

I undeniably learned a great deal about research and writing processes during my graduate studies, but much of my knowledge emerged incipiently, without conscious awareness on my part. Lest the reader infer that academic work—especially writing—has ever been effortless for me, allow me to quash such assumptions before we move further. I have never viewed academic writing as anything but difficult, if not torturous; my attitude hasn't changed appreciably since my student days. Even after nearly 15 years of full-time employment in the academic ranks, I seldom find writing to be a natural or organic process, notwithstanding the inspirational influence of Peter Elbow (1973, 1981) and Frank Smith (1984, 1988).

Still, I chose a career that requires such writing. How did I survive graduate school and endure the rigors of a profession where research and writing for publication are inherent responsibilities? I learned crucial but not-so-obvious lessons—in some instances, not very well. Some lessons were subtly embedded in the routine interactions between my professors and me, in collaborations with peers, in correspondence with editors, in indirect communications with anonymous reviewers, and in all manner of conversations with people in the profession. In the pages that follow, I excavate selected turning points in my autobiography as a novice academic that illustrate my socialization as a reader-researcher-writer-and-teacher in two quite different graduate programs, the first in French literature (where I completed an M.A.) and the second in applied linguistics (where I completed an M.A. and a Ph.D.). I hope that some of these episodes will show that crucial lessons about academic and professional literacy are not necessarily learned through systematic or explicit means (e.g., research methods courses, professional seminars, and the like). Certain fundamental lessons may actually take place in routine encounters with texts and with fellow novices, gatekeepers, and experts—"old-timers," as Lave and Wenger (1991) might call them.

Early Chapters from My Academic Literacy Autobiography

How and why did I choose a career that requires research and writing without actually undergoing formal writing instruction myself? A little pre-history might be useful here. As I have already confessed, I was never formally "taught" anything about writing once I started college. In fact, I don't remember learning much about writing *processes* during my pre-college years, either. I distinctly recall learning about conventional *forms* of academic writing—what I would now call school-based genres. As countless U.S. high school students do, I mastered the much-maligned five-paragraph essay formula, which I learned to manipulate for a range of purposes. It was fun to play with word choice and syntax while subtly pushing at the boundaries of the deductive essay template. I'm sure I experienced brief moments of creativity or "flow" (Csikszentmihalyi, 1997) when crafting less-constrained texts, but most writing tasks were invariably driven by two purposes: (a) displaying content knowledge and (b) demonstrating adherence to an unimaginative but efficient organizational scheme.

It would be fair to characterize my early training as current-traditional in orientation and mimetic in method (Clark, 2003). That is, instruction focused on noticing and adopting rhetorical conventions such as pre-revealing a purpose for writing, formulating thoughtful "thesis statements," crafting explicit topic sentences for each paragraph, presenting suitable forms of evidence, following a "logical" flow of reasoning, and reiterating a "main idea"—while somehow avoiding tedious repetition! Considerable ink has been spilt critiquing current-traditional writing instruction and its shortcomings, yet I can't help but credit my early education with giving me this formal template to work from.

Internal Paradigm Shifts

I began my undergraduate studies at a large, comprehensive state university, where I initially wrote very little. I never took a freshman composition course, and until I reached advanced-level language and literature courses, minimal demands were placed on me as a writer. However, when I settled on a double-major in French and Spanish and progressed to third-year language and literature courses, the rhetorical axe fell: My template stopped working, and my reading and writing strategies stopped working. My writing strategy was to vary the deductive, linear pattern I had transferred from high school English, but the approach resulted in disaster when it came to producing subtler, more sophisticated texts that required asserting my voice in either of my target languages. To that point, my naïve strategy for foreign language writing had functioned well (to a point) because L2 writing essentially amounted to language practice: Content and rhetorical structure for me were simply vehicles for developing linguistic fluency and accuracy.

Learning about Academe and Its Divergent Agendas

I entered the M.A. program in French literature at the same university immediately after completing my B.A. I continued to view my reading and writing largely as exercises aimed at enhancing my fluency and accuracy in French and Spanish, but judgments of my work increasingly depended on the quality of its content; linguistic form no longer mattered as much as it previously had. In fact, professors in the department routinely encouraged graduate students to write their papers in English, rather than in their target languages. They asserted that we were now learning literary criticism and that North American scholars generally published their work in English. I was surprised and disappointed: As a zealous language learner and a card-carrying purist, I had hoped to broaden and polish my L2 writing skills. I also reasoned that, because nearly all of the literary and critical works that I read were in French or Spanish, I might as well write in those languages. The papers that I produced during my French M.A. program actually reflect a range: I wrote several significant assignments in English, but I wrote a majority of exegetical and critical papers in French (and for my Spanish elective courses, I wrote in Spanish). I likewise presented my lengthy M.A. thesis in French, a privilege for which I sought an administrative waiver. I had come to understand that, in the eyes of my professors, the language in which I wrote was subordinate, if not incidental, to *what* I wrote. Nonetheless, I actively pursued the goal of becoming a multilingual writer.

Grappling with the language issue is a significant factor in my academic trajectory, as the covert conflict between my goals, on the one hand, and the expectations of the academic community, on the other, resulted in a crucial shift in my thinking. Early on, my aspirations and conscious choices were incongruent with the expectations of my professors. I wanted to write about literature, literary criticism, and language in order to develop and demonstrate my linguistic competence. However, I gradually came to accept (but not embrace) the premise that my writing at the graduate level, for all practical purposes, should be geared toward sharpening my intellectual and critical skills—with the ultimate aim of becoming a published academic author. I aspired to achieving status through publication (in whatever language), but I also hoped to carve an identity as a multilingual, multiliterate professional. To my chagrin, this latter aim was not a high priority in the discipline, it turned out.

Learning the Rules—Without a Rule Book

Irrespective of the language in which I wrote, I struggled tremendously with the writing process itself as I advanced through my literature courses. Whereas struggle is inherent in the planning, drafting, and editing of a piece of writing, I now believe that some of the more frustrating aspects of academic reading and writing could have been mitigated, if not averted, had expectations and processes been overtly revealed. For example, through most of my coursework as a literature student, guidelines for writing were rarely provided. I might have struggled less with selecting topics, formulating novel ideas, and shaping my texts had I been told what to do and how to do it! Generally, the major assignment for survey courses and seminars was to "write a paper." Model assignments were hard to come by, and even by the time the proposal for my M.A. thesis in French was approved, the only sample material available to me was the vast collection of bound M.A. theses in the stacks at the graduate library. These documents were useful to a limited degree in that they gave me an idea of the magnitude and scope of my undertaking. As end products, however, those nicely edited theses didn't help much when it came to initiating or sustaining the research process, judging the quality of sources, reading mindfully, organizing ideas, or crafting an original interpretation of my topic.

I came to understand that apprenticeship would involve building content knowledge and displaying it by writing skillfully. Successful apprenticeship would necessitate (a) figuring out the expectations of "old-timers"—initially, my professors (the experts and gatekeepers)—and (b) discovering effective strategies for satisfying those expectations. For me, it turned out that step (b) was easier than step (a). In my first round of graduate studies, the gatekeepers' expectations were deeply embedded in their practices and in institutional folklore—not revealed explicitly. In the absence of overt instruction, models, and other scaffolding tools, the most formative lessons for me as a novice researcher and writer were provided through implicit means: There simply was no *How To* manual or *Idiot's Guide to Surviving Graduate School*.

Over time and in different conversational spaces (classrooms, faculty offices, the copy room, the corridor outside of our TA cubicles), I noticed certain refrains that gradually coalesced into coherent, operational messages. One such message was that writing in graduate school wasn't just a pedagogical exercise or a private transaction between student and professor: The process was designed to stimulate the professional conversations in which scholars engage through their publications, editorial activities, and conference presentations. I was slow to catch on, but I eventually captured the principle that a chief goal of graduate school apprenticeship was to produce *public* writing that would contribute to a body of knowledge and perhaps even influence the course of a professional conversation (Casanave & Vandrick, 2003; Hyland, 2004).

My experience in a survey course in modern French narrative might illustrate my point. The course required enormous quantities of close reading (one novel per week) and copious amounts of writing. When

I shyly requested directions for writing or a model assignment, I was politely rebuffed. The prevailing expectation was that students at my level should already know these things: The embarrassing truth is that I didn't know *anything*. However, the professor's unusual teaching method of inducing students to penetrate texts deeply provided instructive clues for me and my fellow students. After inviting selected students to read their essays aloud, he would lead highly engaging discussions by eliciting reactions to our peers' essays, gently critiquing our analyses, and prompting us to revisit the novels we had studied. The samples I had sought came in the form of my peers' essays—there were my models! By taking notes on how my classmates had carefully unpacked thematic material and organized their arguments using textual evidence, I deployed strategies for reading increasingly demanding novels with the clear purpose of writing insightfully about them. After I came to understand the instructional method, I began reading each new novel with the knowledge that I would have to write intelligently about it. I therefore took careful marginal notes as I read, crafting prospective writing topics as I went along. I likewise developed a primitive method for organizing my own writing, largely by imitation. Close, careful, and purposeful *reading* had thus become my *modus operandi* as a student writer.

The final assignment, a long exegetical paper on Émile Zola's epic novel, *La Bête Humaine*, signaled a true turning point: I had somehow figured out some basic rules of the academic literacy game. My professor's global comments on my paper offered constructive criticism, yet they gave me a sense of my new legitimacy as a reader and writer:

> The paper's strength and weakness arise from its ambitious scope. While you try to treat the subject exhaustively, you haven't quite found a way to integrate all of the components into a genuinely linear essay . . . On the positive side, you certainly do an extremely conscientious job of reading and writing, and your sense of fine (as opposed to gross) organization is excellent. You write clearly and with a certain amount of color, and you marshal your material coherently and persuasively. (Your work this quarter has shown great progress, and I very much appreciate your generous contribution to class discussion.)

I selected this excerpt for two related reasons. First, the comment accurately assessed my paper and my intractable tendency to overreach. The remarks about my paper's "ambitious scope" and my effort to treat the topic "exhaustively" is startlingly prescient: Reviewers of my current work would probably attest that I have yet to overcome this inclination. In fact, a discerning editor of this volume made remarkably similar comments on my initial description of this chapter. My professor had recognized in my work habits a penchant for misreading expectations and overstepping boundaries. Second, the lessons woven through my professor's commentary could only have been learned *post hoc*—after my having tried (and initially failed) to appropriate the critical genres of the field. Even if I had been able to study sample papers and experiment with analytic writing strategies, I might not have stretched my reading and composing strategies as much as I had to without concrete tools. My professor's novel method created a sort of rhetorical zone of proximal development, a space in which I discovered and selected new tools for reading and interpreting literature with a degree of autonomy.

Evolving toward Professionalism

That I can still take my French professor's incisive appraisal to heart some 20 years after the fact speaks to the lasting value of "lessons" embedded in dialogue, modeling, expert commentary, and mentoring in graduate school. Some such lessons may seem incidental, although their impact can be truly lasting. I took several other courses with this professor, who also supervised my M.A. thesis, contributing significantly to my growth as a student and future professional. On a seminar paper leading to my thesis proposal, he noted that I had written "a chapter for a book of literary history," suggesting that I wouldn't even "have to bother studying" for my general exams. These encouraging words primed me for the short term as a prospective doctoral student and for the long term as an academic, while subtly reminding me to avoid the pitfall of letting the scope of writing tasks get out of control.

From Intermediate Stages to Launch: Gearing Up as a Pre-Professional

There is no question that such summative and formative feedback served as a crucial mentoring device in my apprenticeship. I don't recall needing much direct "supervision" in the process of completing my first M.A. or during subsequent years as a doctoral student. Nonetheless, as I leaf through my stack of manila folders, I realize that I have cumulatively internalized the incisive comments of numerous professors and applied lessons learned from them. Instructive and constructive commentary, for example, certainly made its mark over time, and my appreciation of lessons learned became more evident when I shifted disciplinary directions, having decided against pursuing a doctorate in Romance literature in favor of entering a Ph.D. program in applied linguistics.

Maturing Expectations

Although it prolonged my education and delayed my entry into the job market, completing my first M.A. was an invaluable preliminary that shaped my expectations about the rigors of my next four years as a doctoral student. By this time, I had few doubts about how graduate school would test me. Even before applying for admission, I knew the requirements: several years of course work in a new discipline, primary research, written and oral exams, a dissertation, a defense, conference presentations, publications, a job search, and so forth. Thanks to my very recent, prior experience in the graduate school game, I had developed a holistic concept of the "how" of graduate school, although I knew that some of my existing strategies would have to be adjusted or replaced by new ones.

A vital expectation that I couldn't have articulated at the time was that, in my new program and discipline, I might not get much more explicit guidance than I had been provided in my previous program. That is, I fully anticipated that I would need to *look for lessons* about how to succeed, rather than assuming that my professors, advisers, or peers would deliver them systematically. Consequently, I actively sought answers to important questions early on, largely motivated by a determination to finish my studies on time and launch my career. Here is a list of operational questions that effectively enabled me to manage as a newcomer to applied linguistics, to a different university, and to an unfamiliar socioeducational setting:

■ How do I excel in my courses?

■ How do I select a dissertation topic, adviser, and committee?

■ How do I pass my qualifying exams and get my dissertation proposal approved?

- How do I write a dissertation?
- How do I get my work published?
- How do I get a job?

Informed by these pragmatic questions (all of which are linked directly or indirectly to reading and writing), I sought lessons in encounters with faculty members, fellow students, professionals outside my program, and the field's text sources. Rather than working through a list of simple answers or helpful hints, I will explore themes around which my "how" questions revolve, in the hope that readers might draw insights relevant to their own professional aims and educational challenges.

Mediated Social Action

Reflecting on the setbacks and moments of growth during my training as a student has led me to conclude that little of my learning in graduate school can be attributed to working in isolation. The knowledge and skills that comprise academic and professional literacy emerge from mediated social action, as well as the interpersonal alliances that develop from mediated activities. By mediated social action, I mean human interaction among "social actors *as they are acting* . . . in the social world" (Scollon, 2001, p. 3). This process naturally occurs "within a dialogical chain of social actions as well as within a hierarchy of simultaneously occurring practices" (Scollon, p. 5). The realization that I needed to orient my writing for a professional readership constituted a significant internal paradigm shift for me. This new orientation led me to view each writing task as an opportunity to produce a text that would be good enough to satisfy a discipline-specific readership and to add a link to the "dialogical chain." At the start of every semester, I would select topics for my research projects carefully, envisioning each paper as a potential publication.

Presumptuous as my strategy may seem, I undertook every course paper with the aim of turning it into a publishable article. Typically, generating work that might ultimately be submitted for publication was my top priority, while earning an "A" for the course was, in fact, a secondary objective. Fairly early in my doctoral program, a couple of my professors explicitly urged me to gear *all* of my work toward publication—and not to wait until I was finished with graduate school. The following end comment on a seminar paper reflects one such professor's effort to steer me toward refining my work to make it suitable for a broader, professionally discriminating audience:

> A nice study with a reasonable discussion . . . If you are interested in publication, I would try to reduce this to a research note or short article. You may want to submit it together with [your] first language study, two short papers to the same journal to be published back to back.

A classmate was surprised and intimidated when she read this comment, as she apparently thought of herself and her classmates as novices not yet ready to expose their writing to the scrutiny and criticism of journal editors and anonymous reviewers. I wasn't surprised, though, and I was grateful (at last) to get some concrete advice about how to reshape and craft my work for purposes beyond my graduate courses. In offering such commentary, my professor did exactly what Lee and Norton (2003) suggested faculty mentors should do, namely, "encourage students to think of themselves as members of larger scholarly communities" (p. 21). As a first-year doctoral student, I looked beyond the short-term challenges of course work and qualifying exams to the demands of the job market: I knew that having publications to my credit before graduation would be not only desirable but perhaps required in order to be competitive.

I now see that the approach I took to my own apprenticeship as a future applied linguist would result from immersion and participation in the activities and practices of the disciplinary community. Guidance similar to that provided in the feedback excerpt above led me to a crucial realization, eloquently summarized by Hyland:

> [A]cademics work within communities in a particular time and place, and . . . the intellectual climate in which they live and work determines the problems they investigate, the methods they employ, the results they see, and the ways in which they write them up. (p. 6)

My professor's end note critiqued my research study and, significantly, endeavored to bridge the gap between the protected environment of graduate school and the wider community of practice that graduate school is supposed to simulate. Research and writing activities in graduate school create a developmental, proximal space in which experts guide novices in constructing their professional identities through interaction that is centered on writing for a broader audience and purpose. My experience with this professor and others helped me learn that "[s]uccessful academic writing depends on the individual writer's projection of a shared professional context" (Hyland, p. 1).

Purposeful Reading and Writing

To survive graduate school and define a publication agenda for the early stages of my career, I cultivated certain work habits, such as viewing every assignment as a prospective publication. A corollary operational principle involved maximizing the work leading to the completion of a project (e.g., a conference presentation, an article, a chapter, a book) so that the preliminary research and legwork would serve multiple purposes. In all of my required and self-selected reading, I discovered the benefits of reading and recording information systematically, with more than one aim in mind. While composing a literature review for an empirical study, for example, I learned to take notes, write summaries, and build electronic databases that I could later use for related projects. I have continued to apply a similar strategy in my current professional work: Although my reading is no longer as broadly based as it was during my graduate school days, I seldom prepare a conference paper or workshop without simultaneously laying the groundwork for a more polished piece of writing, such as a refereed article or book chapter.

Textual Infusion

A related strategy that enabled me to maximize my reading, research, and writing efforts entailed a process that I call textual infusion. A phenomenon that I noticed as a language and literature student was how texts discernibly influenced my reading habits and even my writing style. I assigned a label to this subtle yet significant process of infusion when I first read the work of Frank Smith in doctoral courses on literacy and language acquisition. Particularly striking to me as a struggling student trying to cultivate a professional writing voice was the concept of "reading like a writer," which Smith (1988) based on the simple (though not uncontroversial) premise that "it [can] only be through reading that writers learn all the intangibles they know" (p. 17). Much of my development as a novice writer has resulted from reading—and writing about—the work of other writers, most far more accomplished than I can hope to be. "Everyone who becomes a competent writer," wrote Smith (1988), "must read like a writer in order to learn how to write like a writer" (p. 23).

I was (and am) no exception to Smith's dictum, which points to the tremendous value of viewing texts both as sources of disciplinary knowledge and as models to use in recognizing, analyzing, reproducing, and selectively reshaping textual conventions. In her dialogue with Bonny Norton, Ena Lee noted that "most of the time when I read articles or books, I don't think about the processes the authors went through to get to this point in their writing and publishing careers" (Lee & Norton, p. 18). Unlike Ena, I thought a great deal about the reading, reasoning, and writing processes of the writers whose work I read. In fact, I became so hyper-aware of textual features that the medium at times got in the way of the message. All things considered, however, I can affirm that my excessive sensitivity has produced more positive than negative effects. I still read mindfully by looking for global and local features that seem to recur across texts, often with the aim of expanding my repertoire of academic genres. When I consider a writing project involving an unfamiliar area of expertise or a novel style of reporting, I systematically explore the texts that typify the new domain. As I discovered in graduate school, representative samples of professional products and conduct (e.g., acceptable forms of writing, speech, and social interaction) may be more readily available and perhaps even more useful than traditional forms of explicit teaching, if explicit teaching actually happens at all.

Conclusion

Like many eager students, I had expected my doctoral studies to teach me how to be a scholar, researcher, teacher, and institutional citizen: Graduate school certainly did teach me those things, though not always through traditional, overt delivery methods. I am grateful to have been apprenticed as I was, having learned what it means to work as an applied linguist through mediated action (which consistently took the form of expert feedback on my work), purposeful reading and writing, and the symbiotic process of textual infusion. What graduate school did not do was teach me how to read or write through the explicit means that I had anticipated. Since I began teaching graduate courses myself, I have consistently endeavored to demystify the means and processes of developing professional literacy by acquainting students with strategies for effective reading and writing, clearly outlining criteria for written work, and providing benchmark samples—always with the expectation that students will likely learn more through imitation, exploration, and experimentation than through any *a priori* "lessons" that I might provide. I hope that the retelling of pivotal episodes in my development as a professional and my reflections on these turning points and paradigm shifts will encourage future students to *look for lessons* in their own graduate school apprenticeships. As I have endeavored to demonstrate, some of the most meaningful lessons may be learned not in the classroom but in the student's many interactions with texts, experts, and fellow novices.

JOHN HEDGCOCK, MONTEREY INSTITUTE OF INTERNATIONAL STUDIES

Beginning my M.A. studies in French, I didn't know where graduate school would lead or that success would depend on satisfying unspoken criteria. Embarking on a Ph.D. program in Applied Linguistics, I pragmatically determined what to read, how to read, and how to write. I realized that my apprenticeship would require me to learn lessons about research, writing, and teaching by engaging proactively with faculty, peers, and the wider profession. As a professor in a graduate program, I now share the lessons that I learned with my students to help them discern the sometimes hidden rewards of an academic career.

REFERENCES

Casanave, C. P., & Vandrick, S. (2003). Introduction: Issues in writing for publication. In C. P. Casanave & S. Vandrick (Eds.), *Writing for scholarly publication: Behind the scenes in language education* (pp. 1–13). Mahwah, NJ: Lawrence Erlbaum.

Clark, I. L. (with Bamberg, B., Bowden, D., Edlund, J. R., Gerrard, L., Klein, S., Neff Lippman, J., & Williams, J. D.). (2003). *Concepts in composition: Theory and practice in the teaching of writing.* Mahwah, NJ: Lawrence Erlbaum.

Csikszentmihalyi, M. (1997). *Finding flow: The psychology of engagement with everyday life.* New York: Basic Books.

Elbow, P. (1973). *Writing without teachers.* New York: Oxford University Press.

———. (1981). *Writing with power: Techniques for mastering the writing process.* New York: Oxford University Press.

Hyland, K. (2004). *Disciplinary discourses: Social interactions in academic writing.* Ann Arbor: University of Michigan Press.

Lave, J., & Wenger, E. (1991). *Situated learning: Legitimate peripheral participation.* Cambridge, UK: Cambridge University Press.

Lee, E., & Norton, B. (2003). Demystifying publishing: A collaborative exchange between graduate student and supervisor. In C. P. Casanave & S. Vandrick (Eds.), *Writing for scholarly publication: Behind the scenes in language education* (pp. 17–38). Mahwah, NJ: Lawrence Erlbaum.

Scollon, R. (2001). *Mediated discourse: The nexus of practice.* London: Routledge.

Smith, F. (1984). *Reading like a writer.* Victoria, BC: Abel Press.

————. (1988). *Joining the literacy club: Further essays into education.* Portsmouth, NH: Heinemann.

Chapter 3

Learning to Write a Thesis with an Argumentative Edge

XIAOMING LI

In front of me is the master's thesis I wrote almost two decades ago. It is a relic excavated from my last academic life.

It was written, in Chinese, to meet part of the graduation requirements for the master's degree in Modern English at the East China Normal University. Titled "English Rhythm and Sentence Stress," it purports to "understand the features of English rhythm and sentence stress, the relationship between the two, and the approaches to master them." I selected the topic because I found most Chinese teachers of English at that time were preoccupied with the clear pronunciation of each individual sound, paying little attention to sentence stress and rhythm, which, I believe, are just as essential to effective and intelligible spoken communication. The paper references ten publications on English phonetics, among them, Halliday's *A Course in Spoken English,* Daniel Jones' *An Outline of English Phonetics,* and Gillian Brown's *Practical Phonetics and Phonology* and others, all that I could find in the university library at that time. In the paper, I borrowed extensively the terminology, theory, explanation, and even a good number of examples from those works. Of the entire 36 hand-written pages, the only part that bears my personal stamp is the final recommendation for ways to teach English rhythm and stress patterns to Chinese students. Even there, my suggestions are shielded from controversy: Teach word pronunciation before teaching rhythm and sentence stress; tap the blackboard to maintain a steady rhythm as students read, etc. Although called a thesis, it actually does not have an argumentative thesis statement. I imagined myself as a conduit of knowledge, through which the wisdom of the experts was passed to the Chinese teachers. Why would a conduit argue with its sources?

My agency in the process was akin to that of editor and translator as the thesis simply synthesized the existing knowledge and repackaged it for a Chinese audience. The master's thesis, after all, was part of the rite of passage for a graduate student, a platform on which I should demonstrate to my professors that I had acquired the necessary knowledge. I was not expected to argue for a particular point of view or to evaluate the sources—it would be presumptuous for me, a graduate student, to think that I had the authority or sufficient knowledge to do that. Neither did I acknowledge any diverse views or unresolved issues—it simply never occurred to me that experts would espouse different views and, thus, I did not notice any. Ironically, my inability to evaluate the sources led me to present all that I reported as universally accepted and with a tone of finality and certainty that left little room for further exploration or questioning.

The professors approved my thesis, and, with a master's degree in Modern English, I graduated from the program in two years and started teaching at the same university. The paper was later published in two installments in an educational journal for English teachers in Chinese high schools. It served more than one useful purpose in that particular context at that particular time.

A Chinese *Zhishifenzi* Aligning Herself with a New Intellectual Tradition

Fan Shen (1998), in his widely cited article, claims that, in order to write an English paper, a Chinese writer has to "create an English self and be *that* self (italics original)" (p. 126). I believed Shen was referring to the ethos that the writer creates in the writing, not to the self in its ontological sense, for one could not manufacture a new self as demanded by the occasion. However, a doctoral dissertation, a few publications, and two decades later, I have come to read Fan Shen's claim differently: Writing a thesis with an argumentative edge, I now believe, requires an identity different from the self-effacing, conduit-like subjectivity I assumed when writing my master's thesis in Chinese.[1]

---

[1] The distinctions between the concepts of ethos, self, identity, and subjectivity, though they deserve careful deliberation, are beyond the scope of this chapter. In her book, Roz Ivanič (1998) defines a host of terms employed in the discussions of identity. I use the term *identity* as she defines it, which is to denote one's alignment with certain social groups, ideologies, discourse communities, professional practices, and others. Such alignment can be permanent or temporary, but always of one's conscious choosing. Gee (1999, p. 7) uses the term in a similar fashion.

Somewhere along the way, I learned that an English academic paper is characterized by an argumentative edge. Yet, unlike the fiery speeches of the politicians, the research paper, which is the chief genre of the academic paper, is not necessarily polemical. Objective and non-confrontational in tone, it uses new evidence or new theory to problematize, complicate, extend, reinterpret, or, in times of paradigm shift, challenge or even reject the existing knowledge wholesale. The thesis, in other words, can be, and often is, a modest refinement of the existing knowledge, but it is never a mere reiteration of the accepted. It stakes out the new territory the project ventures into, hence the edge—edging into the risky world of the unclaimed.

Alignment with such a convention requires a stance or attitude that is anything but natural for a graduate student. It is a way of writing that can be learned, but the learning curve can be steep for those of us from non-Western educational backgrounds. In the following pages, I will reflect on my writing the doctoral dissertation at an American university and ponder the identity change it entailed.

Language can tell much about a tradition. In Chinese, the word *intellectual* is translated to *zhishifenzi*, which means, literally, "knowledge members," i.e., people who are separated from the rest of the populace by their command of specialized knowledge. That does not mean that Chinese *zhishifenzis* do not have critical discernment or Western intellectuals do not possess knowledge. The difference is only in emphasis.[2] That difference in emphasis, however, results in distinctly different writing experiences for graduate students apprenticing for the profession.

The ancient Greco-Roman rhetoric, one of the wellsprings of the Western intellectual tradition, calls this process of interrogation and analysis "dialectic." James Berlin (1994) describes dialectic as "the interaction of two interlocutors of good will intent on arriving at knowledge" (p. 15), "a process involving the interaction of opposing elements" (p. 17). It is an open-ended process, in which competing views are being proposed, scrutinized, and debated, endlessly. Ghassan Hage (2003), a Lebanese Australian professor of sociology, who, probably because of his non-Western background, has a keen sense of the uniqueness of this brand of intellectual tradition, describes such inquiry as so open-ended that its

---

[2] Geisler (1994, p. 4) reports that most Americans assume that "the literacy practices of the academic are based on a mix of three kinds of skill: an advanced facility with words, a strong sense of logic, and deep understanding of a specialized domain of knowledge." According to that model, she expounds, one major activity of academics is to put facts together "to construct an argument according to the general canons of logic."

participants should never claim certainty or finality: "Critical intellectuals do not know what certainty is. They judge each other according to how thoroughly, ethically, and interestingly they can keep questioning everything" (p. 105). The sense that truth is always in the making, not made, is crucial to the understanding of the academic discursive conventions in the West. It is based on a world view antithetical to any religious or secular dogma that claims to possess indisputable and unalterable truth. Subjecting all claims to the examination of dialectic is what gives rigor and meaning to the Western academic discourse. Such intellectual process values what Keats called "negative capability," the capacity to remain in doubt (quoted by Berthoff, 1990, p. 33). Seen in this light, no academic paper is worth writing or reading if it does not advance a proposition that has an argumentative edge.

However, for a graduate student to doubt and, further, critique existing disciplinary knowledge is anything but natural, given the lopsided power relation she has with her readers. Roz Ivanič distinguishes two types of writing at the "opposite ends" of the continuum of the power relation between the writer and reader (p. 297). On the one end is "an essay for assessment (italics original), in which the role of the writer is to be a student, an apprentice, still on the margins of community membership." On the other end is "an article for publication, in which the role of the writer is to be an insider with the 'special right to speak': to contribute to the knowledge-making projects of the community" (p. 297). In China, my writing was in accordance with my status in the community: As an apprentice of the trade, I was expected to produce only essays for assessment, and my master's thesis falls squarely in that tradition. Yet, in North America, a graduate student, although marginal in status, has to write as an insider and produce articles that might be considered publishable.

In her study, Ivanič finds that "those who took on social roles of contributors were more highly rewarded than those who took on the roles of students" (p. 298). Bartholomae (1985/2003) comes to the same conclusion when he discusses a placement essay by a basic writer: "The key distinguishing gesture of this essay, that which makes it 'better' than the other, is the way the writer works against (italics mine) a conventional point of view..." (p. 607). And to take such a "negative" stance, Bartholomae advises that writers "must imagine for themselves the privilege of being 'insiders'—that is, the privilege both of being inside an established and powerful discourse and of being granted a special right to speak" (p. 597). In other words, in order to write a good academic paper in English, the student has to exercise a privilege that she does not possess;

perceive herself as an insider when she is on the periphery; assume that she is participating in a public dialogue and writing for publication, although she is writing for a professor; and adopt the attitude that "I know what I am talking about" when she does not know nearly enough to say anything with true authority. All in all, she has to pretend to be a master when she is, in reality, an apprentice. The contradiction between the required self-perception versus her actual status is mind-bending, if not maddening. It is a mind game that requires a good dose of willed make-believe to pull off. Bartholomae (1985), with no tongue in cheek intended, urges students, basic writers no less, to dare to "carry off the bluff" (p. 590)!

In their longitudinal study of more than 400 students of the Harvard Class of 2001 through their college careers, Nancy Sommers and Laura Saltz (2004) describe such contradiction as the "novice-as-expert" paradox (p. 133), which, they suggest, explains the prevalence of the "descriptive thesis" among the students. The "descriptive thesis," unlike an argumentative thesis, merely names or reports on phenomena rather than articulating claims based on an analysis of the evidence. The reason why the "descriptive thesis" is the default *modus operandi* for students writing in the academic setting, the study has found, is that most of the students "have neither the tools to pry open their sources or the familiarity with them to ask 'why' questions instead of 'what' questions" (p. 135).

The Harvard study concludes that learning to write the academic paper calls for not only "dramatic changes on paper," but also "changes within the writers themselves" (Sommers & Saltz, p. 124). Much has been said about the normative or even repressive power of the dominant discourse (Foucault, 1980, p.100). In my case, paradoxically, it was the pressure to *conform* to the traditional discursive conventions in an American graduate school that forced me to come to my own intellectual identity in writing.

Writing as a Western-Educated Intellectual

The doctoral dissertation I produced at the end of seven years of graduate education at the University of New Hampshire (UNH) shows the dramatic changes both in my writing and me. Here are some of the textual features that differ from those in my master's thesis written in China:

1. As a cross-cultural study, my dissertation begins by critically review-ing other cross-cultural studies. I acknowledged the debt I owed to such intellectual predecessors as Alexis de Tocqueville and Shirley Brice Heath, but I also pointed out their limitations and oversights. Words of the authorities were referred to not as the ultimate truth, but as textual evidence that helped me to establish my niche (Swales, 1990, p. 158), or that served dialectical or explanatory purposes.

2. Instead of borrowing from published sources, I collected around 50 teachers' comments on a set of students' papers and interviewed the four teachers who assigned those papers. Then I sorted out the data thematically and then grouped them along the line of the participants' nationality, highlighting the differences between the Chinese writing teachers and their American counterparts to advance the argument that criteria for good writing are not universal, but culturally specific.

3. To make sure that the findings would withstand scrutiny, I deliber-ated carefully on the methodology of the study. As the issue of repre-sentation was hotly debated at the time, I studied various approaches and their theoretical underpinnings. After much reading and thinking, I rejected the traditional realistic model and adopted the multi-vocal ethnographic approach designed by Tobin and his colleagues in their cross-cultural study of pre-school education (1989). Such an approach brings together diverse perspectives into layers of conversations, which generated a multitude of interpretations. The result diffuses, to a good extent, the researcher's interpretive dominance, distributing the power more equitably among the researcher and the researched.

4. When discussing the findings, I owned up to my subjectivity, admit-ting that the ethnographic study, despite its exhaustive "thick descrip-tion," is not objective. My subjectivity nudged out other perspectives not just because my interpretation comes last as final words, but also because the writer has the sole power to edit the raw data. "Selection is power, and decision as to what to include and exclude are inevitably tainted by the researcher's vision of reality" (Li, 1996, p. 6).

The dissertation was later published by SUNY Press under the title "Good Writing" in Cross Cultural Context. The book was written when I was a graduate student and revised when I was untenured. My marginal status left clear marks on the result: I tried to blunt the argumentative edge even though I knew I should not. In the book, instead of confront-ing arguments of individuality, I mentioned only in passing that "it is tempting…to conclude that 'good writing' is just a matter of personal taste" (1996, p. 111). But I found myself enmeshed in the dialectic anyway. Contrastive rhetoric came under criticism soon after my book was published for creating cultural stereotypes. At a conference, a panelist mentioned my book as an example of dichotomizing cultures. I had to defend my thesis publicly and even modify it to some extent (Li, 2005; Li & Casanave, 2005). However, this need to defend myself turned out to be a blessing in disguise. That my thesis was noticed and debated certified me as a legitimate player in the game, a status that usually takes years for a novice to achieve.

What Does It Take to Write a Thesis with an Argumentative Edge?

First and foremost, one has to dare to "stick her neck out." Unlike writing a descriptive thesis, which reiterates what has already been argued and accepted, writing an argumentative thesis means exposing the writer's limitations and biases in public. The questions I chose to pursue, my assessment of the existing knowledge, the significance I assigned to some data instead of others, the subtexts I brought to light, all bore the stamp of me, my presumptions, perspectives, ethics, as well as my cognitive, linguistic, and rhetorical sophistication—or the lack of it. It was scary, and the desire to hide was strong. Yet, I could hedge, qualify, or triangulate, but in the end, to be in the game, I had to stake out a position and then brace myself for the inevitable controversy, should anyone take note of my participation.

However, it takes more than just nerve to write a thesis with an argumentative edge. A few other things, in retrospect, steered me away from writing a "descriptive thesis." First, I did not start with a topic, such as sentence stress and rhythm, but with a question. The question for my dissertation project eventually became part of the book title, What is good writing? It is a question that I had been turning in my head for years when I was teaching writing to undergraduates at UNH and struggling with as I wrote my own papers for various graduate courses. I could not find satisfactory answers as the topic was never brought up in the Teaching Assistant training sessions, as if it were one of those things in life that one could learn only by being around long enough. When my dissertation director, Prof. Tom Newkirk, advised me not to write a grammar handbook, the project I proposed initially, but to take advantage of my bilingualism and bring something new to the table, I jumped at the invitation to explore something I wanted to know (Li, 1999). Since the project sprang from my desire to know, searching for answers, not displaying knowledge, was the main driving force behind the project— although, let's face it, a public act can never not be a performance at the same time. This desire fueled me for the next two years, during which I struggled with dead-end correspondence, trans-continental travels, hours of transcription, sorting and resorting of data, and, at last, the slow and painstaking construction of the book-length report.

Second, I chose a project that capitalized on my education and teaching experience in two cultures, my proficiency with both Chinese and English, and my personal contacts with teachers in both countries. That gave me an edge and a good degree of real authority. Looking back, it was not sheer serendipity that landed me in a cushy spot, as I first thought. Prof. Newkirk forced me out of my comfort zone toward doing what I was uniquely positioned to do. Knowing my own strengths and weaknesses, likes and dislikes, also helped. Since I had been trained in linguistics and literature, I chose to mix interviews with textual analysis. I stayed away from the popular process-oriented protocol analysis and the "scientific" quantitative approach, which I did not think all that scientific but deadly boring. I was not insulated from the pressure to follow the "fad," however. To ensure that my project would pass muster, I included a small-scale quantitative study, which ended up only weakening the result. One reviewer of my manuscript described it as "a weak quantitative attempt in a strong qualitative study."

Third, read, and read as a peer. Peter Elbow (1985/2003) describes writing as "an act of finding and acknowledging one's place in an ongoing intellectual conversation with a much larger and longer history..." (p. 495). To find that place, he points out, one has to read—and read a lot. When reading, he urges, we should treat the texts as written by "fellow writers—as fully eligible members of the conversation, not treat them as sacred" (p. 491). No one told me that in my first academic life. I always regarded the printed words of the specialists as ultimate truth and tried to absorb all. Flower (1999) pairs reading for "knowledge-getting" with writing as "knowledge telling" (p. 252). In both cases one's subjectivity is being suppressed: An individual functions like a dock where vessels of knowledge would anchor and, then, leave. A dock, I was, but I wanted the vessels to leave the goods behind before they sailed for another destination.

To formulate a thesis with an argumentative edge presupposes a different relationship with printed words than I had been familiar with at the time I wrote my master's thesis. I started to put question marks, exclamation marks, or simply check marks in the margins to keep track of my reaction to the ideas on the page. Indicative marks grew into fragmentary and elliptical remarks scribbled in the margins to link the "nodes" of the author with those of my subjective world.[3] Soon margins were not wide enough for my reaction, and I had to use post-its, and eventually a ubiquitous notebook would lie around whenever I read. Writing continues those conversations that started from the reading notes. I have become a peer conversing with equals, not a loading and unloading dock in the transportation of knowledge.

An Evolving Self, an Evolving Community—I Hope

I have actively apprenticed and practiced the Western academic conventions for the past two decades, and I have certainly changed in the process. Although my friends have always known me as an assertive, or, some would say, stubborn and opinionated person, I rarely displayed the same attitude in writing. Yet, the change did not simply align my public self with the private. The new public self is textually mediated; committing myself in printed texts, the new self is more deliberative, reflective, open-minded, and open-ended, willing to take a controversial stand and to read and to listen to opposing views. This new way of writing and being is not entirely different from the old, private self; it is an expanded self.

As luck would have it, I have, in the last few years, moved to a more visible perch, speaking regularly at various academic forums and published on a range of topics. The competence to write academic papers, like an ID card, has granted me entrance to a community that I always wanted to be part of (Wenger, 1998, p. 153), yet I am far from feeling at home. In fact, the feeling of alienation has often stopped me cold in my tracks. I had a dry spell of two years after the publication of my dissertation partly because I did not like the feeling of being an imposter "carrying off the bluff." I wanted to read what I should

---

[3] According to Flower (1999), "The links between a group of nodes might reflect causality, or subordination, or simple association, or a strong emotional connection" (p. 243).

know to become an insider so as to write as an insider. To my dismay, however, I found that for a non-native speaker of English who reads and writes in English slowly, there were simply not enough hours in a day to keep up with all the new publications, while teaching a full load and parenting a teenager at the same time. Worse still, often, after I have spent days hatcheting my way through prose as thick as brush and dry as sawdust, I found familiar clichés wrapped in new jargon. Although tenured now, I continue to perceive myself a peripheral participant as my participation has been punctuated by non-participation or selective participation. I am comfortable with my partial membership, but I wish the game could be different and I could participate fully. I wish graduate students could have more time to learn the existing knowledge before being obligated to contribute their own. I wish faculty could be judged more on teaching than publication; I wish writing in the discipline were not driven by tenure or promotion anxiety, as it often is now, but by genuine intellectual curiosity and the spirit of exploration. Further, I wish that the relentless negativity and the pursuit of the next "cutting edge" could be balanced with affirmation and respect for the traditional values and practices that have served us well.

Despite my misgivings, I have to say I am drawn to the game. I like to read and be read, and feel more alive when thinking and writing, and yes, even arguing and debating. Writing has freed me from the small cocoon of here and now, letting me participate in a stimulating conversation and putting me in touch with my still-evolving intellectual self. That self is what it takes to write a thesis with an argumentative edge.

XIAOMING LI, LONG ISLAND UNIVERSITY, BROOKLYN CAMPUS

My beeline education to the top, expected by two largely self-educated Chinese parents, was interrupted and re-oriented by two events: first, the Cultural Revolution, which closed all schools, forcing all youngsters to receive "re-education." I worked on a state farm for five years and then entered university as a worker-peasant-soldier student to "reform the super-structure dominated by the bourgeois intellectuals"; second, years later as I was teaching at a university after finishing a master's degree, receiving a scholarship from the World Bank for one-year study in America. When the scholarship ended, I stayed and went on to earn a Ph.D. in Composition and Literature. I now teach English to urban immigrants in New York.

REFERENCES

Bartholomae, D. (1985/2003). Inventing the university. In V. Villanueva, Jr. (Ed.), *Cross-talk in comp theory: A reader* (pp. 589–620). Urbana, IL: National Council of Teachers of English.

Berlin, J. (1994). Contemporary composition: The major pedagogical theories. In G. Tate, E. Corbett, & N. Myers (Eds.), *The writing teacher's sourcebook* (3rd ed.) (pp. 9–21). New York: Oxford University Press.

Berthoff, A. E. (1990). *The sense of learning.* Portsmouth, NH: Boynton/Cook.

Elbow, P. (1985/2003). Being a writer vs. being an academic: A conflict in goals. In V. Villanueva, Jr. (Ed.), *Cross-talk in comp theory: A reader* (pp. 589–620). Urbana, IL: National Council of Teachers of English.

Flower, L. (1999). Rhetorical reading strategies and the construction of meaning. In L. Ede (Ed.), *On writing research: The Braddock essays* (pp. 242–259). Boston: Bedford/St. Martin's Press.

Foucault, M. (1980). *Power/knowledge: Selected interviews and other writings 1972–1977.* New York: Pantheon Books.

Gee, J. P. (1999). *An introduction to discourse analysis.* London: Routledge.

Geisler, C. (1994). *Academic literacy and the nature of expertise: Reading, writing and knowing in academic philosophy.* Hillsdale, NJ: Lawrence Erlbaum.

Hage, G. (2003). *Against paranoid nationalism: Searching for hope in a shrinking society.* London: Merlin Press.

Ivanič, R. (1998). *Writing and identity: The discoursal construction of identity in academic writing.* Amsterdam/Philadelphia: John Benjamins.

Li, X. M. (1996). *"Good writing" in cross-cultural context.* Albany: State University of New York Press.

———. (1999). Writing from the vantage point of an outsider/insider. In G. Braine (Ed.), *Non-native educators in English language teaching* (pp. 43–56). Mahwah, NJ: Lawrence Erlbaum.

———. (2005). Composing culture in a fragmented world: The issue of representation in cross-cultural research. In P. K. Matsuda & T. Silva (Eds.), *Second language writing research: Perspectives on the process of knowledge construction* (pp. 121–131). Mahwah, NJ: Lawrence Erlbaum.

Li, X. M., & C. P. Casanave (2005). Introduction: Multiple perspectives on L1 and L2 academic literacy in Asia Pacific and diaspora contexts. In X. M. Li & C. P. Casanave (Eds.), *Special issue on multiple perspectives on L1 and L2 academic literacy in Asian Pacific and diaspora contexts. Journal of Asian Pacific Communication, 15*(1), 7–13.

Shen, F. (1998) The classroom and the wider culture: Identity as a key to learning English composition. In V. Zamel & R. Spack (Eds.), *Negotiating academic literacies* (pp. 123–134). Mahwah, NJ: Lawrence Erlbaum.

Sommers, N., & Saltz, L. (2004). The novice as expert: Writing in the freshman year. *College Communication and Composition, 56*(1), 124–149.

Swales, J. M. (1990). *Genre analysis: English in academic and research settings.* Cambridge, UK: Cambridge University Press.

Tobin, J., Wu, D., & Davidson, D. (1989). *Preschool in three cultures.* New Haven, CT: Yale University Press.

Wenger, E. (1998). *Communities of practice: Learning, meaning, and identity.* Cambridge, UK: Cambridge University Press.

Chapter 4

Dissertation Writing and the (Re)Positioning of Self in a "Community of Practice"

MAYUMI FUJIOKA

It was late November. I was sitting at one of the tables at the second floor atrium at the school of education building. My eyes were following people passing by in the hallway, but I was not really watching them. I didn't know how many minutes (or hours?) I had passed sitting there. When I realized, I saw someone sitting beside me; it was one of my classmates, a woman from Taiwan. She did not say anything to me but started resting her chin in her palm with her elbow on the table. She also made a serious expression and sighed deeply. I immediately knew that she was imitating me. She made me realize how funny I was looking to other people. Yes, I knew I was looking very funny, but I didn't care about that. The only thing I cared about at the moment was my dissertation. Before I came to this table, I was in Dr. Anderson's office, talking about my proposal. When I got out of her office, I was devastated by how our meeting went; I was totally at a loss, being unable to figure out how I should work on my dissertation from now on.

A week later, I was walking toward the main library on campus, feeling the cold winter wind on my cheeks. When I was waiting for the traffic light to change just in front of the library, something flashed in my head. I stood there for a few minutes, thinking about what had just come up in my head. The next moment, I turned around and started walking to one of the buildings on campus. I was saying the following words in mind, "OK, this is going to be my new dissertation topic. I have to talk about this to Dr. Brown."

Introduction

The scenes described above are the moments when I decided to change my dissertation topic and advisor in a U.S. graduate school. Those moments still come back to me as a flashback even though ten years have passed since then. Now I am an associate professor at a university in Japan, dealing with various responsibilities I have, teaching, doing research, and being engaged in committee work. During my daily life, I occasionally remember the days when I was a graduate student in the U.S. Looking back on my academic acculturation process as a graduate student, I see it was "participatory practice" (Casanave, in this volume); I gained a membership in various academic communities of practice in which I constructed my identity and shifted from the position of a novice to a beginning academic professional through interactions with the other members of the communities in relation to specific academic literacy activities.

A process of writing a doctoral dissertation is indeed participatory practice. Besides producing the text itself, students as writers need to be engaged in various academic communities of practice: the research paradigm, disciplines and subdisicplines in relation to their chosen topics, and their dissertation committees, to name a few. Regarding students' engagement in dissertation writing and its preparation practices, a growing body of research focuses on a wide range of aspects including advisor-advisee relationships (Belcher, 1994), dealing with the research paradigm (Belcher & Hirvela, 2005), and the advisor's responses and the student's revisions (Prior, 1994). However, few studies document students' decisions to select their advisors and committee members, let alone their decisions to dissolve the existing committee and form a new one.

Change of dissertation topic and advisor/committee members does happen. More than that, taking a close look at what actually happens in the change process tells us a lot about the intricacies of students' participatory practices in the academy. Thus, in this chapter, I would like to share with readers my own experience of changing my dissertation topic and committee members, in the hope that it will help students who are preparing for their dissertations in their decision-making on the topic and committee selection. I will narrate my experience by focusing on three themes: topic development, committee selection, and changing the topic and committee members. I will then discuss what my experience means in terms of students' participatory practice in academe, drawing on the framework of the "Communities of Practice" (Lave & Wenger, 1991; Wenger, 1998).

Topic Development

During Doctoral Course Work

I studied at a large midwestern state university in the U.S. After receiving a master's degree in TESOL and applied linguistics, I switched to the school of education for my Ph.D., majoring in foreign language education. I felt the same way to a certain degree as Casanave (in this volume) felt toward the course work in the school of education, feeling isolated in relevant social science discipline courses including anthropology and psychology. However, I always had someone to talk to from the same major in taking courses outside my major, and in fact I enjoyed connecting viewpoints and perspectives from relevant social science disciplines to my major. Another major influence on me during my Ph.D. course work came from inquiry courses. For inquiry training, both quantitative and qualitative research methodology courses were required.[1]

These inquiry courses offered me very different experiences of encounters with the research paradigms. Since many of us in the statistics course, both U.S. and international students, had concerns about understanding statistical concepts and doing well on the quizzes and exams, we formed study groups, met frequently outside the class, and studied together. We felt we were learning together and were helping each other. This helped me alleviate my initial concerns about dealing with statistics, and as a result I was able to do well in the course. During the course, I actually enjoyed the processes in which such concepts and terms as *the alpha-level, significant differences,* T-test, and ANOVA, began to make sense, though they were simply mysterious words and symbols for me before.

In contrast, in the qualitative inquiry course, I think I was lost. At first, I was really confused as to why those pieces of writing that we had to read,

---

[1] For language education majors back then, taking three inquiry courses, at least one from each research paradigm, was a minimum requirement. I fulfilled the requirement by taking beginning and intermediate statistics courses and an introductory qualitative research course. Regarding the two statistics courses, here I report on the intermediate-level course, which was the core course for quantitative inquiry training.

including someone's diaries, and narratives, would constitute research. Such concepts as personal experience, feelings, and stories seemed to contradict the criterion of "objectivity," the concept of research that I had learned during my undergraduate and master's training. In addition, the style of writing in qualitative research was confusing to me; I thought that clear-cut structures such as introduction, method, results, and discussion in the quantitative research were a lot easier for readers. Qualitative research struck me as a "fuzzy genre" (Belcher & Hirvela), at least on my first encounter with it. Moreover, in the inquiry course I took, I felt we were so isolated; besides discussing the required readings, we were mainly engaged in our own research projects and had few chances to talk about our projects outside the class. This contrasted sharply with my experience in the statistics course, and at the end of taking the inquiry courses, I felt I was much more oriented toward quantitative research.

After completing the required courses, both in my major and inquiry training, I was engaged in a research project under the supervision of one professor in my major. The purpose of the project was for doctoral students to conduct an independent study, choosing a topic of their own and using a research methodology based on what they had learned in the inquiry courses; in other words, it was a chance to conduct a preliminary study for a possible dissertation topic and methodology. I chose the topic of English academic writing, investigating non-native English-speaking graduate students' experience with English writing prior to coming to the U.S. and problems they encountered in writing in their U.S. graduate schools. I was interested in the topic of non-native English-speaking students' development of English academic writing skills because I had been always curious about how my own experience was similar to or different from those of other non-native students.

For my project, I chose to use both quantitative and qualitative methodologies. Although I did not feel a strong commitment to qualitative research based on my experience in the inquiry course, the dominant idea in my department, at least at that time, was that a good dissertation study would consist of a combination of quantitative and qualitative methodologies. I collected data through a questionnaire from more than 50 participants in the school of education and conducted an analysis of descriptive statistics for the first stage of the study. Then for the second stage, I conducted interviews with a small number of participants selected from the first stage based on their responses in the questionnaire. I received a good grade and positive comments from the professor who guided me in my project. She was not an expert on writing studies, and her comments mainly focused on my research methodologies and data analysis. Being oriented toward quantitative study, she gave me more comments on the statistical analysis than on the analysis of the interview data. Still, I was satisfied with her comments at that point and thought that I had made a big step toward my dissertation study.

The Dissertation

Based on my experience from my research project, I decided to continue to study academic writing for my dissertation. However, when deciding on a specific topic, I made premature and hasty decisions. Those decisions came from practical reasons, which concerned time and money. By the time I started working on my dissertation, I had finished a three-year position as a Japanese-language teaching assistant at the university where I was studying. Since the position was not extended, I had to rely on my parents financially after the completion of my course work. Out of pressure to alleviate this great burden from my parents, I decided to complete my dissertation under an easily manageable topic and within a relatively short period of time. Thus, at this point, I opted out of doing a solely qualitative dissertation that would have had an extended period of data collection such as field work.

With this practical decision, the topic I developed was analyses of textual features and writing processes of the introductory parts of my fellow Japanese graduate students' term papers in English for their graduate courses. I decided to focus on only introductions because it would be easier and manageable to select only one section of research papers. In addition, based on the background reading for my study, I was fascinated by Swales's (1990) model developed for describing research article introductions, and thus I decided to base my analysis on his model. The following are specific research questions that I posed in my draft of the dissertation proposal:

1. To what extent are Japanese graduate students aware of the text structure of the introductory statement of research papers (the CARS model by Swales) in English?
2. What are discourse and linguistic features of the introductory statement of research papers in English written by Japanese students?

3. What patterns of writing are present in Japanese students' development of introductions for their research papers?

4. Are there any differences between master's and doctoral students in terms of textual features and writing processes of the introductions of their research papers?

Regarding the research methodology, I intended to use a combination of different methods, for example, using an elicitation task for Question 1, collecting the term papers that my participants had already written for their courses for Question 2, and asking the participants to answer questions in a questionnaire for Question 3. With these specific research methods in mind, I thought that I would be able to collect and analyze data within a relatively short period of time.

Committee Selection

When selecting my dissertation committee, I made a practical decision again; I thought about who could serve best in order to help me complete my dissertation as soon as possible. I based my decision on my previous experiences: doctoral courses I had taken with different professors and my experience in the research project. I also utilized information from my fellow doctoral students in the same program as to what they knew about each professor, who was working under which professor, and what their stories were. Among three members on my committee that I needed from my major, I decided on two quickly. One was Dr. Anderson,[2] who orally agreed to be my main advisor (committee chair). She was the one under whom I did my research project on academic writing, and I had taken a course in addition to the research project with her. Although she was not an expert on writing studies, she was familiar with a wide range of topics in language education. In addition, based on my experience working with her, I learned that she was prompt in responses to students' questions over email and she was skilled in guiding students to complete their work within a proposed time frame. This was the most important factor for me to choose her to be my main advisor. The other professor, whose course I had taken once, was not an expert on writing studies, either. However, he was also recognized as being very prompt

---

[2] All the professors' names reported in this chapter are pseudonyms.

in responding to students' questions and helpful in aiding students to complete their dissertations in a timely manner.

After asking Dr. Anderson to be my main advisor, I started working with her on my dissertation proposal. As I proceeded with my proposal, however, I began to feel that my style of working and hers did not match; I felt that I was not getting enough dialogical, face-to-face interactions with her, given that she seemed to prefer a rather hierarchical and impersonal style of communication through email. I thought I knew how I should interact with her based on my prior experience in the research project, but the experience I was going through was different from the previous one. In my research project, I did not have critical questions to ask regarding my study, and I was satisfied whenever I received Dr. Anderson's quick replies to minor questions that I had over email. However, in my dissertation proposal, I encountered critical questions as I read more sources and thought about my research methodology. Although I became eager to talk with Dr. Anderson in face-to-face meetings, she mainly stayed with email conferencing. In addition, I began to feel that she was more eager to make me complete my dissertation as soon as possible than I was; she knew about my financial problems because I had told her about that when I asked her to be my advisor. Although I understood that she was trying to help me, I began to feel that she was almost sending a message that she did not care about the quality of my study as long as I could finish it within the proposed timeline. This made me begin to question her attitude because I thought that I should still maintain a certain level of quality in my study although I knew I was the one who had put a priority on the timeline. At the same time, I started seriously doubting if the topic I was proposing was the topic that I would really like to explore. Even so, I kept writing my proposal as the deadline that Dr. Anderson and I had agreed on was approaching.

Changing the Topic and Committee Members

A month after I started working with Dr. Anderson, I had almost completed a draft of my dissertation proposal. At that point, I had to choose a third member on my dissertation committee, and I decided to ask Dr. Brown. I had taken Dr. Brown's course only once but did not have a lot of interaction with her until that point. The main reason I asked her to be on my committee was that among doctoral students, she was recognized as being the best person to ask for help with a dissertation as she would offer a great deal of assistance whether she was a main advisor or a committee member. The slight concern that I had about Dr. Brown was that she was more oriented toward qualitative research, which was the main reason it took more time for me to decide to ask her to be on my committee compared to the other two professors. I wrote a two-page prospectus based on my dissertation proposal, submitted it to Dr. Brown, and made an appointment with her, being eager to hear from her that my topic was acceptable.

However, the response I received from Dr. Brown was contrary to my expectations. Having read my prospectus, she told me that I should rethink my topic and methodology as well. I still remember the words she said to me at our meeting, "I don't see elements of a good dissertation in your prospectus." First, she pointed out that my focusing on only the introduction of a research paper was too narrow in scope and too limiting. Second, she said I was not being critical enough as I treated Swales's model as something to be followed without considering whether it was right. Third, she found problems with my methodology. She did not think that using an elicitation task or a questionnaire would be an effective way to investigate students' understanding of research paper structures and their writing processes. Instead, she suggested that I look at students' processes of writing papers from reading sources and making outlines to the final submission by interviewing them and collecting multiple drafts with revisions of their papers. When I heard her suggestions, I said in my mind, "That's a qualitative study. It's going to take a lot of time only for data collection. No, I can't afford the time and money," though I did not say that to Dr. Brown. Instead, I just told her that I would rethink my topic and left her office.

On the following day, I went to see Dr. Anderson, reporting to her about what Dr. Brown had told me. In fact, I even do not quite remember the details of the conversation that Dr. Anderson and I had at that meeting. The only thing I remember was that I did not think I received help from her; she either left everything to me, including changing the topic and methodology, or suggested I stay with my proposal if wanted to finish my dissertation within the proposed timeline. Another thing I remember was that I felt devastated when I left Dr. Anderson's office and went to sit at one of the tables in the hallway, the scene described at the beginning of this chapter.

For the following few days, I could not think about anything. I was totally at a loss and even thought that I might have to leave the U.S. without starting my dissertation. I now do not recall if I talked to anyone about the problem I encountered; I probably did not. I knew Dr. Brown was right. I knew the problems she pointed out in my proposal could not be solved unless I totally changed the topic, focus, and the research methodology. While days went by, at one point I realized that I should go back to the beginning in order to get out of this plight and asked myself what I really wanted to study without thinking about time or money. I knew that I had always been interested in how other students' academic writing experiences and specific writing processes were similar to and different from mine. When I started thinking about this topic, I had a lot of thoughts coming up in mind. At the same time, I looked at the paper I wrote for my research project on academic writing again, the reports of the interview data in particular. I included interviews in my project simply because I wanted to add a qualitative research methodology, although I mainly focused on the statistical analysis in the paper when I talked with Dr. Anderson. However, when I looked at the interview data more carefully, I saw that my participants were telling me a lot about their writing problems and writing processes. I was even relating their experiences to my own, which had not happened when I finished writing that paper.

After reading my project paper again, I realized that I actually wanted to see other students' writing processes, not based on the information through questionnaire responses. In order to do that, the most effective way was taking a qualitative approach, following students' writing processes over months by conducting interviews during various stages of their writing processes, and analyzing emerging drafts with revisions and the final submissions. At this point, the reservations I had about qualitative research due to my inquiry course experience did not prevent me from choosing to switch to a qualitative dissertation. I was desperate. I now knew that the best paradigm to pursue my new topic would be qualitative research. I had no other choice. My decision-making coincides with some of the cases of participants writing qualitative dissertations as reported in Belcher and Hirvela in that they chose a qualitative method-ology because their topic required it, although they did not initially find the qualitative paradigm especially appealing or attractive.

The realization for my new topic and the best research paradigm to pursue it became clear and concrete to me at one moment, the second half of the scene described in the beginning of this chapter. I also real-ized that I should work with Dr. Brown if I wanted to pursue the new topic. In fact, Belcher notes that in selecting a mentor, a critical factor may be to find someone "who can inspire enough trust and admiration in students to encourage the risk-taking entailed in challenging and attempting to contribute to the established knowledge of a community" (p. 32). In retrospect, this is probably the point I considered in my decision to work with Dr. Brown instead of Dr. Anderson. I went to talk with Dr. Brown, who was surprised at my quick decision to change the topic but kindly agreed to be my main advisor. At the same time, I was faced with the task of telling Dr. Anderson and the other professor about my topic change and the decision to form a new committee. Although I was fortunate in that I had not officially formed my committee yet by obtaining their signatures, the task of talking to the two professors, Dr. Anderson in particular, was very difficult. I thought that I was in danger of hurting and offending her. Yet, I decided to take the risk mainly because I now knew what I wanted to study and I knew this was going to be MY dissertation, not anyone else's. Fortunately, I received understanding and even encouragement from both professors for my topic change.

For the new topic, I broadened the scope of students' writing processes. I added social and cultural aspects and decided to conduct case studies of both American and Japanese graduate students' writing processes in writing papers for their graduate courses. The social and cultural aspects that were added for investigation included students' understanding of professors' expectations about writing assignments, asking for friends' or tutors' help on revising drafts, and analyses and observations of U.S. academic practices and Japanese students' comparison of them to the academic practices in their own culture. Under this new topic, I wrote a new dissertation proposal, and much to my surprise, it won the best dissertation proposal award in the school of education that year.

My new dissertation process with Dr. Brown went smoothly. She always gave me face-to-face conferencing whenever I had questions about my study or my writing. Since my new topic was a qualitative study, I invited two professors who were both qualitative-oriented researchers to my committee. Based on Dr. Brown's suggestions, I met with all the committee members when I finished one stage and was moving on to another, including writing the literature review, finishing the data collection, and analyzing the data. In addition, I let all the committee members know what comments I received from each member. Thus, everyone knew the progress I was making and the kinds of comments I was receiving from each committee member. My whole dissertation process took almost two years. In the meantime, I managed to solve the financial problems, and eventually I completed my dissertation successfully.

Communities of Practice

My experience shows that I participated in various "Communities of Practice" (CoP), (Lave & Wenger) including classrooms, research paradigms, disciplines and subdisciplines, and dissertation committees. A CoP is defined as a group of people engaged in social practice under a joint enterprise (Wenger). A community is not constrained by physical boundaries nor is social practice limited by physical actions or tangible objects. The concept of practice here includes "tacit conventions," "specific perceptions," "underlying assumptions," and "shared world views" (Wenger, p. 47). In my engagement in various CoPs during my graduate studies, I experienced different kinds and levels of "Legitimate Peripheral Participation" (LPP) (Lave & Wenger), and gradually moved toward fuller participation in a dissertation community where my work was supported. Lave and Wenger's main assertion is that LPP, which refers to a learning process, takes place when novices, or newcomers to a community, move from the periphery toward fuller membership through participation in practices of a community consisting of members of differing levels of expertise. According to Lave and Wenger, "peripherality" is a positive term for viewing newcomers' potential degree of involvement in a community as open and flexible. Reflecting on my experience with my former dissertation advisors, I see a clear connection between my learning processes and the CoP and LPP framework, but would like to point out that a simple conceptualization of this framework does not match the complexities of lived experiences within an educational setting such as graduate school.

A simple interpretation of the CoP and LPP framework, that is, an "apprenticeship-like" process in which novices gain increasing expertise by participating with experts in the practices of a community, may appear to capture the dissertation process nicely. In this view, the dissertation writer as a novice learns to conduct and write a dissertation through the advice and guidance from the committee members, who could be viewed as experts embodying the accepted practices of the academic community. However, a smooth transition of a novice from the periphery to fuller participation in the practices of an educational community, a characterization that has been contested by some authors (e.g., Lea, 2005), did not happen in my case. Belcher points out that one of the critical differences that determine the success of students' dissertation experiences is whether they fit in the research community of practice of their chosen fields—whether there is an intellectual match. In the case of my initial efforts at planning the dissertation, obviously I did not fit in the research community of practice in terms of topic interest and methodology choice. However, the more critical factor that made my experience particularly difficult was the social aspect of the participation in the dissertation CoP on the part of both myself and my former advisors.

In a dissertation CoP, the advisor and the advisee participate in multiple kinds of activities and it is their patterns of participation that shape the CoP. For example, in addition to gaining content knowledge and putting appropriate research methodology in practice, students are engaged in the activity of navigating the dissertation processes with careful planning and effective time-management as well as in the activity of seeking advice and guidance from their advisors. Advisors are also engaged in the activities of fostering students' intellectual development by sharing their expertise, helping them with the navigation of the dissertation process, and responding to the students' questions and needs. In other words, both students and advisors are engaged in intellectual and social participation in their dissertation CoPs.

Intellectual participation in a dissertation CoP can go beyond the boundaries of a particular dissertation committee, where the expert-novice dichotomy may not characterize well the realities of the participants' knowledge of content and practices. In terms of content expertise, students cannot be categorized as total "novices" because they have already acquired a certain degree of expertise when they start their doctoral dissertations, given that they have already done extensive reading in a focused area. It may also be the case that advisors are not necessarily experts on the students' chosen topics, which happened in my case and also in other graduate students' cases that I was familiar with. Moreover, students can increase their content expertise by participating in other CoPs, such as research communities where they interact with other students and professors outside their dissertation committees who share the same academic interest with them and have more knowledge on their chosen topics. As Wenger notes, individuals can be members of multiple CoPs at the same time.

Regarding social participation in a dissertation CoP, it has a direct impact on shaping the community because students and advisors interact with each other within the boundaries of their communities. As reported in Belcher, advisors' mentoring styles seem to affect students' degree of success in their dissertation processes. However, advisor-advisee relationships cannot be treated from the unidirectional viewpoint of the advisors' fixed mentoring styles with their advisees. In order for advisor-advisee interaction to be successful, negotiation of the personal relationship between them may be critical; both students and advisors need to learn to understand the most effective, productive, and comfortable way of interacting. In my case, the difficulty came at the point where my main advisor and I were not moving toward fuller participation together in the dissertation CoP. I became clearer on my need for certain kinds of guidance from my advisor and on the most effective and comfortable interactional style for me with her. However, I did not find that my advisor was moving toward my goal with me. There may be cases where good dissertation studies are produced even though students and advisors stay on the periphery in their participation in their dissertation CoPs, such as students who do not seek much help and guidance from their advisors and advisors who do not respond to students' inquiries and requests for help. However, if we focus on the dissertation process as an instance of a CoP, the degree of mutual social participation between students and advisors in the practices of the CoP can be a crucial factor in determining the success of students' dissertation processes.

Another issue arising from my experience that can be considered a social aspect of participation in a CoP involves power relationships between the advisor and the advisee. Although Lave and Wenger do not fully explore power relationships between novices and experts in their CoP and LPP framework, there are obviously many cases where power imbalances among the members of a CoP influence their patterns of participation in the CoP, and a dissertation CoP is certainly one of them. Although I mentioned earlier that the expert-novice dichotomy may not be so simple in a dissertation CoP, status imbalances between students and the advisors are obvious. Because of status imbalances, I could not request that my former advisor change the style and mode of interaction with me, from impersonal email conferencing to face-to-face dialogical interaction. Furthermore, power imbalances became a problem in my transition from the former dissertation CoP to the new one. The main reason I felt so burdened emotionally about the changes in my topic and committee was that although I was the status inferior, I had decided not to follow through with the personal commitment that was once agreed upon with someone who had more power than I. I thought that this decision would be sufficient reason for the advisors to get offended or upset, thus jeopardizing my personal relationship with them and possibly the progress of my dissertation as well. From the advisors' perspective, however, students' change of committee members may not be so much of a problem; I found that my former committee members understood my decision to change. Nevertheless, dealing with power relationships with advisors is probably difficult for all graduate students, regardless of their cultural background, as I discovered from my experience with the educational practices in the U.S.

Before coming to the U.S., I had had a stereotypical image of Americans as open and assertive and as a result I had visualized American students as not being hesitant to tell professors what they needed to say. However, throughout my graduate studies in the U.S., I learned that graduate students, both American and internationals, felt highly vulnerable to professors, whom they saw as embodying authority in the academy. I observed that American students were also sensitive to power relationships with their professors and that they were as careful as international students in terms of what to say and how to speak to their professors. Thus, I believe that changing advisors in the dissertation process is difficult for all students in great part because of the difficulty of dealing with status imbalances. Although there may be cultural influences on international students' perceptions of what the accepted practices are with their advisors, to me, the difficulty of graduate students changing their advisors seems to be connected with questions of how to handle these status imbalances in their social participation in a dissertation CoP. This challenge affects graduate students from all educational and cultural backgrounds.

Now that I have written about my painful experience of changing my dissertation topic and committee members, I can see that I learned a lot and gained a lot. I now recognize that the greatest gain I received was that I realized what I really wanted to do and found a way to pursue it. I could have stayed with my old dissertation topic and still received a Ph.D. degree, but in that case, I would not have the sense of attachment to my study that I enjoy now. I remember the words that Dr. Brown, my dissertation chair, said to me at my defense, "I can see your excitement about your study through your writing." Even now, every time I go back to my study, I enjoy what I found and what I learned. Moreover, my dissertation gave me a continuing intellectual interest; when I go back to my study, I find more things that I could not fully explore at the time I completed my study. In fact, I have been working on a publication in which I look at parts of my dissertation data and analyze them with a different theoretical framework from the one I used in my dissertation.

I now feel grateful that I have this sense of strong, life-long attachment to my study.

Another important experience from my dissertation process is that I learned to act in my best interest. The important point for me in working with my advisors, the main advisor in particular, turned out to be personal relationships. Those included my sense of trust and admiration for the advisors, but most importantly whether I felt comfortable with the style of interaction between us. I learned that I needed to consider the advisors' personal qualities in interaction with my own. I also learned that I should not be afraid of making changes in order to pursue my best interest. It turned out that I did not experience any disadvantages as a graduate student by changing my dissertation topic and committee members. Although I still think that it would be wise to be cautious and careful when changing committee members, which I believe I was, the gain by changing my topic and committee members was much greater than the potential risk that I had envisioned.

Engaging in a dissertation probably brings the image of only the process of academic accomplishment, that is, students becoming experts on their chosen topics with the help of more experienced advisors and then receiving a diploma, to most people's minds. This scenario fits the simple understanding of the CoP framework. In my case, however, the dissertation process was more complex for a number of reasons, not the least of which was that it gave me the chance for personal and social as well as intellectual growth. Certainly the CoP framework has helped me interpret my experiences during those difficult times, but the simple expert-novice dichotomy of learning to participate in dissertation practices does not sufficiently capture the nuances of my lived experiences.

MAYUMI FUJIOKA, KINKI UNIVERSITY, JAPAN

My old friends from high school and university have often commented that they never envisioned me being so adventurous and courageous to study for a Ph.D. in the U.S. I am also sometimes surprised at the major decision I made in my career development. Despite difficulties, what I gained from my graduate life in the U.S., the sense of accomplishment by pursuing a Ph.D. in particular, has given me power and energy to deal with various difficulties I encountered in my professional life, and I know it will continue to do so in the future.

REFERENCES

Belcher, D. (1994). The apprenticeship approach to advanced academic literacy: Graduate students and their mentors. *English for Specific Purposes, 13*(1), 23–34.

Belcher, D., & Hirvela, A. (2005). Writing the qualitative dissertation: What motivates and sustains commitment to a fuzzy genre? *Journal of English for Academic Purposes, 4,* 187–205.

Lave, J., & Wenger. E. (1991). *Situated learning: Legitimate peripheral participation.* Cambridge, UK: Cambridge University Press.

Lea, M. R. (2005). 'Communities of practice' in higher education: Useful heuristic or educational model? In D. Barton & K. Tusting (Eds.), *Beyond communities of practice: Language, power, and social context* (pp. 180–197). Cambridge, UK: Cambridge University Press.

Prior, P. (1994). Response, revision, disciplinarity: A microhistory of a dissertation prospectus in sociology. *Written Communication, 11*(4), 483–533.

Swales, J. M. (1990). *Genre analysis: English in academic and research settings.* Cambridge, UK: Cambridge University Press.

Wenger, E. (1998). *Communities of practice: Learning, meaning, and identity.* Cambridge, UK: Cambridge University Press.

Chapter 5

"You Are Beginning to Sound like an Academic": Finding and Owning Your Academic Voice

TRACEY COSTLEY

I first saw a poster very similar to the "Uncle Sam Needs You" poster tacked to a tree on the campus of Northern Arizona University, where I was enrolled as an international student in an M.A. programme. A very serious Uncle Sam was looking intently at the viewer, a finger pointed directly at me. The text surrounding it read: "Are you a first-generation student? You need us! Come to the writing office…." Being British, my knowledge and understanding of Uncle Sam are not as well developed as an American student's might be; however, the image, accompanied by *you need our help*, communicated the idea that whoever these *first-generation students* were, they needed to do something and they needed to do it quite urgently. Although I understood the connotations of Uncle Sam, I was completely unfamiliar with and bemused by the term *first-generation university student*. I did not know who "they" were or why they might be in such urgent need of help.

I went home to the house I was sharing with an American friend and asked if he was a first-generation university student, and he, quite firmly, with a tone indicating a level of offence, replied *"Hell No!"* I then asked what the term meant, and I was told that it referred to students who were the first person in their family to go to university—the first generation. This clarified things for me in some sense, but I still could not work out why these students *in particular* would need to go to the writing workshop. Adding to my confusion and growing sense of discomfort was the fact that, by this definition, I am a first-generation university student. Neither of my parents, for a multitude of reasons, went to university. My sister, three years before me, was the first person in our family to go. Both of us, however, had made it through the process without ever thinking about being first generation. At no point in my entire undergraduate career in Britain did anyone single me out or label me in such terms, and at no time did my sister or I think that our background would mean that we were in need of some sort of special help.

The Power of Labels

My friend's reaction to the idea of being a first-generation university student was one that conveyed a real sense of stigma and suggested that students whose parents didn't go to university are somehow disadvantaged, both socially and academically. This view took me completely by surprise, and to this day in fact I remain troubled and somewhat disturbed by it. It may sound somewhat dramatic, but this was the first time that I had ever come across such labels and, more important, the first time that I had, under these terms, officially been seen, labelled, and/or identified as being deficient in some way. I do not mean to suggest that I have been an A grade student who sailed through school with constant praise, as this has not been the case, but it was the first time that my family background had ever been brought to bear upon my academic identity.

The experience left me feeling like I had just stumbled across some sort of skeleton in my closet that was known to everyone but me. I felt that I was walking around carrying a big sign for the entire world to see: "I'm a first generation student...I need help!" I became very conscious of this and thought that people would be making assumptions about me, my life, and my academic abilities, an entirely unpleasant feeling to say the least. A more searching question that I began to ask myself was the following: What does the act of entering academia and becoming a student, whether undergraduate or postgraduate, entail that one's social background, ethnicity, and very personhood are taken to be markers of academic potential, or the bases for predictions about one's potential? I found myself wondering about what the "right" type of background might be and whether you could get by without it if you didn't have it.

For reasons utterly unrelated to my being a first-generation student, I did not finish my M.A. in Arizona but transferred to King's College London where I completed a different M.A. and where I am currently in the third year of my Ph.D. Ever since that afternoon in Arizona, I have continued to hear references made to the relationship between social background and academic performance. In England there has been much press over the last five years about "widening participation,"—that is, increasing student recruitments from sociocultural and ethnically diverse backgrounds. There are regular announcements in the press about the underachievement and drop-out rates within the non-traditional (working class and ethnolinguistic minority student body), and it is not uncommon to hear reference to this in and around the university.

The idea of using social class as a means by which to understand students' struggles, problems, and achievements at university is an idea that I had spent most of my early twenties being blissfully unaware of and an idea that of late I have become increasingly more sensitised to. The idea of being a first-generation student, and more generally the labels that are applied to students in relation to academic writing and overall academic performance, are topics that I remain very much interested in, not only in terms of my own research[1] but also in relation to how I see myself and some of the barriers I feel that I have experienced. I am sharing these feelings and experiences for a number of different reasons that I hope to explore in this chapter.

I want to draw from my own experiences as a postgraduate student to explore some of the learning processes I have experienced in relation to acquiring and developing, through writing and speaking, my academic voice and identity. In the course of this exploration, I highlight some general assumptions that I have encountered in regard to ideas about my social background and the impact these have had on my own academic performances. I also talk about how my sense of self has developed, or emerged, through the process of being and becoming a postgraduate student. I am not writing this chapter with the presumption that I have the answers or that I have "mastered" grad school, but I hope that through sharing my experiences I will be able to highlight some of the strategies I have found helpful in terms of acquiring and developing my own voice. I hope to offer some sort of assurance that whilst being a challenging and at times brutal process, finding your academic voice is not an impossible task, whatever generation you might belong to.

To return to my opening anecdote, it is necessary for me to say that in Britain the term *first generation* university student does not really exist

---

[1]   My own research focuses on English as Additional Language Students (EAL) and how they navigate the language and literacy demands of the English National Curriculum in state school classrooms in England.

and is not used. This is not to suggest that we do not label students in a similar way. Our weapons of choice, so to speak, are class and ethnicity and as such, the term *non-traditional student* is one that is widely applied to students. This term is generally used to describe ethnically diverse, multilingual and/or working-class students. My sense is that the two terms, *non-traditional* and *first-generation students*, are essentially the same and do an almost identical job. The terms take their meaning from the binary oppositions they create. If there are non-traditional students, there must be traditional ones. Equally if there are first-generation students, there must be second-, third-, fourth-generation ones and so forth. Ultimately, the dynamic that results is that there are students who at enrolment are considered, on the basis of their socio-economic and ethnic backgrounds, to be in deficit and those who are considered to be "in credit."

Nature vs. Nurture and Novice vs. Scholar

I have received a number of wide-ranging comments about my writing both during my time in the U.S. and also back in England. One of the most significant questions I have been asked was posed to me in relation to a piece of my writing for my Ph.D. The question went as follows: "What in your educational background has caused you to write like this, Tracey?" This was followed by, "Do you remember a teacher or someone telling you that this is the way to write?" This question still resonates with me today, but fortunately no longer sends me to my bed in tears. When asked this question, I was struck to my core, thinking there must clearly be a sign attached to me. My writing had betrayed some sort of first-generation-ness and non-traditional-ness. I felt as though I had been busted, my cover blown, exposed as a parochial charlatan who should go back to the educational void from whence I came. I felt floored (indeed flawed), because not only was my writing style seemingly a million miles away from what was required, but it also apparently revealed some sort of problem in my educational background.

Returning home to the house I shared with friends I had questions galore spinning through my head. How could my writing prompt such questions? What was it revealing about the type of education I had, and who am I kidding about being able to do a Ph.D.? I spent a number of days trying to think about how my schooling may have so spectacularly ill-prepared me for my current academic endeavour. I wallowed in how mortifyingly embarrassing it was to have handed in such a flawed piece of writing to such well-respected and established academics. How offensive it was that someone like me was trying to do something like them.

As for my educational background, I attended the local primary and secondary schools in my home town, which was the norm. I grew up in a relatively small (approximately 50,000 people) East Anglian town. This may not mean very much to an audience outside England, and rest assured, it doesn't really mean much in an English context either. It is not a particularly high-profile area, with my home town's biggest claim to fame being that it is the most easterly point in the U.K., a fascinating fact little known even to most of the U.K.'s residents. The schools that I attended were, and still are, the local state comprehensive schools that serve the area that I lived in. My parents never really felt the need to consider other schools, such as private schooling, as the local schools were generally considered to be sufficiently capable of providing a quality education.

I found myself thinking that I could explain my problems with writing on the grounds that I did not go to a private school and that my parents didn't go to university. This neatly explained why I was having such difficulty, and I should have realised that it was all a simple misunderstanding and I was the wrong person trying to do a job meant for someone else. Although convenient, this view of the world served to make me more miserable, and in particular it made me deeply uncomfortable as it did not fit with the view that I have of the world. I have always held the belief that as an individual I am, within reason, able to do and be pretty much anything I want if I put my mind to it and want it enough. I found it hard to believe that going to a private school and having university graduates for parents were the requisite criteria for being a successful Ph.D. student. It didn't make sense to me and just wasn't something that I could believe.

Even though there seem to be somewhat entrenched ideas about the relationship between socio-economic background and academic performance, there is something almost Darwinistic about the essentially determinist proposition that having a certain educational background and parents would help me to successfully write my literature review. There is something fallacious in the cause-and-effect relationship that such a view propounds. The danger for me in such a suggestion is that it can be easy for people to buy into it and to believe it is true. It comes to work as some sort of Marxian social class determinism in that having a certain socioeconomic background determines your cultural position in life.[2] I had a number of conversations with my close friends and family around this time in which I lamented my lack of ability and talked about how I couldn't do it and should drop out and save everyone involved anymore time and money. They wanted to know what had happened to make me talk in such a way, and when I recounted the questions that had prompted such introspection, the responses ranged from confusion to abject horror: "They said what!?...What does that mean?"

I found myself asking more and more how having parents who had been to university, studying whatever they may have studied (based on their careers, perhaps something in the field of engineering and emergency health care), would help me in doing a Ph.D. that arises out of interests and experiences from my own professional background (teaching English in South East Asia). I began to think more critically of the idea that social background and academic success are causally related. From both my undergraduate and postgraduate studies, I have friends from a range of socio-economic and educational backgrounds. There are many who fit the profile of the traditional student but who struggle with writing and academia in general. At the same time I know many so-called non-traditional students whose standard of writing and whose academic voices are something to which I can only aspire.

Through some very honest conversations with my tutor, as well as those with my family and friends, I came to realise that I had bought in to the idea that success at university is some sort of socio-economically determined given. I had taken comments about my work personally, too personally, and had missed the point somewhat. I realised that I needed to step back and reassess the comments and critiques that I had received in relation to my work, and indeed my ways of working, and begin to look at feedback in terms of what it was that comments from my tutors were directing me to *do* rather than what I thought they were directing me to *be*. What I had taken to be questions directed at my ability were in fact questions about work that I had or had not done. For example comments such as "inappropriate use of reference," "unclear rhetorical stance," and "how clear are your notes on this," are not comments of an existential nature. They do not require me to be someone different; they require me to take action and to do something different.

During this period of review and reflection, I could feel myself becoming re-engaged and re-motivated. I felt that a light had come on, and I

---

2   For some discussion, see Medway, Rhodes, Macrae, Maguire, and Gerwitz (2003); National Audit Office (2002); and Woodrow and Yorke (2002).

realised that academic success is not determined by birth, genetics, or whether or not my parents went to university. My tutors and colleagues who I consider to be academics do not write, speak, think, and do academic "stuff" well because of their breeding but because they have learnt to do it. Being a postgraduate student is about tapping into and learning the ways in which things need to be done. Realistically people do not arrive at grad school being able to write perfectly—why would they be there if they could? It is a process that involves being trained, acquiring the appropriate skills, experiences, attitudes, and dispositions. It is about taking or adopting the relevant stance in the same way that professionals do in any other field of employment. To detail all of these points is beyond the scope and intent of this chapter, so I use the following space to highlight what I think have been the most positive and constructive shifts in my ways of working and overall approach (or mindset) to my studies.

Learning How To...

Creme and Lea (1997) use the metaphor of a foreign country to try and capture the sociocultural dynamics of academia and how one might feel upon arrival. This metaphor is useful in terms of getting at the role or position that I found myself adopting. I tried to stand back from all that was going on around me and began to take a look at what people were doing to see if I could understand what was going on, just as a tourist might do. In this light, everything becomes a learning opportunity. I realised that I usually sat in seminars and conference presentations concentrating on *what* was being said as opposed to the *how* of what was being said. I realised that I paid no real attention to the language and techniques people use to structure and present their ideas. As I began to listen for more than just content I began to hear the ways in which people pose questions, make references to publications, and generally take control of the topic in hand.

Similarly I started to make comparable observations in texts. Instead of reading for content alone, I started to look at the different devices people use to structure their work and present their arguments. For example, how do writers make reference to other texts and how do they use references to make their own stances and positions clear? How are arguments signposted, supported, and developed across texts and, how do people introduce the theoretical backgrounds from which they are drawing? This focus on form raised my awareness of the ways in which both writers and speakers handle the literature and concepts they are using and how these formal features are used to scaffold their ideas and ultimately their voices. I found these types of activities most useful in relation to the concept of voice in that, for me, they have highlighted how *"writers create an impression of themselves—a discoursal self—through the discourse choices they make as they write, which align them with socially available subject positions"* (Ivanič, 1998, p. 32, italics added).

There are many things that I have learnt from these observations but perhaps the two key things for me have been (1) recognising the similarities between academic speaking and writing and (2) understanding that a central part of academic voice is the control that one has over the text, whether this be spoken or written. An example that might help to illustrate this is in relation to writing this paper. At a conference in the U.S. I was talking to people about this book, describing what it was that I was hoping to do. I presented my ideas in the following way: *"I am exploring academic writing from the perspective of a non-traditional student."* My interlocutor asked the following question: *"In what way are you non-traditional?"* I remember being quite taken aback by this, and the conversation went on to include a question about whether or not I was *"working class."* This brought a lot of thoughts and feelings to mind, but mostly I felt that here I was again encountering funny assumptions about my background and couldn't really understand why people would ask such questions.

What I realise now, however, is that the way in which I described what I was hoping to do left me wide open for such questions, and in fact actually demanded those questions. The way that the initial description was set up essentially says that *"I am a non-traditional student and I am going to tell you all about writing from such a perspective."* This ultimately focuses the discussion on me, my non-traditional-ness, and my experiences. Such a stance requires me to elaborate upon how I conceptualise non-traditional-ness and moreover how I see myself as constituting a "non-traditional" student. Rephrasing the description something along the lines of "I am interested in the ways in which labels are attributed to students within higher education and how this may influence academic writing" sets up an entirely different conversational dynamic. The focus is no longer on me and how I have come to represent or embody a non-traditional student; the point of engagement for my interlocutor now concerns the impact of labels on student achievement in writing.

Key for me has been understanding that the ways in which writers phrase and sequence their ideas is the means by which their audience pieces together or maps out their particular stance or attitude. I have recognised how important it is to see that academic speaking and writing is the medium through which you draw connections between ideas and concepts, and that you need to be aware of how these connections may be taken up and "heard" by your audience. Central to this is the idea of clarity. By this I do not necessarily mean the lucidity of the language being used but the clarity with which you are using particular terms, concepts, theoretical frames, and so forth. For me an integral part of academic discourse is being clear and explicit about the ways in which I am both conceptualising and framing my research and ideas. In many ways these discourses of clarity and explicitness also apply to the "academic audience." As reader or listener, there is something of an obligation to seek the same level of clarity and explicitness from the texts that you are encountering.

Understanding the role of clarity and control has, I would say, been the biggest lesson for me and is part of an ongoing learning process. I find myself eternally drafting and re-drafting sentences that I write, mentally scripting and re-scripting sentences I plan to say, in order to make sure that I pay attention to the types of assumptions, connections, and interpretations I am placing on ideas and materials. I try to anticipate and see what a particular sentence, term, and concept may establish or invoke in my audience. Obviously it is not possible to predict and measure audience responses in their entirety, but for me it has become part of an essential process of stepping outside my work and ideas to gauge what it is I am saying and how my voice might sound and, more importantly, be understood by my audience, whether this is my tutors or a conference audience. Through these processes I am beginning to gain control not only of the material and ideas that I am trying to express, in the sense that I am better informed as to the traditions and/or schools of thought from which certain ideas or theoretical approaches emerge, but also in the sense that I feel that I have increasing control of the voice, my voice, with which I am doing it. In short, I am more familiar with the conventions and stylistic devices that others use to achieve this, and I am coming to understand what counts and is considered to be "appropriate" in the field within which I am working.

A concept that has been very powerful for me, not only in terms of my own research but in terms of understanding my academic identity is the following: to 'pull off' an 'X' doing 'Y' (e.g., a Los Angeles Latino street-gang member warning another gang member off his territory, or a laboratory physicist convincing colleagues that a particular graph supports her ideas). It is not enough to get just the words right, though that is crucial. It is also necessary to get one's body, clothes, gestures, actions, interactions, symbols, tools, technologies (be they guns or graphs), values, attitudes, beliefs, and emotions right as well, and all at the right places and times" (Gee, 2005, p. 7). For me, Gee's notion of identity fits in with the foreign culture metaphor as it too highlights the need for students to focus in on and acquire understanding of the day-to-day, moment-by-moment "stuff" of interactions whether these be face-to-face or texts. As the quote suggests "pulling off" a particular identity or "successfully" participating in a social event and practice often requires more than just an understanding of the language being used.

At this point I feel that it is necessary to stress that these are things that have been key for me in terms understanding the puzzle that is doing graduate school. I do not want to suggest that I am now a model academic or that my experiences and coping mechanisms are universal or that they will mesh with your own experiences. There are many moments when I do not get things "right" or get them in the "right" places. At times the identities that I have (e.g., the Tracey that presents at academic conferences and the Tracey that chats with her friends in the pub) do not "maintain" in quite the way they should; I do not produce "perfect texts," and there are slips in my discourses. But where these seemed to be more frequent and more obvious during my first few years of postgraduate studies, they are becoming less so and I am now aware of things that do not read or sound quite right. I feel that I am closer to "pulling off" my academic voice because the degrees of distance between "me" and "them" is less. As the time passes and I experience more of what it means to be a postgraduate student, the more I become socialised and enculturated into the practices and traditions of my field and department.

One of the things that I have learnt, and this may seem like something of a cliché, but everybody finds their own way of learning to do graduate school. What I feel I can say with some degree of confidence is that everyone struggles with the process, and this is where your peers are of the utmost importance. Doing graduate school can be a very lonely and somewhat isolating experience. The social aspect of my postgraduate career has been quite different from my undergraduate one. I have spent a lot of time assuming that everyone else was happily moving along at pace with his or her work, doing alright and getting good grades, and that it was just me who was struggling. This assumption has of course turned out to be a complete myth. My peers and cohort have all experienced, in varying degrees, the same problems, concerns, and crises that I have. Whilst I do not celebrate the fact that others are unhappy, there is something very reassuring about the commonality of experience. In this respect your department, fellow students, and tutors become a vital source of support and help. There is something very distinct about the process of graduate school that in many ways is difficult to capture in words. Those who are going through it or who have been through it are those most likely to be able to identify and sympathise with you. It is from each other that you can draw (and offer) help, advice, and encouragement.

"Pulling off" my university identity for me is as much about confidence as anything else. This is not, obviously, to be mistaken with arrogance, but refers to a confidence that is based not only on the degrees of familiarity I have with my subject, department, and wider field, but also on the belief that I can and should be doing what I am doing. In her work on academic writing, Ivanič makes the salient point that one of the greatest challenges that face students at university is that they *"have to adopt a voice which they do not yet own"* (Ivanič, p. 86). This is a really powerful (and in many ways empowering) statement for me. It highlights the fact that success is not necessarily about innate abilities and talents or educational and class commodities. University, whether undergraduate or postgraduate, is a process of adoption and adaptation in which we must identify and learn to own the discursive traditions of our subject areas. One of the biggest compliments I have received during my time as a postgraduate student came recently when my tutor said, *"You are beginning to sound like an academic."* My journey is by no means complete, but comments such as these make me realise just how far I have come and give me the confidence to continue and the reassurance that the hard work is paying off.

Summary of Key Points and Strategies

Below are some summary points that I would like to add to this chapter. Some of the comments reiterate points that I have already made, and others are pieces of advice that I have been given and are, I think, valuable to anyone involved in the process of learning to do graduate school.

1. Academic writing and speaking is not an innate skill. The relative level or "brilliance" of your writing and speaking is not determined by your brain size or some kind of essential quality. It is something that you learn to do. It is something you learn to do in a particular way that is in line with your field, audience, institution, funding bodies, supervisors, and whoever else may be involved in your work. But it is also determined by you and what you bring to it, the richness, diversity, and cumulative experiences that you have and that shape, colour, and orient your work.

2. Be prepared for comments on your writing that verge on being harsh. Expect to write and re-write a piece a million times. One of the most striking comments I heard was in the meet-and-greet session run by our department for new Ph.D. students in which our head of research said that writing a Ph.D. involved the ability to *"kill your own children."* The message was that thousands of words that you have spent days, months, and even years sweating over stand a good chance of never making it into your final thesis. Great chunks of text that you know by heart will have to be culled, but this is quite simply part of the process. You cannot get from point A to point Z without going through all the other letters of the alphabet.

3. Embrace being a pedant. Finding the right mixture, tone, balance, and structures in academic writing and speaking is a time-consuming process. I may spend hours reviewing whether I meant *but* or *however, performance* or *enactment, constituted* or *constructed.* Such attention to words and their meanings is for me a fundamental step toward understanding the craft of academic writing and speaking. It is a process that I have come to enjoy.

4. Be prepared to interrogate who you are, what you are doing, and why. But keep in mind that your background, experiences, and understandings of the world shape and define you and are valid and valuable. These are resources that provide you with a perspective that will be unique and something that you can voice to your field, department, and colleagues.

5. Look upon seminars, conferences, and peer interactions as sources and resources. These moments provide content knowledge, but they also reflect or provide access to the means, the "knowing how," and the practices of the academic community of which you are a part. Take opportunities to talk to colleagues and peers. It is through a range of both formal and social events that discursive traditions are modelled.

Talking in and across these contexts helps you to become comfortable, not only with talking to professors and "famous people," but also in how you handle and present yourself. Talking, speculating, and thinking aloud are all highly valuable processes in the development of your own voice. These acts of sharing have forced me to find ways of conveying my thoughts, feelings, and interpretations in a way that fits in with the required setting and all its expectations.

6. Keep reading. Not only does reading serve as a means of developing your knowledge base, but it provides examples of the ways in which writing in and around your subject is done and presented. Focus on the different ways in which data and ideas are presented in books, articles, and journals. Such observations not only help to develop an understanding of the scope of your field, but also they are a means of attuning yourself to the ways in which different audiences require different forms and modes of presentation.

7. Be prepared for ups and downs. Be sure to put the downs in context, learn from them, and move on. Enjoy the highs and recognise the moments in which you find yourself becoming more confident, capable, and at ease in the community in which you find yourself. Recognising and celebrating your progress is a right that you will have earned!

TRACEY COSTLEY, KING'S COLLEGE, LONDON

I still find myself being surprised when people ask me what I do and I say I am doing a Ph.D. I never seriously thought it would be something that I would do. People's responses equally surprise me: "Oh, you must be really clever." "It's all right for some...isn't it about time you got a job?" "A Ph what?" And my favourite: "And I thought I was boring!" For me it is a hard and at times brutal process but one that has been made possible through the support, encouragement, and inspiration I have received from those around me and from the privilege of knowing that every day brings new ideas and new challenges.

REFERENCES

Creme, P., & Lea, M. (1997) *Writing at university: A guide for students*. Buckingham, UK: Open University Press.

Gee, J. (2005) *An introduction to discourse analysis: Theory and method (2nd ed.)*. London: Routledge.

Ivanič, R. (1998) *Writing and identity: The discoursal construction of identity in academic writing*. Philadelphia: John Benjamins.

Medway, P. , Rhodes, V., Macrae, S., Maguire, M., & Gerwitz, S. (2003). *Widening participation by supporting undergraduates: What is being done and what can be done to support student progression at King's*. London: Dept. of Education and Professional Studies, King's College London.

National Audit Office. (2002). *Improving student achievement in English higher education executive summary*. London: HMSO.

Woodrow, M., & Yorke, M. (2002). *Social class and participation: Good practice in widening access to higher education. The follow-up report to 'From elitism to inclusion'* (1998). London: Universities UK.

PART 2

Mentors and Mentees

Chapter 6

Mentoring as a Long-Term Relationship: Situated Learning in a Doctoral Program

STEVE SIMPSON AND PAUL KEI MATSUDA

> *Learning cannot be designed:* it can only be designed *for*—that is, facilitated or frustrated.
>
> (Wenger, 1998, p. 229)

An important part of professionalization in graduate school is working with faculty members. The faculty-student relationship in graduate school is institutionalized in many ways, including: teacher and student in graduate seminars; advisor and advisee in independent study courses; researcher and research assistant; and thesis or dissertation committee member and advisee. While these institutionalized relationships are essential components of the graduate school experience, what is often more important to the professional socialization process is the mentoring relationship that takes place outside these formal structures. The mentoring relationship can be especially important at the doctoral level, where the student is not only trying to enter the profession but, in many ways, learning to do what faculty members do.

In this chapter, we—the co-authors of this chapter—describe our mentoring relationship during the first two years of Steve's doctoral studies. First, we contextualize the relationship by describing Paul's approach to mentoring and the institutional arrangement. We then discuss our mentoring relationship, focusing on two of the key issues in mentoring, including the issue of overcoming the initial barrier in establishing a mentoring relationship, and the issue of identifying and negotiating tasks that facilitate the mentee's professional development. We conclude this chapter by reflecting on the long-term nature of the mentoring relationship and by sharing some thoughts on how to make the relationship healthy and sustainable. We should also note that we relate our experience in several voices: We use a joint voice in the introduction and conclusion, but we switch to our individual voices when narrating our individual perspectives on the mentoring relationship.

We acknowledge that our experience is not necessarily representative of a typical mentoring relationship. Our relationship has been more deliberate than usual because of our common theoretical interest in situated learning. Yet, by sharing our experience, we hope to show what a productive mentoring relationship could look like—to provide a point of reference as mentors and mentees at other institutions reflect on their own mentoring relationships and as prospective mentees look for appropriate mentors for their own professionalization.

An Approach to Mentoring: Paul's Perspective

In the late 1990s, when I was completing my Ph.D. with emphases on both rhetoric and composition and applied linguistics at Purdue, the number of doctoral programs that had faculty members specializing in my field of specialization—second language (L2) writing—seemed few and far between; as Dwight Atkinson put it rather pessimistically, the field of L2 writing was "dying before our eyes" because there were not enough Ph.D. programs producing specialists in the field (Santos, Atkinson, Erickson, Matsuda, & Silva, 2000, p. 2). Since I was interested in contributing to the development of L2 writing as a field, mentoring the next generation of L2 writing researchers at the doctoral level became one of my important professional goals. For that reason, I was determined to obtain a faculty position at an institution with a nationally-known doctoral program and worked toward building my professional profile with that goal in mind.

My previous institution, the University of New Hampshire, where I worked with Steve, provided an institutional context conducive to my professional agenda—to mentor the next generation of L2 writing specialists. It had the national reputation to attract strong graduate students. When I arrived at UNH, I already had two doctoral students who were interested in L2 writing, and have been able to collaborate with both of them on a number of projects (e.g., Knoblauch & Matsuda, in press; Matsuda & Cox, 2004; Matsuda, Cox, Jordan, & Ortmeier-Hooper, 2006; Matsuda, Ortmeier-Hooper, & You, 2006). The doctoral program was small enough to allow me to play a central role, participating in the admission decision, offering graduate courses regularly, and working closely with individual graduate students. My current institution, Arizona State University, also provides opportunities for me to work closely with doctoral students in Rhetoric, Composition, and Linguistics as well as Applied Linguistics, and to teach an advanced graduate seminar on second language writing on a regular basis.

I am quite explicit about my approach to mentoring, which draws heavily on situated learning—the idea that learning is facilitated by various forms of participation in real or realistic activities (Lave & Wenger, 1991; Rogoff, 1990)—and activity theory—the idea that people's activities are intertwined with the object of the activities and are facilitated or mediated by various cultural tools such as language that they learn to use in the process (Leont'ev, 1978; Vygotsky, 1978, 1986; Wertsch, 1991, 1998).

In the classroom, I resort to what Freedman and Adam (1996) have called, "facilitated performance" (p. 399; cf. Rogoff). My graduate seminars are organized around activities that involve realistic tasks and contexts; I provide lectures and readings to help create the context or to provide tools for completing the activity, and use discussion to facilitate reflection and sharing of insights. I take Wenger's idea seriously—that "one can design a curriculum but not learning" (p. 229). Although I do provide a detailed list of learning objectives on the syllabus, it is phrased in broad terms to allow for incidental learning based on what students are ready to learn. To me, the purpose of the classroom instruction is to provide controlled exposure to ideas and practices in the field—to serve as a catalyst for further learning through participation in various professional activities.

The most important part of mentoring, it seems to me, happens outside the classroom, where I strive to provide opportunities for "attenuated authentic participation" (Freedman & Adam, p. 399; cf. Lave & Wenger). That is, I invite promising graduate students who have indicated some interest in working with me to take part in my professional activities. It is attenuated in the sense that I choose, in consultation with each individual collaborator, an activity that is somewhat challenging yet manageable. It is authentic in the sense that the activities are what I normally do; they are, for the most part, not modified for the purpose of teaching. It is participation—rather than mere performance—in the sense that the outcome of the activity has real professional implications and consequences. In general, my role as a mentor involves the following: (1) creating opportunities for attenuated authentic participation; (2) providing resources and support to help my collaborators succeed; (3) providing examples by sharing what I have done or by inviting mentees to observe what I do; and (4) introducing my mentees to the social network of professionals in the field.

Having a well-situated faculty member who is interested in mentoring graduate students is one important pre-condition for a successful mentoring relationship, but that is not sufficient. A mentoring relationship does not just happen; it needs to be initiated by someone and taken up by another. Initiating the mentoring relationship might be one of the most formidable challenges for graduate students. It is true that some graduate students actively seek these mentoring relationships while researching possible graduate programs. For instance, when I was looking for a doctoral program, I visited Purdue and met with Tony Silva, who became my mentor and colleague, to ask about the future of the program and the field. Yet, others may find initiating a relationship with a faculty mentor rather intimidating. In the following sections, Steve describes some of his experiences in his first few years of doctoral work.

A Mentoring Relationship in Action: Steve's Perspective

Overcoming the Intimidation Factor

As Casanave demonstrated in the first chapter of this book, learning to "do" graduate school entails a movement from the periphery of a community of practice toward fuller participation within it. Participation, according to Wenger, involves acquiring a community of practice's shared repertoire of tools such as language and artifacts to engage in "actions whose meanings [members] negotiate with one another" (p. 73). Participating in this way, however, requires learners to construct and negotiate their own unique identities within the existing community (p. 76). That is, new doctoral students need to fashion for themselves an image of what it means for them to *be* participants in their field. For most—if not all—new doctoral students, there are moments early in the professionalization process when it becomes painfully clear (to themselves, at least) that they lack the language and tools necessary to engage others in the community, and that their attempts to participate fall short of the community's expectations. *Some* students—the exceptionally brave ones—are not deterred by this period of acculturation. Others—and I would put myself in this category—are petrified, or at least they are overly conscious of their shortcomings and intimidated by others in the community who seem to know what they are doing. For this reason, it can be very difficult for some of us to take that first step toward "doing" graduate school.

In my case, I knew I wanted to work with Paul before applying to UNH, and I had considered emailing him or introducing myself at conferences numerous times, but frankly I felt a little intimidated by Paul's accomplishments, and perhaps a bit awkward, too. I have always had trouble knowing just *how* I should introduce myself in academic contexts, as I fear coming off as too effusive (i.e., "I *really* like your work; I've read everything you've ever written!") or too pretentious (i.e., "In my *own* research on such-and-such..."). In fact, I missed a perfect opportunity to discuss my work with him at a conference a year before starting school at UNH. I was giving my very first conference presentation at the 2003 Conference on College Composition and Communication (CCCC) in New York City. I had presented second on a fairly eclectic panel of relative newcomers to the field of L2 writing. Mere moments after I finished presenting, the rear door of the auditorium opened and a very tall Japanese man in a trim suit strode in purposefully and sat quietly in the back row. Somehow, I knew this was Paul, and I can remember mentally running through all the ways I might initiate a conversation with him afterward. Granted, I would have benefited from talking to Paul about the presentation; my project, while provocative, was methodologically unorthodox and not very well situated in the field. However, I was oddly relieved that Paul had missed my presentation, and I declined the chance to introduce myself. As an inexperienced researcher, I simply lacked the confidence to *perform* academically before an established member of the field, and as a somewhat introverted person, I felt hesitant to start a conversation I was not sure I could properly sustain.

Paul was the one who eventually initiated our mentoring relationship after I had been accepted to UNH. In April 2004, he emailed everyone who had been accepted to the program that year to congratulate them. We exchanged a couple emails and eventually agreed to meet for coffee after I had moved to New Hampshire. We met officially for the first time at a coffeehouse in Durham on a hot August day, and I can remember thinking, as the two of us sat at a table out on the sidewalk, that Paul did not look quite so tall when he was sitting down—he seemed to be talking, both literally and figuratively, at my level. The casual nature of this encounter removed the pressure of having to *perform* for Paul. Instead, we could speak more frankly about the program, about my research interests, and about life in Durham, in general. While I might have been intimidated by Paul initially, I soon found him to be welcoming and eager to step into the mentor role.

That same summer, Paul emailed all the new doctoral students to ask if we were interested in chairing a session and staffing a booth at the Symposium on Second Language Writing, which he was organizing at Purdue University. In exchange, he offered a registration waiver and assistance in finding a crash space. I was among the three students who had accepted the invitation. In addition, because Paul knew Joleen Hanson (another new doctoral student who had written an M.A. thesis on L2 writing under Paul's guidance) and I were interested in L2 writing, he invited us to work as his paid research assistants in the fall. I took up this invitation and became one of his research assistants before my first semester at UNH even started.

Identifying and Negotiating Appropriate Tasks

A major challenge in mentoring is identifying and negotiating appropriate tasks. In Paul's case, I noticed that he tries to line up a series of tasks designed to move his mentees toward increased participation in the field, but he knows when doing so that the exact trajectory of a mentees' development cannot be predetermined, as the professionalization process is not codifiable. In many cases, the nature of the tasks he assigns is based on the individual mentees' interests and their strengths and weaknesses as scholars and researchers. Throughout the mentoring relationship, however, Paul and his mentees regularly assess both their progress and their professional goals and renegotiate the nature of the tasks accordingly.

The first of Paul's tasks for me involved copyediting the final proofs of *Second Language Writing Research (SLWR)*, a collection of papers from the 2002 Symposium on Second Language Writing (Matsuda & Silva, 2005). It exposed me to the field's major research concerns, to key scholars and seminal works in L2 writing and composition, and to accepted genres and discourse conventions. To some extent, the act of copyediting, even at such a late stage in the publication process, demystified the act of academic writing for me. The thought of having to publish—of crafting an essay *good enough* to be accepted by the academic community—was often paralyzing to me because my impression of the process was shaped largely by the final, *published* versions of academic writing (see Casanave, 2005, this volume; Matsuda & Silva). In particular, I realized that the polished nature of published research removed traces of all the collaboration that went into their composition. As I proofread the chapters, I imagined how the *SLWR* contributors might have solicited the thoughts and feedback of their friends and colleagues as they planned their papers and conference presentations; how they might have asked other professionals in the field for comments on earlier versions of their drafts; and how they *might* have even accounted for the questions and criticism they received from 2002 Symposium participants or from the *SLWR* editors.

Through this experience, I realized that writing an academic article was a process, and that the authors knew that they could rely on the constructive support of the community—they were not just throwing scraps of meat to the wolves. I have mentally revisited this experience countless times as I have taken on other copyediting jobs and as I have drafted my own papers. This experience helped me feel at least a little more confident about putting my own ideas into print. Furthermore, by participating in this process, I became personally invested in the finished product and the impact it would have on the field.

From this first task, Paul noticed my inclination toward detail-oriented work. For a follow-up project, he asked me to transcribe a conversation he had had with Dwight Atkinson (Matsuda & Atkinson, in press). The transcribed conversation in which Paul and Dwight discussed the future of contrastive rhetoric research would later be edited for inclusion in *Contrastive Rhetoric: Reaching to Intercultural Rhetoric* (Connor, Nagelhout, & Rozycki, in press). Since I have an interest in both qualitative research methods and in L2 writing research, the transcription task had several immediate applications for me. Naturally, the task familiarized me with the transcription process itself and many of the problems associated with putting human speech into writing. From the content of the conversation, I learned numerous unfamiliar terms and concepts that would eventually factor into some of my own research interests, such as "distributed cognition," the notion that thought and knowledge are not situated in an individual mind but are distributed across an array of mediating tools, people and places (Salomon, 1996). I also encountered names and terms that I had seen in print many times but had never heard used in conversation, such as *ki-shoo-ten-ketsu* organization of Japanese prose and "William Grabe." I must have replayed Paul and Dwight's reference to "Bill Grabe" 20 to 30 times trying to figure out who they were talking about. Unfortunately, "Bill Grumpy" was the best I could do at the time. Later, I learned that, contrary to my expectations, the *e* in Grabe is not silent.

Most importantly, eavesdropping on Paul and Dwight's conversation allowed me to hear how they articulated their own ideas on what has become a highly sensitive yet critical topic in our field, how they incorporated and synthesized others' works, and how they responded to and even critiqued each other's ideas in a manner that preserved their relationship as colleagues and as friends. In a portion of the dialogue that did not make the final cut, Paul and Dwight entered into a debate on the extent to which it was possible for a professional in our field to position herself or himself within both the fields of composition/rhetoric and ESL/applied linguistics. From the start of this debate, I realized that it had a *very* long history, that each man had a professional and personal stake in the conversation, and that they were not likely to settle their differences at that juncture, nor would they have to. As a future professional in the field, I knew I had stumbled upon a pivotal insider conversation that I would probably enter myself at some point in my career, a conversation that forces participants to explore the field's purpose, boundaries, and definition. I came to understand the importance of having scholars approach such issues from different perspectives. Paul and Dwight, I realized, were friends and colleagues, but they have their differences on a number of issues. Further, they knew from the onset of the conversation that these differences would emerge at some point. However, they also knew that by participating in (and publishing) this dialogue, they were entering into a collaboration that *could* produce new ideas and perspectives, new theoretical approaches, and new directions.

The project that has had the most significant impact on my socialization into the field was my work with a long-term, meta-disciplinary study of research in second language studies, which I presented in a poster session with Paul and Joleen at the 2005 CCCC in San Francisco. This project benefited me in numerous ways: It exposed me to a wide range of research in second language writing, and it granted some legitimacy to my participation in the field, which according to Wenger is crucial if a newcomer's "inevitable stumblings and violations" are to be "opportunities for learning" (p.101). Most important, it gave me the opportunity to dialogue with others in the field, an opportunity I had been too timid to accept at my first conference presentation two years earlier.

Much like my first presentation, this presentation had its share of bobbles, though I now had the opportunity to bumble in full view of people who could gently point out my errors, and in the guidance of a mentor who could mitigate the "damage." The most educative part for me came when a well-known scholar in composition and rhetoric (whom I will refer to as "Dr. Smith") visited our booth and asked about our project. I recall launching into a spiel I had prepared on the plane to San Francisco only to find that Dr. Smith already knew everything I was telling her, and that I was not really answering the question she had asked, at least not to her satisfaction. A bit rattled, I attempted a few more explanations, none of which satisfied Dr. Smith's curiosity. I remember thinking that I had no shortage of information; my studies and my work on previous tasks had given me a broad overview of major issues in the field. At this point, my problem was with the *synthesis* and *use* of this information—the ability to discern which information was needed as background information, which information I could assume my audience knew, and which information might best drive home my point in this instance.

Eventually, Paul stepped in, and I watched him as he carefully attempted to address Dr. Smith's concerns. Later, Paul confided in me that even he found her questions hard to answer, as he was not always clear what her *specific* concerns were. Nonetheless, watching Paul interact with Dr. Smith taught me much about the importance and collaborative nature of academic dialogue and helped me more rationally examine my academic "performance" anxiety. Dr. Smith's questions, I realized, were not intended to dismantle me. Rather they were simply inquisitive and constructive—they were meant to engage my ideas and further the knowledge-making process I had entered into with my colleagues. Like the conversation I had transcribed between Paul and Dwight, my exchange with Dr. Smith was a collaboration. In a sense, I was presenting *with* her, and not necessarily *for* her.

Reflecting on the "Layered" Learning Experience

While these projects marked only the beginning stages of our mentoring relationship, I feel that the "lessons" I learned from them have become a significant foundation for subsequent learning in the field. In fact, I continue to learn from these experiences. To me, learning to become a professional has been a gradual process involving engagement in a series of tasks and, more importantly, continual reflections. There was not a single glorious moment over the past two years when everything "clicked" and I understood completely the "big picture." Rather, I learned these aspects of graduate school gradually, and it has largely been through opportunities such as writing this chapter that I have had the occasion to take stock of my experiences and evaluate my progress. That is, my learning has occurred in layers. While completing a task, I would sometimes notice only the more immediate applications (e.g., the transcription process), but after further reflection—and after embarking on new tasks that forced me to draw from my previous experiences—I was often able to see the subtler aspects of the field to which these tasks exposed me (e.g., the various ways one collaborates with other professionals, and the reasons for doing so).

My reflections on the process of "doing" graduate school have also highlighted for me the intricate relationship between learning and identity construction, and the layered nature of my own developing professional identity (Wenger; Casanave, 2002). In *Communities of Practice*, Wenger describes identity as a temporally-situated learning trajectory. According to Wenger,

> We are always simultaneously dealing with specific situations, participating in the histories of certain practices, and involved in becoming certain persons. As trajectories, our identities incorporate the past and the future in the very process of negotiating the present. . . . They provide a context in which to determine what, among all the things that are potentially significant. A sense of trajectory gives us a way of sorting out what matters and what does not, what contributes to our identity and what remains marginal. (p. 155)

In this vein, it has been through my varying degrees of participation with others in my discipline—whether it be with my professors, my fellow graduate students, or others with whom I have collaborated—that I have been able to see how others situate themselves within the field and how they identify as professionals. My own learning trajectory, then, has involved identifying and, to some degree, appropriating *pieces* of others' identities (i.e., research interests, professional habits, etc.). Thus, by working closely with Paul, I have not simply *become* Paul, but certain aspects of his professional identity have become an integral part of my own. For example, Paul's use of situated learning and activity theories in his teaching and mentoring has fascinated me, and in turn

I have not only incorporated these ideas into my own teaching, but I have taken them on as research interests. Further, I can identify certain elements of my professional identity that have developed from working closely with Christina, Michelle, and Joleen at UNH, and from working peripherally with other graduate students at Purdue or San Francisco State University. In short, I credit Paul for nudging me deeper into our discipline's network of activities, which has facilitated the development of my professional identity.

Working closely as Paul and I have, however, does not come without its share of hitches, particularly with regard to the negotiation of working styles. Right off the bat, we noted some significant differences in work habits. For example, Paul, a night owl, prefers working late at night into the early morning, while I prefer to work from late morning to early afternoon; Paul tends to work fairly quickly and multi-tasks well, while I like spending more time on fewer simultaneous tasks; Paul seems to favor collaborative environments and is adept at networking on projects, while I tend to approach tasks from a very "individualist" point of view.

These differences in working styles do complicate the mentor-mentee relationship from time-to-time. While I like keeping pace with Paul, for example, I often find that when trying to do so, I take on more than I can handle at any given time, and I find myself frustrated when I fall short of what I believe are Paul's expectations. In one case, when Paul and I sat down to work on this book chapter, I was a bit perplexed to find that Paul had drafted a fairly sizeable chunk of text in the time it took me to revise four small paragraphs. Through working together, however, one does find ways to negotiate these differences, and in my case, to better understand these differences. While Paul appears to work quickly, he has since told me that he is by nature an "excruciatingly slow" writer, and that, when given the choice, he prefers to work independently. The ability to multi-task and to collaborate were work habits he learned out of necessity as he delved further into the profession—a process I am going through.

Conclusion: A Long-Term Relationship

As we have tried to show through our collaborative reflection on our mentoring relationship, mentoring at the doctoral level is a long-term relationship, one that is developed over five or so years. Mentors who collaborate with their graduate students in early stages of professional development may be able to draw the distinction between experienced and inexperienced peers more easily (Ferris, 2005). With doctoral students, however, the boundary between experienced and inexperienced is not so clear-cut because being a doctoral student, to many, is the last phase of being a student and the first phase of being a professional (Matsuda, 2003). They are in the process of becoming their mentors' experienced peers—if they are not already. Eventually, the relationship will turn into that between colleagues in the same profession.

Again, the transition from being a student to being a professional does not happen in a flash; as Steve's experience suggests, becoming a professional is a gradual process that requires an ongoing involvement in multiple tasks and reflections. Although the series of tasks that Steve has gone through may seem to work seamlessly in retrospect—partly because we have had to construct a coherent narrative for this chapter—it is not always possible to come up with a series of tasks that can take a mentee from one stage of professional development to another smoothly. As Wenger points out, the tasks cannot be pre-designed; there can be no prescribed mentoring curriculum. Instead, it has to emerge from the ongoing relationship between the mentor and the mentee. The best kinds of tasks cannot be created; they can only be carved out from what projects the mentor happens to be working on at any given moment. The nature and scope of each task also needs to be negotiated based not only on what the mentor needs to have accomplished but also on what the mentee is interested in, capable of, and is ready to learn.

In order to identify appropriate tasks, the mentor needs to have many different projects going on at any given point. The mentor and mentee also need to build a strong working relationship in which their needs and concerns can be expressed freely so that the mentor is aware of the mentee's interests, development and strengths and weaknesses. The relationship also needs to be healthy and sustainable. That is, both parties need to benefit mutually from the experience—and feel that they do. One way to accomplish the sense of mutual benefit is to identify tasks that have some immediate incentives for both parties. When Steve copyedited a book for Paul, for example, it was clear from the outset that the task was something Paul needed to have done, and that Steve would receive a stipend in addition to gaining a glimpse into an aspect of the profession. In another case, Steve did not receive any financial compensation but gained professional recognition as a co-presenter of a poster session at a conference.

Although it is important for each task to have some immediate incentives for both parties, not all the benefits can be instantly clear to either of them. While Steve was always aware of some of the immediate benefits of each task, the long-term implications did not become evident until much later—until when he found himself applying the set of skills he had learned in a previous task or when he reflected on the process through, for example, writing this chapter. It is also important to keep in mind that the mutual benefits do not always correspond one to one. Sometimes one gives more than the other, but in the end, the benefits may balance out. In the initial stage of mentoring, what the mentor can provide—by way of opportunities, guidance, support, and resources to help the mentee get established—may outweigh what the mentee can produce. Later in the relationship, however, the mentee might take on more for the mentor in the process of gaining independence. At this stage, the mentor's role, and challenge, is to trust and encourage the mentee and to be less hands-on, or even to let the mentee take the lead.

For this type of relationship to work, both the mentor and mentee need to see the relationship not just as a short-term bartering of services but as a long-term investment—both for themselves and for the field.

STEVE SIMPSON, UNIVERSITY OF NEW HAMPSHIRE
Since starting my Ph.D. in composition studies at the University of New Hampshire, I've learned the importance of collaboration in academia. Not only have I had professors who have nurtured my professional development, but I've benefited from other students in the program who have shared with me their knowledge, their time, and their encouragement. As a community of learners, we mentor each other, regardless of our year in the program. Upon completing my Ph.D., I hope to secure a position at a university where I can foster this sort of community among grad students I work with.

PAUL KEI MATSUDA, ARIZONA STATE UNIVERSITY
I have been blessed with mentors with a wide range of mentoring styles at various stages of my professional development. Although each of my mentors has had a profound impact on me, I realize that none of them alone could have provided everything. As a mentor now, I find myself constantly reflecting on my own experiences with my mentors as a way to guide my interactions with my mentees. In addition to playing multiple mentoring roles, I strive to create opportunities for my mentees to network and collaborate with others.

Acknowledgments

We thank Matt Schneider for providing insightful comments that stimulated our thinking and helped us consider our audience. We hope observing the whole process of writing this article has been valuable in his own professionalization process. We are also grateful to Michelle Cox, Joleen Hanson, Aya Matsuda, and Christina Ortmeier-Hooper for their helpful reader responses.

REFERENCES

Casanave, C. P. (2002). *Writing games: Multi-cultural case studies of academic literacy practices in higher education*. Mahwah, NJ: Lawrence Erlbaum.

―――. Uses of narrative in L2 writing research. In P. K. Matsuda & T. Silva (Eds.), *Second language writing research: Perspectives on the process of knowledge construction* (pp. 17–32). Mahwah, NJ: Lawrence Erlbaum.

Connor, U., Nagelhout, E., & Rozycki, W. (Eds.). (in press). *Contrastive rhetoric: Reaching to intercultural rhetoric*. Amsterdam: John Benjamins.

Ferris, D. (2005). Tricks of the trade: The nuts and bolts of L2 writing research. In P. K. Matsuda & T. Silva (Eds.), *Second language writing research: Perspectives on the process of knowledge construction* (pp. 223–234). Mahwah, NJ: Lawrence Erlbaum.

Freedman, A., & Adam, C. (1996). Learning to write professionally: "Situated learning" and the transition from university to professional discourse. *Journal of Business and Technical Communication, 10*(4), 395–427.

Knoblauch, A. A., & Matsuda, P. K. (in press). First-year composition in the 20th century U.S. higher education: An historical overview. In P. Friedrich (Ed.), *Teaching academic writing*. New York: Continuum.

Lave, J., & Wenger, E. (1991). *Situated learning: Legitimate peripheral participation*. Cambridge, UK: Cambridge University Press.

Leont'ev, A. N. (1978). *Activity, consciousness, and personality*. Englewood Cliffs, NJ: Prentice Hall.

Matsuda, P. K. (2003). Coming to voice: Publishing as a graduate student. In C. P. Casanave & S. Vandrick (Eds.), *Writing for publication: Behind the scenes in language education* (pp. 39–51). Mahwah, NJ: Lawrence Erlbaum.

Matsuda, P. K., & Atkinson, D. (in press). Contrastive rhetoric: A conversation. In U. Connor, E. Nagelhout, & W. Rozycki (Eds.), *Contrastive rhetoric: Reaching to intercultural rhetoric* (pp. 00–00). Amsterdam: John Benjamins.

Matsuda, P. K., & Cox, M. (2004). Reading an ESL writer's text. In S. Bruce & B. Rafoth (Eds.), *ESL writers: A guide for writing center tutors* (pp. 39–47). Portsmouth, NH: Boynton/Cook Heinemann.

Matsuda, P. K., Cox, M., Jordan, J., & Christina Ortmeier-Hooper (Eds.). (2006). *Second language writing in the composition classroom: A critical sourcebook.* Boston: Bedford St. Martin's.

Matsuda, P. K., Ortmeier-Hooper, C., & You, X. (Eds.). (2006). *The politics of second language writing: In search of the promised land.* West Lafayette, IN: Parlor Press.

Matsuda, P. K., & Silva, T. (Eds.) (2005). *Second language writing research: Perspectives on the process of knowledge construction.* Mahwah, NJ: Lawrence Erlbaum.

Rogoff, B. (1990). *Apprenticeship in thinking: Cognitive development in social context.* Oxford, UK: Oxford University Press.

Salomon, G. (Ed.). (1993). *Distributed cognitions: Psychological and educational considerations.* Cambridge, UK: Cambridge University Press.

Santos, T., Atkinson, D., Erickson, M., Matsuda, P. K., & Silva, T. (2000). On the future of second language writing: A colloquium. *Journal of Second Language Writing, 9*(1), 1–20.

Vygotsky, L. S. (1978). *Mind in society: The development of higher psychological processes.* Cambridge, MA: Harvard University Press.

———. (1986). *Thought and language.* Cambridge: The MIT Press.

Wenger, E. (1998). *Communities of practice: Learning, meaning, and identity.* Cambridge, UK: Cambridge University Press.

Wertsch, J. V. (1991). *Voices of the mind: A sociocultural approach to mediated action.* Cambridge, MA: Harvard University Press.

———. (1998). *Mind as action.* New York: Oxford University Press.

Chapter 7

Finding One's Way into Qualitative Case Studies in Ph.D. Thesis Research: An Interactive Journey of a Mentee and Her Mentor

YONGYAN LI AND JOHN FLOWERDEW

Introduction

This chapter takes the form of dialogue between a Ph.D. student, Yongyan, and her supervisor, John. A research project that lasts for a number of years probably never proceeds along a well-charted path from the beginning to the end. A project conducted in the qualitative research paradigm illustrates this aptly, with qualitative researchers having to undergo "a research process that puts a premium on thinking that is emergent, research contexts that are natural, and researchers who are self-reflexive and socially sensitive" (Belcher & Hirvela, 2005, p. 202). For novice researchers committed to a qualitative research project in a Ph.D. programme, such a research process is one of learning and finding one's way into the details of what shape one's thesis will take. Mentor-mentee relationships can crucially contribute to the discoveries that will be made.

A major part of Yongyan's Ph.D. thesis took the form of multiple qualitative case studies, focusing on how Mainland Chinese doctoral Science students write up their research for publication in English-language journals. However, the qualitative case study format, as it emerged, was not envisaged from the outset. In this chapter, we illuminate how Yongyan found her way into the intricacies of the qualitative case studies through an interactive journey with her mentor, John. We highlight Yongyan's discovery of the value of a qualitative case study approach, the role of theories in such case studies, coming to grips with particular theories, and adjusting her plan by reacting to the data and contingencies, all the while in interactions with John. Our story will be told by quoting from the email correspondence between Yongyan and John; in addition, quotes are also taken from Yongyan's research proposal submitted to John during her application to the programme, and Yongyan's research journal, which recorded her difficult process of conducting and writing up her research.

Beginning the Research

Yongyan:

My Ph.D. thesis topic on investigating Chinese doctoral science students writing for international publication started as an evangelical goal on my side many years ago. In the Mainland Chinese university where I was teaching, writing for publication in international journals had been set as a graduation requirement for doctoral science students for years; however, there was no academic writing course at the university (or generally, in other universities in Mainland China) specifically geared to assisting the students in meeting the requirement. ESL writing, teaching and research in China has always been focused on the writing of undergraduate-level compositions typically required in English tests. I decided a foundation of empirical research would be a useful and perhaps necessary step toward initiating some pedagogical support for doctoral science students in my university.

In my research proposal submitted to John during my application to City U's Ph.D. programme, 16 months before my actual entry to the programme, it can be seen that I was obsessed with a scheme of doing predominantly text-based work. Among others, I wanted to do genre analysis of the students' texts to find out about their "genre knowledge" and search for linguistic features that may have cultural and socio-psychological implications. I also proposed to do genre analysis of journal protocols and email correspondence between student writers and the gatekeepers of international journals.

John:

The situation Yongyan has described is fairly typical of students from Mainland China who apply to do a Ph.D. (which is largely by thesis research in Hong Kong, following the British system). That is to say that she was motivated by a professional goal and the theoretical and methodological aspects of the proposed research were heavily influenced by the limited literature available to her in Mainland China (in Yongyan's case Swales and Bhatia's books on genre analysis [Bhatia, 1993; Swales, 1990] and some of my own publications about writing for scholarly publication that she had been able to obtain [Flowerdew, 1999 a&b; 2000; 2001]).

Questioning Case Studies

Yongyan:

In my first appointment with John at City U, after listening to my lengthy report of a "blueprint" with much patience, he said: "It seems you have many ideas in mind, now you need to sort them out." Then in the appointments that followed this one, early in the research process, he proposed his expectations for me in the thesis research: to treat the research topic in a "multidimensional" manner, in particular, by triangulating different perspectives and methods of data collection. He illustrated the ideas by pointing to a chart in one of his manuscripts (see Flowerdew, 2005, p. 68). In addition to the idea of multidimensionality, John advised to the effect of "you should pull out issues from case studies," "case studies will explicate the issues in your thesis," and "in your conclusion you summarize the issues and compare across the cases." While I seriously noted down every bit of his advice (perhaps partly in my typically Chinese respect for teachers' teaching), I did not feel he intended to impose his advice on me as "guidelines," neither was I immediately receptive to his advice.

In the research proposal submitted to John as part of my application, I did also include a plan of investigating cases of individual students' process of writing for publication. Nevertheless, I was not psychologically ready to commit to the case studies. Instead, I was hoping to circumvent this step or minimize the commitment somehow, and focus on text-based work, which, as I started my Ph.D. at City U (September 2003), seemed to have acquired a logistical justification, given that I was geographically separated from my research subjects.

John:

Looking back at Yongyan's initial Ph.D. proposal sent to me some time before she was accepted into the programme, I notice that, as Yongyan said above, there was a strong emphasis on text-based study. However, what interested me most in her proposal was one dimension of the proposed research which Yongyan expressed as follows:

> Research Question 2 is answered through ethnographic case studies and textual analysis. A number of doctoral students (both male and female) representing several science disciplines are selected on a voluntary basis. The case studies should last over several months to around a year, covering each participant's writing and publication stages. The researcher will interview the participants regularly (including email exchanges) during their process of writing a paper (or papers), inviting them to reflect on their progress, specific problems, strategies, and their interaction with their fellow students or supervisor. The participants' supervisors are also interviewed at some intervals, to provide observations on their supervising pattern with the students and their perception of the students' progress in writing.

While I am indeed interested in text-based research, the more naturalistic case study approach expressed by Yongyan here attracted me, I suppose, because I had at that time recently done some similar work with academics writing for publication in Hong Kong. My approach in this work had been multi-dimensional (Flowerdew, 2005) and I thought Yongyan could replicate this approach, perhaps including some of the methodologies that I had had in mind when I did my own research, but never developed. For example, one of the dimensions involves think-aloud protocols. As it turned out, Yongyan tried this method, but it was of only limited success and she did not include it in her thesis. We will return to this issue again in a later section.

Yongyan:
   In retrospect, I was conceptualizing case studies differently from John at the time. A few months into the programme, I was still holding to a text-based plan of my thesis (from what I had written in my research proposal); to me case studies were a part but should not be a central part of the thesis (partly as a result of the logistical challenge involved in conducting case studies, as noted above). If John was visualizing case studies as a central part, I was suspicious of the capacity of case studies to fulfill this central role. I said in an email to John: "I have in mind all the time your reminder that I should 'pull out issues from the cases.' But what I'm concerned is will the data be rich enough to allow me to

pull out some issues strongly?" (Email, 22 Dec 03) I also felt insecure to be committed to case studies: "I need to go beyond 'case': relying on it solely is dangerous—methodologically failing to be 'multidimensional'; and logistically running a risk." (Journal, 28 Dec 03) And I was firm that textual analysis should be an important part in the thesis, although I was puzzled over what texts to analyze, for what purpose, and how to make textual analysis and case studies a coherent picture while pointing to some worthwhile "issues." So in an email to John I said:

> Immediate evidence [of issues] that may emerge could be from (1) the contextual description (which I think I've done quite a lot already, with my preliminary writing-ups and ongoing data collection); (2) their texts— but this will probably demand some rigorous linguistic textual analysis, e.g., using Hallidayan approach (as you suggested). The submission stage (analogous to your study of Oliver) [Flowerdew, 2000] is also in my consideration—but correspondence over "scientific" papers could be much less interesting than the situation in your case study. Separate 'genre' analysis of some sort seems meaty and attractive, but again it does not seem straightforwardly 'covered' within 'cases', I felt. (Email, 22 Dec 03)

John wrote back:

> Regarding the problem of potential conflict between qualitative case studies and more linguistic/genre approach, maybe you can follow . . . [name of a staff member in the department who had just finished a Ph.D.] and do what she calls thick and thin description. In your case the "thick" description (although I have a problem with that term—we can discuss) will be the qualitative cases and the "thin" description will be the discourse/linguistic analysis of the texts produced or processed by your subjects. Hope that gives you something to think about. (Email, 23 Dec 03)

I followed-up with a response expressing doubts of being able to conduct fruitful analysis of case students' individual texts, noting this could also exclude efforts in the spirit of contrastive rhetoric or genre studies (which I had held to since my pre-programme research proposal):

> Earlier you suggested I can combine "thick" and "thin" description—that's exactly what I've been hoping to do. But I wonder: how to make "thin" description of the Astronomy text or Physics text that my cases process/produce? I think . . . [the staff member John mentioned in his email] can make "thin" analysis of the "literature reviews" (which made up a corpus) of her research subjects (who are mostly students in this dept it seems) and combine it well with "interviews". . . .To me my science students' stories are similar and quite routinized (less interesting than I previously thought)—I'm not sure what issues I can pull out. Building everything on case studies also seems to rule out space for more or less independent and thorough treatment along the line of contrastive rhetoric or genre studies. (Email, 1 Jan 04)

Now with the wisdom of hindsight, I can perhaps claim that before I actually started to conduct a case study, my imagined problems or possible routes to take could be endless. The key is to begin a case study and see what happens and take it from there. Indeed, I started data collection for my first case study (with Chen, a physics student) when I was very anxious. It took me two years to go from data collection (December 2003) to having it accepted for publication (December 2005) (Li, 2006). I had only cleared away my earlier imaginings and pulled out reasonable issues through reiterative data collection, data analysis and writing-up (see more on this case study later in this chapter).

John:

At that time, close text-based analysis, possibly using a Hallidayan framework, was still considered to be one of the dimensions of the research, perhaps as one of a number of case studies. Later, when Yongyan tried to code a case student's (i.e., Chen, the physics student mentioned above) textual revisions across drafts using a scheme within such a framework (a la Gosden [1995]), as both Yongyan and I agreed, it turned out to be somewhat problematic, for above all, the coding was dense and very hard to read. When I gave feedback to Yongyan on this work, I think we both agreed perhaps that her greater strength lay in the qualitative interview-based data analysis, drawing on relevant theories, where appropriate, as is clear from Yongyan's next comment.

Discovering the Role of Theories

Yongyan:
    Early in the programme, I had in mind a range of theoretical concepts, such as: Centre vs. Periphery (Phillipson, 1992), discourse community (Swales), legitimate peripheral participation and community of practice (Lave & Wenger, 1991; Wenger, 1998), genre knowledge (Berkenkotter & Huckin, 1995), disciplinary enculturation (Prior, 1995), and social construction of scientific knowledge (Knorr-Cetina, 1981). I thought I might need to write an early chapter covering all these concepts to pave the way for the rest of the thesis, including case studies. The problem in the case of my thesis was, as I realised later, even if with an early "theory chapter," such a list of theoretical concepts does not adequately cover the subsequent case studies, though they can be part of a general theoretical background. My case studies (altogether four eventually)—each in an individual chapter—needed their own theoretical/interpretative frameworks respectively. I realized this when I was looking at the "Qualitative Research Guidelines: Case Study Research" of *TESOL Quarterly,* upon finishing the first draft of my case study on a chemistry student, Yuan. The guideline says the report of a case study should have a "theoretical context"; but my case report on Yuan did not have one. I emailed John:

> So far I don't feel any one/two of the theoretical concepts I have had in mind can capture the 'findings' nicely. Previously I didn't think of giving a theory part; now seeing the need (or do I have to?), I find it hard to supply a suitable theory part. I also thought that the findings, which are mainly based on "process logs," perhaps are not rich enough to support some theory? (Email, 22 Nov 04)

John replied:

> Seems sensible. I think you do need the theory part. It seems obvious to me. You need to explain what others have said about cognition and practice [two concepts I highlighted in the 'findings' part of the case report draft at that point] and what you mean by these terms/theories in your study. (Email, 24 Nov 04)

In retrospect, I wondered why I had not realised earlier that an individual study (such as a case study) should preferably have a theoretical context—perhaps because it was not in my previous training or writing experience. Hence I had to learn the lesson anew even though I had previously been guided by Xiaoming Li and Christine Pearson Casanave through laying out the theoretical background for an earlier case study report, which was later published in an issue of *Journal of Asian Pacific Communication* guest-edited by them (Li, 2005). I had also read John's (and some others') observations regarding the role of theory in qualitative research. For example, in Flowerdew (2002, p. 238), John said:

> The researcher starts with as few preconceptions as possible about what is likely to be found. In practice, however, there will always be some implicit theory with which the researcher is working.

With a realisation that I needed "theory," I also realised that the "issues" I could pull out from a case study—which in my mind amounted to the "theme" of a case study (though Stake [2005] distinguished between "issues" and "theme")—should be able to be interpreted by the theoretical context I would adopt for the case study. Nevertheless, in practice, perhaps as is the case for any other qualitative researcher (though my novice researcher status must have exacerbated the twists and turns involved!), I had not been able to take a straightforward step from theories to issues. With my four case-study chapters, without exception, I only came to the theoretical frameworks eventually adopted in the chapters gradually, through cyclic procedures. Collecting data, analyzing data with assistance of a tentative theoretical perspective, then often running into a dead-end, thus trying an alternative/adjusted theoretical lens, collecting further data, analyzing and writing-up, but then seeing new problems, so mending the theoretical framework and examining/selecting the data again. The process was reiterated until a harmonious match was achieved between data, theories and issues.

John:

As indicated in my previous comment, this reiterative process of relating theory to data is where Yongyan's main strength probably lies. By this time, I think we had both accepted that the Hallidayan textual analysis was not needed and that the focus of each of the cases could use a similar methodology of interview, text-based interview, and other relevant artifacts (such as participants' correspondence with journal editors) but that each would draw on different theories in highlighting and explicating the issues involved. The result was that there would be more triangulation of theory than method as had been initially envisioned.

Coming to Grips with Particular Theories

Yongyan:

With a case study on a physics student, Chen, for a long time, from my data collection (December 2003) till my early version of the chapter (March 2004), I had a textual orientation toward the case. This seemed natural, considering that I had collected all the major five drafts of Chen's paper and "genre analysis" was dominating my mind. On the basis of analyzing the textual revisions across the drafts of Chen's paper, and the role of Chen's two supervisors as well as that of a few referees in contributing to the textual revisions, I tried to illuminate a case of "social co-construction of science"—which I took as my "theoretical background," and which I tried to lay as my groundwork in the introduction of the case report through a review of literature. However, when I submitted this case-study chapter as a paper to the journal of *English for Specific Purposes (ESPj),* the referees were critical. One referee explicitly asked: "What is the politics of editing and reviewing?" So I went back to Christine Pearson Casanave's article (2003), which called for more "sociopolitically-oriented" case studies in second language writing research. However, while I knew that this "sociopolitical" concept may be appropriate and in fashion—see all those articles and books on critical pedagogy!—probably because of my personal background, I did not feel very comfortable adopting this approach. I wrote in my journal: "I suspect part of my difficulty in grasping the term comes from the fact that in Chinese we don't have an equivalent for the concept in the context of literacy research (if I'm correct). I suspect we would be at a loss trying to put a term like 'the sociopolitics of writing' into Chinese while preserving the term's implication in English. Although everyone knows what 'politics' is." (Journal, 7 July 04)

John:

I remember several meetings where we discussed the meaning of the term "sociopolitical" and how this could fit into the paper Yongyan was trying to get published (the data had the potential to raise issues concerning power inequality between the research subject, Chen, his doctoral supervisors, his institutional context, and the gatekeepers of his target journals in the Centre). Yongyan had difficulty in getting to grips with this concept, with its central concern with power. I tried on various occasions, on the one hand, to explain the meaning of this term and how it might be present (if occluded) in Yongyan's research data, and, on the other hand, to encourage Yongyan to include a "critical" dimension (in the sense of e.g. Benesch [2001] or Pennycook [1997]) to her analysis in the thesis. I think the difficulty here was possibly a cultural one. Coming from Mainland China, Yongyan's academic training had not been "critical" in the Western sense of the term and the concept of criticality was alien to her as a person coming from a country with a different political ideology. I think that by the time Yongyan had finalised her thesis she had come to grips with this concept, but even now, my feeling is that it is something that perhaps does not come naturally to her. I must admit to feeling slightly uneasy about this aspect of academic enculturation. It seems that writing in a Western-style university may mean taking on (or borrowing, for the purpose of passing the thesis examination) a Western identity, an identity strongly influenced by dialectical thought and criticality.

Yongyan:

Despite my difficulty in grasping the notion "sociopolitical," I believed this was the right angle to take for that particular case study on the physics student, Chen. I told myself: "To portray this publication story from a Western theoretical perspective is a twisting of my normal apolitical mindset. I'm willing to do the twisting though, because I believe this angle is right." (Journal, 7 July 04) After much reading, soul searching and discussion with John (and some enlightening from Christine Pearson Casanave and Xiaoming Li through emails!), I eventually resolved this problem of how to make the case study "sociopolitical." This new theoretical orientation was settled upon alongside further data collection and analysis and re-writing of the case report (from May to October 2005), following the first round of review at *ESPj*. The re-orientation was successful, for the resubmission was accepted for publication by that journal (Li, 2006).

With the other three case-study chapters, I have undergone similar time-consuming yet eventually rewarding reiterations. It seems to me that if conducting and writing up a case study is to attempt an "awkward marriage" between "narration and exposition" (personal communication with Xiaoming Li, Sep 05), the awkwardness is only ironed out by the researcher-writer working toward a harmony among theories, data, and issues.

John:

As Yongyan worked on her four case studies, I noted with satisfaction that she was growing in confidence. I remember telling her at the beginning of her case study work that issues have a habit of turning up, even if in the beginning there does not seem to be anything of great interest in the data. These issues, to my relief, did indeed start to turn up, as Yongyan tried to apply various theoretical constructs to her data. In passing, it is worth pointing out that supervisors, like students, are not always confident of outcomes, although they may have to give the impression that they are. It seems that once Yongyan had seen how one case study was able to be resolved, she was more confident about interpreting the other case studies to her own satisfaction.

Adjusting the Plan of the Thesis by Reacting to Data and Contingencies

Yongyan:

As John noted earlier in his comment (under "Questioning the Case Studies"), an expectation of his for me at an early stage was that my case studies should triangulate research methods, with the idea, for instance, of one case study using interviewing, and another think-aloud protocols.

With the think-aloud in particular, although I felt it could produce interesting data, intuitively I knew it would be hard to be implemented: Evidence of its difficulty, for example, can be found in research on scholarly writing (e.g. Rymer, 1988, on native-English-speaking scientists).

Yet I made special efforts early on to find someone to do think-aloud. To every potential case I explained about this method. All expressed hesitation at the thought, saying that to think aloud while writing would make the writing difficult. They emphasised that they did not just sit down and write, but that writing a draft might drag on for a very long time. They also mentioned that they often conceived of ideas at places other than sitting at a desk. One or two agreed to collaborate, but later gave up, even though I proposed various compromises, such as letting them tape-record by themselves without my presence, and write only part of a paper.

Amidst frustration, I felt I probably had to give up on the method and just proceed to obtain whatever data I could from my research participants. I said to John: "The best seems to be adjusting plan with data. Do you agree?" (Email, 11 Nov 04) John had no objection but was more concerned with the overall picture:

> In general, I agree that you have to be flexible and adapt your plan according to the data you can get (but, on the other hand, you shouldn't organize the thesis in a particular way because you have certain data). (Email, 12 Nov 04)

Months later, when I had already long given up on the method of think-aloud and indeed had been on the track of collecting data largely in view of the contingencies of the particular case students, I was nevertheless still concerned that I was not achieving a triangulation of methods with the cases as I thought John had hoped me to. In an email to John I said:

> The starting-point, that of triangulating methods in different case-study chapters, is in some difficulty. Except the one on Yuan is primarily based on "blog"; the other chapters are not particularly characterized by one method. The one I gave you (Min's) has used a little of "discourse-based interview"; Chen's chapter was more ethnographic perhaps. The in-planning textual-borrowing chapter again will draw upon various sources of data I suppose. Is this OK? (Email, 25 May 05)

John's reply reiterated his earlier response:

> Regarding the triangulating case study issue, I think you need to keep your eye on maintaining some sort of coherent development to the thesis, even if it is not based on the different methodologies. A set of individual disparate chapters will be a problem. (Email, 25 May 05)

Thus in a natural course of action, with John's approval I strayed away from the original plan of triangulating particular methods across cases. In retrospect, I saw that what data collection methods will be used with a particular case indeed seems to depend largely on the particular students. A "process log" approach may not work with many students, due to the difficulty of having someone maintain an ongoing diary, as John himself has suggested (Flowerdew, 2005). But it did work in the form of web logs (blogs) with one of my cases, Yuan, who had a pleasant personality, was particularly understanding and supportive of my research, and importantly, had always been enjoying keeping blogs. In other words, hitting upon the method of blogs with Yuan was a matter of "contingency."

So, based on the contingencies of the particular case studies, have my four case study chapters (each featuring one student's case) eventually become "a set of individual disparate chapters" or have they made a coherent picture that fits into the overall argument of my thesis? I believe that the cases form a coherent picture. Although each case has its own protagonist and context, a salient theme, its own theoretical implications, its own connections to the literature, and its own interpretive power, each one at the same time throws a different light on the central problem—how Chinese doctoral science students go about writing for publication. Moreover, I framed the four case-study chapters, with John's advice, within a narrative that gave coherence and interconnection to the case studies.

Conclusion

In this chapter we have illustrated how one doctoral student, in negotiation with her supervisor, came to discover the value of a qualitative case study approach and the role of theories in her case studies, and how she came to grips with particular theories and adjusted her plan in reaction to the data and contingencies. As Yongyan read John's comments in the foregoing parts, she was surprised to see that John knew her better than she had thought. John's comment that "supervisors, like students, are not always confident of outcomes, although they may have to give the impression that they are" somewhat amused her, but enhanced her understanding of the Ph.D. process as a negotiated, learning experience, for the student primarily, but perhaps also, to some extent, for the supervisor. For John's part, he learned that supervision is a process of not only testing his tentative research beliefs on the subject matter, but also of getting to know what could eventually work out for the supervisee, given the latter's intellectual inclinations, the research conditions, and various contingencies throughout the research process. We were both surprised and pleased that reflecting and writing on the graduate school experience, as a pair of contributors to this book, has been quite illuminating in itself.

YONGYAN LI, NANJING UNIVERSITY, P.R.C.

Pursuing a Ph.D. in Hong Kong was perhaps my way of escaping the flourishing ELT scene in mainland China. My (biased) perception of what I was expected to do in the Chinese context was to collect data through questionnaires from students (who were too innocent to be uncooperative) and boil everything down to statistics—a prospect that tortured me to think about. No one said that I was a good student during my M.A. years there when I felt bogged down by that (biased) expectation. But at the end of my Ph.D. program in Hong Kong, John said I had been one of his most successful students. The compliment will be with me all my life.

JOHN FLOWERDEW, UNIVERSITY OF LEEDS

For more than 16 years I worked at City University of Hong Kong, where I was Yongyan Li's Ph.D. supervisor. I enjoyed supervising Yongyan, as I did all of my Ph.D. students in Hong Kong. When I was a graduate student myself, I was advised that a good way to structure a thesis/dissertation is according to chapters that might be publishable in the future. Yongyan certainly learned this lesson, as I am now finding it hard to keep up with her publication rate.

REFERENCES

Belcher, D., & Hirvela, A. (2005). Writing the qualitative dissertation: What motivates and sustains commitment to a fuzzy genre? *Journal of English for Academic Purposes, 4,* 187–205.

Benesch, S. (2001). *Critical English for academic purposes: Theory, politics, and practice.* Mahwah, NJ: Lawrence Erlbaum.

Berkenkotter, C., & Huckin, T. N. (1995). *Genre knowledge in disciplinary communication: Cognition, culture, power.* Mahwah, NJ: Lawrence Erlbaum.

Bhatia, V. K. (1993). *Analysing genre: Language use in professional settings.* London: Longman.

Casanave, C. P. (2003). Looking ahead to more sociopolitically-oriented case study research in L2 writing scholarship (But should it be called "post-process"?). *Journal of Second Language Writing, 12,* 85–102.

Flowerdew, J. (1999a). Writing for scholarly publication in English: The case of Hong Kong. *Journal of Second Language Writing, 8,* 123–145.

———. (1999b). Problems in writing for scholarly publication in English: The case of Hong Kong. *Journal of Second Language Writing, 8,* 243–264.

———. (2000). Discourse community, legitimate peripheral participation, and the nonnative-English-speaking scholars. *TESOL Quarterly, 34,* 127–150.

———. (2001). Attitudes of journal editors to nonnative speaker contributions. *TESOL Quarterly, 35,* 121–150.

———. (2002). Ethnographically inspired approaches to the study of academic discourse. In J. Flowerdew (Ed.), *Academic discourse* (pp. 235–252). Harlow, UK: Longman.

———. (2005). A multimethod approach to research into processes of scholarly writing for publication. In P. K. Matsuda & T. Silva (Eds.), *Second language writing research: Perspectives on the process of knowledge construction* (pp. 65–77). Mahwah, NJ: Lawrence Erlbaum.

Gosden, H. (1995). Success in research article writing and revision: A social constructionist perspective. *English for Specific Purposes, 14,* 35–57.

Knorr-Cetina, K. D. (1981). *The manufacture of knowledge: An essay on the constructivist and contextual nature of science.* Oxford, UK: Pergamon Press.

Lave, J., & Wenger, E. (1991). *Situated learning: Legitimate peripheral participation.* Cambridge, UK: Cambridge University Press.

Li, Y.-Y. (2005). Multidimensional enculturation: The case of an EFL Chinese doctoral student. *Journal of Asian Pacific Communication, 15,* 153–170.

———. (2006). A doctoral student of physics writing for international publication: A sociopolitically-oriented case study. *English for Specific Purposes, 25,* 456–478.

Pennycook, A. (1997). Vulgar pragmatism, critical pragmatism, and EAP. *English for Specific Purposes, 16,* 253–267.

Phillipson, R. (1992). *Linguistic imperialism.* Oxford, UK: Oxford University Press.

Prior, P. (1995). Tracing authoritative and internally persuasive discourses: A case study of response, revision, and disciplinary enculturation. *Research in the Teaching of English, 29,* 288–325.

Rymer, J. (1988). Scientific composing process: How eminent scientists write. In D. A. Jolliffe (Ed.), *Advances in writing research, volume two: Writing in academic disciplines* (pp. 211–250). Norwood, NJ: Ablex.

Stake, R. E. (2005). Case studies. In N. K. Denzin & Y. S. Lincoln (Eds.), *Strategies of qualitative inquiry (3rd ed.)* (pp. 134–164). Thousand Oaks, CA: Sage.

Swales, J. (1990). *Genre analysis: English in academic and research settings.* Cambridge, UK: Cambridge University Press.

Wenger, E. (1998). *Communities of practice: Learning, meaning, and identity.* Cambridge, UK: Cambridge University Press.

Chapter 8

From Expectations to Empowerment: How a Mentor and a Dissertation Writer Negotiated the Intricacies of a Qualitative Results Chapter

ALAN HIRVELA AND YOUNGJOO YI

Introduction

Under the best of circumstances, the writing of the results chapter of a doctoral dissertation can be a daunting task for both students and their advisors/mentors. This may be especially true with respect to the qualitative paradigm and non-native English-speaking (NNS) writers. As Belcher and Hirvela (2005) have reported, writing about qualitative data may be perceived as a significant obstacle by some NNS dissertation writers, thus steering them in the quantitative direction as a means of avoiding the qualitative experience. However Belcher and Hirvela's research has also found that, once attempted, such qualitative writing can become a meaningful and powerful experience for NNS dissertation writers. As Youngjoo herself noted in one of our email exchanges (8/15/05) that helped in the preparation of this chapter, the "qualitative paradigm was never intimidating" to her from a research perspective; rather, because of its "way of viewing the world and of understanding knowledge and phenomena," qualitative research enabled her to embark on a more valuable quest for insight into her dissertation topic.

On the other hand, as she noted: "If there is something *intimidating* about the qualitative paradigm, it could be the *writing side* of a qualitative dissertation" (email, 8/15/05). She went on to relate how one of her NNS professors had discouraged students (NS and NNS) in her courses from attempting qualitative dissertations because of the writing difficulties she had witnessed in students employing the qualitative paradigm. Youngjoo's anecdote leads to a related point, especially with respect to the writing of qualitative results chapters: that some advisors are uncomfortable supervising qualitative studies.

Let's face it: Writing about qualitative data in results and discussion chapters can present major problems. Particularly frustrating for many students is the fact that there is no script or template to follow in such a chapter as there appears to be for quantitative writers. When these challenges are combined with the dissertation writer's attempts to identify and respond to the advisor's and the academy's sometimes perplexing expectations surrounding a qualitative results chapter, the process of producing a quality version of such a chapter takes on even deeper levels of complexity.

In this chapter we explore how Youngjoo, then a doctoral student from Korea, constructed a successful qualitative, case-study-based results chapter, particularly through the lens of her interaction with Alan, her advisor, and with the various expectations (visible and invisible) surrounding the dissertation process. We focus on two themes that emerged from our extensive review and analysis of the writing of Youngjoo's case study chapter: (1) differences in our expectations for this chapter and our attempts to negotiate those expectations, and (2) how Youngjoo was eventually empowered by the case study writing experience. We believe that these themes are relevant to the experiences of other dissertation students and their mentors.

Background

At the heart of this chapter is Youngjoo's dissertation, *Immigrant Students' Out-of-School Literacy Practices: A Qualitative Study of Korean Students' Experiences* (2005). Specifically, she explored the out-of-school reading and writing activities and practices of five Korean 1.5 Generation high school students in the United States. Working, as she put it, as a "researcher, tutor, sister" with each of them (to varying degrees in each relationship), she examined the types of literacy activities they engaged in, the purposes for which they undertook them, the medium they used (print or screen based), and the language they selected (Korean and English).

Her data were gathered in several ways: through face-to-face interviews, email and instant message exchanges, field notes arising from social and instructional (tutorial) interactions, and checklists (compiled by the participants) of their literacy activities. She wrote a total of six chapters and organized her dissertation as follows: Introduction (Chapter 1), Literature Review (Chapter 2), Methodology (Chapter 3), Results based on checklist data (Chapter 4), Results based on case studies (Chapter 5), and Discussion/Conclusion (Chapter 6).

Of these chapters, Chapter 5, where she created five individual case studies of her participants, is the one we will focus on in our chapter in this volume. That chapter underwent significant changes from its first version, where Youngjoo presented her case studies thematically and included very few references to herself and no accounts of her experiences with her participants, to the version we ended up including in the completed dissertation. This final version was narrative in nature and brought Youngjoo directly into the data presentation as a participant in her study as well as its researcher and author. It was this agonizing but ultimately empowering transition from the thematic to the narrative iteration of Chapter 5 that we believe others can learn from, just as we did.

While working on this paper, we drew from several sources of information: a long post-dissertation defense discussion that we audiotaped and transcribed; email exchanges and telephone conversations that also occurred after the defense; and Youngjoo's dissertation writing diary as well as her copies of emails she and Alan sent each other as she wrote her dissertation. We reviewed all of these sources and identified the themes we felt were most pertinent for the purposes of this chapter. Drawing upon those sources, we explore the two most valuable themes in the next section of this chapter.

Before moving to our discussion of these themes, we want to comment briefly on the affective domain of Youngjoo's dissertation experience. As we hope would be the case for any student and advisor, we experienced many memorable moments as we played our roles in constructing Youngjoo's dissertation. There were also some difficult moments, and certainly we made some mistakes. We share some of these in order to enhance the learning process for others, but it's important to understand that we *accepted* deep emotions and reactions as the experience unfolded and worked in a spirit of cooperation and a willingness to learn from each other during the writing process.

Theme 1: Negotiating Expectations

What are the expectations for a qualitative results chapter in a dissertation? Where do they originate, and which expectations should be most important to the dissertation writer? Those of the advisor (and committee members)? Of the genre of the dissertation? Of qualitative research as a research paradigm? Those of the dissertation writer herself? Whatever the answers to these questions, it seems safe to say that addressing them satisfactorily is one of the major challenges facing a qualitative dissertation writer.

One vital lesson we learned (the hard way) is how essential it is to articulate expectations clearly from the very beginning of the writing of such a chapter. In Youngjoo's case, she had developed a certain notion of how to proceed based on research courses she had taken and her reading of various dissertations: "My definition of case study...was more thematic. I thought I have to write in a thematic way instead of more narrative" (discussion, 7/14/05). As a result, she wrote an initial 87-page draft of the case study chapter that was organized around the presentation of important themes that arose within and across the studies.

At that point there had been no discussion between us as to how the chapter could or should be organized. In retrospect, that was a crucial mistake as well as a perplexing one. How could we have missed such an initial planning and writing step that is in fact so important? The truth is that we simply assumed we had developed the same notions about qualitative results writing. At any rate, when Youngjoo submitted the initial (thematic) draft, her feeling was: "I guess I was quite satisfied with the organization and those themes. Like—that really looks like a qualitative study. But then, that's *my* notion of case study, I guess" (discussion, 7/14/05).

When she received an email from Alan describing his reactions to that thematic draft, she was stunned by his overall assessment: "I didn't enjoy this draft as much as I expected to." As she described her reaction: "I was devastated. I was frustrated. . .I was angry—I had anger a little bit. I don't know toward you [Alan], or toward the situation, or toward me, maybe. . . .Maybe toward you first. . . .But at the end, that's when the anger was more toward myself. You know, 'You're so stupid. How didn't you know about it?'"(discussion, 7/14/05).

What had happened was that Alan had developed a different notion of how her case studies could be told, one centered on the view of

Youngjoo as an intensely involved *participant* in her research. This led to expectations on his part for self-representation in her case study writing, as reflected in the following (post-dissertation) comment he made: "When I was reading it [thematic draft of Chapter 5], I kept saying to myself, 'But where's Youngjoo? I don't really see you here in the way that I saw you throughout the study'" (discussion, 7/14/05). That is, he had assumed she would prefer to *narrate* the case studies, with heavy use of "I" and accompanying details that provided context, such as "When I was instant messaging with June late one night. . . ." That, in his mind, was a more natural qualitative turn to take for Youngjoo's study. And so, seeing no "I" or narrative-type details in the thematic draft, he felt that crucial elements of the story were missing and that the chapter had not fulfilled its potential.

Here we want to once again draw attention to what Youngjoo later referred to as "our miscommunication or lack of communication, of the expectation of what is meant by case study" (discussion, 7/14/05). In fact, there had been no initial negotiation, no sharing of definitions or perspectives, despite the complexities inherent in case study writing. It wasn't until shortly after Youngjoo had received Alan's feedback on the first draft, when we met in a coffee shop near campus, that expectations were finally dealt with explicitly and a clear plan for how to proceed began to be laid out. Until that turning point conversation, Youngjoo was left to cope with her severe disappointment and her anger over what she perceived as the failure of the first draft, as well as moments of self-doubt as a writer: "I kind of. . .I tried to figure out what's wrong with me, and with the chapter" (discussion, 7/14/05). What it boiled down to, from her perspective, was that "I didn't know I was supposed to reveal a little bit of me. . . .Because my understanding of case study was different from yours at that point" (discussion, 7/14/05).

The words "supposed to" above are especially important in turning our attention to the "negotiation of expectations" theme of our story. We now had to deal with the writing of the next version of the chapter, and that meant deconstructing what "supposed to" actually meant. In her initial reactions to Alan's comments on how the chapter could be rewritten, there seemed to be an assumption or belief on Youngjoo's part that she was *expected* to incorporate Alan's suggestions into the chapter. For example, while she found the coffee house discussion useful and "a starting point in terms of revising Chapter 5" (email, 8/19/05), subsequent email comments from Alan represented a "discussion that was still one-way communication because you sent me your messages, and

I tried my best to get your point" (email, 8/19/05). In other words, she still saw what she regarded as an expectation to reshape the chapter as recommended by Alan, i.e., she considered suggestions as commands and found herself feeling "quite passive dealing with your feedback" (email, 8/19/05). She recalled the initial response experience as follows: "When I received the first written feedback on the thematic draft from you, I was puzzled. At that time, I didn't think that I was in a situation where I could negotiate something" (email, 8/19/05).

Eventually, though, some negotiation of expectations did take place as we discussed ways of incorporating Youngjoo's presence into the case studies as well as the nature of qualitative research itself, and Youngjoo gradually developed a sense of control over the chapter:

> Fortunately, some of your very specific guidelines (mostly examples) were very helpful in terms of how to rewrite the chapter. I immediately followed your directions, but I had control (freedom) over how to reorganize the chapter, and the negotiation seemed to take place here (email, 8/19/05).

This does not mean that there was a complete meeting of the minds as to how the case studies could best be presented, but the fact that we were finally discussing such key issues as researcher/author, self-representation seemed to reduce the weight of advisor expectations/suggestions somewhat. Indeed, as we will see later in this paper, Youngjoo eventually experienced a considerable sense of empowerment as a writer as she recast the chapter. On the other hand, the failure to foreground and review ideas about and expectations for case study writing, before the writing began, had caused unnecessary suffering of a kind that we hope will be prevented when others attempt such writing, though it's also important to point out that learning took place in the way that we approached the situation. Still, Alan, as advisor or mentor, could have taken the lead in initiating discussion of how the chapter could be written, and Youngjoo, as the author, could have sought Alan's opinions or recommendations before she began writing the chapter.

The lesson in the recounting of this experience is clear: Communication before attempting a task as complex as writing case studies is essential. And, as we learned, this does not simply involve laying out an organizational scheme for the chapter, but also discussing the nature of qualitative research itself and the various ways in which qualitative data can be shared effectively with an audience. Our experience seems to us to demonstrate that advisees and their mentors need to create meaningful time and space to share and negotiate expectations for qualitative results writing.

Theme 2: Empowerment through Narrative Writing

Here we move to what might be considered the second part of our story, because Youngjoo's case study chapter underwent extensive changes when she shifted to a narrative approach that to some extent revealed her data through descriptions of her interactions with her participants. She did not entirely abandon her thematic draft, but she reconceptualized and reorganized the chapter significantly. Just as importantly, if not more so, she altered her composing style dramatically. After reflecting on Alan's feedback on the thematic draft and subsequent discussions between us about how to revise the chapter, she returned to her data and reexamined it from a participant-researcher perspective. She also returned to her original thematic description of her case studies, eliminated all of her subheadings and other markers that were thematically oriented, and began writing to some extent as a *narrator*. She committed herself to telling the five very different *stories* that her dissertation research had produced, partly by narrating her researcher/tutor/sister relationship and interaction with each participant rather than developing themes, and partly by constructing, for each of the stories, an organizational strategy that worked best for that particular story. Hence, each of the five stories unfolds differently and has its own flavor and nuances. As a result of these changes, Youngjoo felt *empowered* as a researcher/writer.

One of the obstacles confronting Youngjoo in the course of changing her approach was her awareness of a certain bias against qualitative research, and more specifically against narrative writing. Though she had long considered herself to be a qualitative researcher, this bias against narrative had subtly influenced her thoughts about qualitative writing, as she discovered when she talked with a friend of hers who had read various qualitative dissertations utilizing a personal, narrative style of writing. Her friend reminded Youngjoo of how interesting it could be to read such accounts. Youngjoo's response, as she recalled it, was:

> And I remember that. That's true [about it being interesting reading]. But then, I guess I didn't want my dissertation to sound like that. . . .That's interesting to read; however, I guess I was worried that, what if it's not regarded as good as, I don't know. . . .We have a notion of scientific study, scientific writing. (discussion, 7/14/05)

In fact, Youngjoo had found (to her surprise) traces of a positivistic side of herself as a researcher. And so, when she had organized and drafted her thematic version of the chapter:

> I thought that if I include myself in the writing too much, I would seem like a very self-centered, egotistical researcher. . . .I guess that's why maybe I decided not to include myself, or it never occurred to me that I should have, or that it would be better for me to include my story. (discussion, 7/14/05)

Also crucial to Youngjoo's transformation during the revision of Chapter 5 was her adoption of a very different notion of audience. As is probably the case with most dissertation writers, a guiding concern for her was producing writing that would be considered satisfactory by her advisor and her committee members. This concern had been firmly in place while she wrote the thematic draft of Chapter 5. Our coffee house conversation that introduced into our negotiations Alan's "Where is Youngjoo?" question that captured his disappointment with the thematic draft also produced our first significant conversation about *audience*. As Youngjoo noted:

> More importantly [than asking "where is Youngjoo?"], you suggested that I should picture my 'audience' who could benefit from reading my dissertation. This sense of audience/purpose of writing was an important theme throughout my study; in addition, we learned so much about it from the second language writing literature. However, I guess I kept this point in my mind very vaguely. (email, 7/18/05)

Alan's suggestion that she should give more consideration to audience issues reminded Youngjoo of how much she had enjoyed and learned from the process of reading other dissertations in preparation for researching and writing her own. This, in turn, reconnected her to her desire to enable others to learn from her dissertation:

> I recalled other dissertations that I had already read, especially dissertations written in narrative form. Based on my memory of those dissertations, I created a story that could be most beneficial to the future audience, not limited to three committee members. I finally started visualizing my expected future readers, especially doctoral students who prepare for dissertation research. (email, 7/19/05)

Youngjoo then began revisiting her data from the "my story" perspective as well as the desire to reach a wider audience and eventually turned to presenting the data in these new ways in her revision of the chapter. She also adopted a new attitude toward her writing, one that was in a sense liberating for her and that produced, from both her and Alan's perspective, a more compelling rendering of the case studies. It was this shift in attitude that allowed her, as a researcher and a writer, to engage her data quite differently and thus envision new writing possibilities for herself. This is how Youngjoo described her new attitude following her consideration of Alan's response to her first draft and the new perspectives on writing that we had negotiated through our discussions:

> And at that point. . . .How can I explain? I guess I didn't really care about anything. I didn't care about you, I didn't care about me, I just said: "Okay, write whatever I want!" And that's why I didn't care about the length, I didn't care about the organization. (discussion, 7/14/05)

What happened here is what hopefully will happen to any qualitative dissertation writer: Youngjoo took control of the writing process. While writing the earlier thematic draft, her attitude was "I didn't really have a strong feeling that this is my story and this is *my, my, my* work. I guess, instead of that, I felt, 'This is a dissertation. And I have passion, but this is a requirement, this is what every doctoral student does'" (discussion, 7/14/05).

When she began revising her first case study, Youngjoo's commitment now was to her data and her five stories, as well as to the wider audience she was now more cognizant of. What this meant to her as a writer is reflected in the following observation, which captures her state of mind as she moved from her first case study to her second: "So I moved to June [a participant], and while I was writing June, I emailed you. I was inspired. No, I was empowered" (discussion, 7/14/05). This feeling grew as she continued to rewrite the chapter: "I was confident in rewriting those case studies: 'Okay, I'm rewriting once, why not twice? It's only a matter of time.' That's what I meant by empowered" (discussion, 7/14/05).

Looking back on the experience, Youngjoo recognized that it may have been somewhat unique: "I don't know how many doctoral students have such freedom to write. Or if the students are brave enough to write something they want to say" (discussion, 7/14/05). Fortunately, Youngjoo finally wrote with a sense of freedom and the courage of her convictions in telling her stories as she wanted them to be told. She and Alan had, after Alan's lukewarm reaction to the first draft of the chapter, found a way to constructively negotiate the possibilities for rewriting the draft. Through a meaningful coffee shop discussion (and here the value of advisor and advisee meeting in a more informal setting than a faculty office provides should be noted) and subsequent email exchanges that stressed what Youngjoo could do instead of what she shouldn't do or what she was expected to do, that is, through successful *communication* between us, Youngjoo found the writing voice she needed. Now, in contrast to how she felt while writing her first draft, she could say, "Yes, this is *my* dissertation" (discussion, 7/14/05). What had happened is that we had found a way to conceptualize what the key notion of "my story" meant with respect to Youngjoo's approach to her research and her strengths as a writer. Other qualitative dissertation writers and their mentors may likewise want to examine what "my story" means when the time comes for the qualitative data to be shared so as to break the stranglehold of expectations and facilitate the development of empowerment in the writing process.

Conclusion

Whatever forms it takes, academic writing is bound up in a constellation of expectations. Casanave (2002) captures this point powerfully in her use of the analogy of "writing games" to describe the intricate interplay between graduate student writers and the "academy" that stands in judgment of their writing. Advisors, committee members, graduate schools, and graduate students all have their own perspectives on what constitutes success in the realm of academic writing. With respect to the abundantly rich and often mysterious high stakes genre of the qualitative dissertation, the writing games may be played out in especially complicated ways, as our story of the writing of Youngjoo's results chapter illustrates. As Judith Meloy observes in her book, *Writing the Qualitative Dissertation: Understanding by Doing* (2002), qualitative dissertations pose unique challenges to the academy because qualitative researchers are "conscious, interactive sensemakers—that is, what makes sense to one may not be an exemplar for another. The choices and subsequent decisions made are grounded in the individual's perception of his or her focus and overall research purposes, that is, what will work 'for me' " (p. 13). She notes, too, that "we are still in the process of identifying ways of communicating exemplary qualitative research" (p. 18).

In telling our story about Youngjoo's creation of a mutually satisfying case study chapter, we have attempted to explore the complex nature of dissertation-related expectations and the ways in which they can impact on the results writing process. In writing the thematic draft of her chapter, Youngjoo felt she was meeting the commonly held expectations of the qualitative research paradigm and aligning with her own definition of case studies. Meanwhile, Alan was developing different expectations or hopes for her chapter based on his interpretation of her research experience and how it could best be represented in her writing. At the same time, as her advisor he felt he had to take into consideration institutional expectations for dissertation writing as well as what he believed would be well received by the members of Youngjoo's dissertation committee. As this web of expectations surrounded us and shaped the writing process that was unfolding, we failed to communicate about what we expected and assumed, and so the expectations became a barrier to success. This is why, in our experience, advisees and mentors need to conduct frank, open, and ongoing discussions about their expectations so that these expectations can play a constructive role in the writing process rather than impeding it.

As we've seen, Youngjoo experienced a liberating sense of empowerment as a qualitative results writer once we created the conditions necessary for negotiating our expectations for her chapter and for our different kinds of involvement in it—Youngjoo as the writer, and Alan as respondent/mentor. In developing this feeling of empowerment, Youngjoo also gained a deeper sense of ownership of her dissertation that we hope every dissertation writer experiences. She had generated a powerful degree of control (and possession) over her data, as well as her role as a participant-researcher in her study, and narrating her story successfully took on for her a deeply personal level of commitment and identification that extended far beyond meeting the requirements for her degree. When that happens, as it did for her, the dissertation becomes for the qualitative writer, particularly those NNS writers who feel both drawn to and intimidated by qualitative composing, the kind of personally fulfilling genre we believe it can and should be for all doctoral students. That fulfillment need not be confined to the student, either. As Alan recalled, when Youngjoo informed him that she had become empowered during the narrative writing phase of her chapter:

> I remember when you told me that. I would say that was my very favorite moment of your whole dissertation experience, when you said that. I remember thinking, "*Now* we've achieved something. This is what it should be." (discussion, 7/14/05)

We close with this comment because, ideally, the dissertation experience is significant and moving for the advisor as well as the advisee, and this is perhaps most likely to occur in the results section of the dissertation, since this is where the essence of the study is captured. When both advisee and mentor engage this sense of empowerment, the dissertation experience is the transformative one we believe it should be, and in the unfolding of our story, it was the result of communicating about and coming to terms with the intricate expectations that are part and parcel of qualitative results writing.

ALAN HIRVELA, OHIO STATE UNIVERSITY

Having received some wonderful mentoring throughout my career, particularly during my formative years as a faculty member at the Chinese University of Hong Kong, I have come to feel special appreciation for the many mentoring opportunities I experience in my current position at Ohio State University. I feel both privileged and humbled as I guide doctoral students through their apprenticeship into academe and witness their growth as readers, writers, researchers, and thinkers. I'm also struck by what a continual learning process mentoring represents. Every mentoring situation is different, and it is the ongoing process of adjusting to shifting expectations and needs and seeing students evolve from novices to experts that makes this kind of experience so rewarding. I'm extremely grateful to the doctoral students I've worked with thus far and have learned much from them.

YOUNGJOO YI, UNIVERSITY OF ALABAMA

During my graduate studies, two groups of people helped me believe that I was a writer who could not live without writing. *My mentors* taught me that perhaps all of us in academia are writers to some extent. They helped me build up confidence as a writer (not necessarily as a second language writer). *Adolescent English Language Learners* who shared their out-of-school literacy lives with me for my research helped me broaden my view of literacy and see myself as a writer. Though negotiating and forming this writerly identity has been a long journey, it's been a worthwhile experience. I look forward to continuing on this path.

REFERENCES

Belcher, D., & Hirvela, A. (2005). Writing the qualitative dissertation: What motivates and sustains commitment to a fuzzy genre? *Journal of English for Academic Purposes, 3,* 187–205.

Casanave, C. P. (2002). *Writing games: Multicultural case studies of academic literacy practices in higher education.* Mahwah, NJ: Lawrence Erlbaum.

Meloy, J. (2002). *Writing the qualitative dissertation: Understanding by doing* (2nd ed.). Mahwah, NJ: Lawrence Erlbaum.

Yi, Y. (2005). *Immigrant students' out-of-school literacy practices: A qualitative study of Korean students' experiences.* Unpublished doctoral dissertation, Ohio State University, Columbus.

Negotiating the Dissertation Literature Review: The Influence of Personal Theories

WEI ZHU AND RUI CHENG

Introduction

The doctoral dissertation represents an important step in graduate students' participation in discursive activities in their disciplinary communities, and as such, has attracted the attention of researchers of academic literacy (e.g., Belcher, 1994; Dong, 1998; Paltridge, 2002). The dissertation poses a challenge for doctoral students in general because of the complexity of the task and the multitude of knowledge and skills required of the writer. However, the literature review of the dissertation may be a particularly demanding task: It entails the analysis and evaluation of a vast amount of information; it is intricately related to other chapters of the dissertation and is thus essential for its conceptualization; and its scope and structure are less well defined, compared with other chapters of the dissertation.

This chapter focuses on the experience of a non-native English–speaking doctoral student (Rui) and her interactions with one of her major professors (Wei) on the dissertation literature review. The literature review writing process was very challenging for Rui, who described it as "full of confusion, frustration, struggle, self-denial, and eventually satisfaction." In the sections below, through the lens of "personal theories" (McCutcheon, 1992) we describe the understandings of the dissertation literature review that we each brought to the dissertation process, the influences our personal theories had on our practices concerning the dissertation literature review, our reflection on and negotiation of our personal theories, and the learning and revision resulting from our interaction and negotiation.

Personal Theories about the Dissertation Literature Review

The term *personal theories* has been used quite extensively in teacher education research. In the context of teacher education research, teachers' personal theories refer to "sets of beliefs, images, and constructs about such matters as what constitutes an educated person, the nature of knowledge, the society and the psychology of student learning, motivation, and discipline" (McCutcheon, p. 191). Developed over a period of time and influenced by the teachers' knowledge, the teaching contexts and the teachers' experiences, teachers' personal theories are often tacit but underlie teachers' classroom practice and are open to change (Pape, 1992; McCutcheon; Ross, Cornett, & McCutcheon, 1992). These same ideas can apply to students' beliefs as well. In both cases, we do not refer to "theory" in the large sense of abstractions and philosophies of disciplinary knowledge, but to contextually influenced personal visions and understandings.

"Personal theories" offers a useful lens through which to examine our experiences. We brought quite different personal theories about the dissertation literature review to the dissertation process. Our personal theories consisted of beliefs, understandings, and assumptions of the purpose of the dissertation literature review, the criteria for the successful dissertation literature review, the role of the theoretical framework, and the role of the author in the literature review. Our theories were unarticulated in the early stages of Rui's literature review writing process but nevertheless influenced our approaches to her literature review as writer and reader respectively.

Rui's Vision

I regarded the purpose of the dissertation literature review as displaying knowledge I had mastered on the dissertation topic through reflecting on and synthesizing information and detecting gaps in the existing literature so that my study would address previously unaddressed issues and make contributions to the field. For me, dissertation literature review writing provided an opportunity as a doctoral student to showcase the skills and expertise that I had acquired in the years of study and to prove to the committee members that I was ready to enter the larger discourse community beyond the program and institution. The guiding principle rooted in my mind to ensure a successful literature review was to be complete in the information presentation. I saw the dissertation literature review as a thorough summary of previous research and studies on related topics to give the reader a clear idea of the history and current situation of the field and possibly the direction for advancement. When I first began writing the literature review, I believed that points from different schools of thought and diverse research findings were all worth mentioning in the interest of being complete. I regarded the theoretical framework as a necessary component of any literature review and believed that inclusion of comprehensive and popular theories would increase the merit of the study. As the author of the dissertation study, I perceived my role mainly as the objective information organizer of all relevant information, which was consistent with my understanding of the purpose of the review as a display of knowledge. At the same time, I attached great importance to demonstrating critical thinking skills. My understanding of being critical when conducting the research was to find the weaknesses or problems of previous studies so that my own study could stand out by compensating for the weaknesses and solving the problems.

My personal theory as described above was mainly formed through the training I received as a doctoral student at the coursework stage under the influence of instructors, writing experiences, and classroom activities. My beliefs were initially developed in one of my research courses designed to familiarize students with basic research concepts and components of research papers. The literature review in general was discussed intensively, and writing one was taken by the instructor as the measure of success in the course. One of the most important messages I received in this course was that a good literature review needed to contain all the related key studies. Although research findings may vary and experts tend to advocate different views, I was told not to purposefully avoid any studies related to the topic. I and other students in the class were required to write literature reviews as comprehensively as possible in lieu of an exam. Also from this class, I started to form my understanding of the role of the theoretical framework in the literature review and in research studies. The instructor presented different approaches in which a theoretical framework could be incorporated in the literature reviews and emphasized the importance of currency. I sensed that every research study had to have this part and that the basic requirement for a good theoretical framework was to be comprehensive and current. As author, according to what I learned in many courses I had taken, my role was to organize and present all this information objectively and critically.

What I learned about the literature review in this course had an impact on my future attempts to write literature reviews. Since then, I have gradually treated literature reviews as forums for my knowledge display. My experience in writing literature reviews for various assignments seemed to have supported my initial understandings of the literature review.

Wei's Vision

My personal theory of the dissertation literature review was quite different from Rui's. I saw the primary purpose of the dissertation literature review as advancing an argument and rationale for the proposed dissertation study. Given that the dissertation is undertaken as the final research project before the doctoral student enters his or her discipline as a scholar and researcher, I believed that displaying relevant knowledge of the research topic and the field was necessary. However, I saw knowledge display as secondary to and embedded in the argument being advanced in the dissertation literature review in support of the dissertation study. I believed that a successful dissertation literature review ought to contain an argument developed through analysis, synthesis, and evaluation of theory and research relevant to the specific dissertation *study*, rather than be a thorough report of the research on the dissertation *topic*. In this regard, I shared Maxwell's (2006) emphasis on the *relevance* of information in the dissertation literature review.

My views concerning the role of the theoretical framework in the dissertation literature review and in qualitative research were in alignment with those of researchers who see theory as playing a fundamental role in conceptualizing the study and in guiding decisions on research focus and data collection, analysis, and interpretation in qualitative research.[1] I considered the theoretical framework a necessary part of the research design (Yin, 2003; Maxwell, 2005) and expected the theoretical framework and the other components of the research design to be connected.

---

[1]   Anfara and Mertz (2006) provide an excellent discussion on the different views concerning the role of theory in qualitative research.

Consistent with my conception of the dissertation literature review as an argument for the dissertation study and my understanding of the context of the dissertation study, I saw the author of the dissertation literature review as an emergent expert who would analyze and evaluate the information included in the literature review in addition to presenting and organizing the information. My personal theory about the dissertation literature review was developed through my experience working on various research and academic writing projects, through readings on research methodology, and through experience working with doctoral students and other members of students' dissertation committees.

Personal Theories and the First Draft of the Dissertation Literature Review

Theory in Practice: Writing the First Draft (Rui)

After my efforts to follow the completeness principle in the literature review in my course work proved to be somewhat successful, I was ready to apply the same principle when I was working on my dissertation literature review, although I realized it would be more difficult and complicated. When I was writing the literature review of my dissertation, I felt I was ready to enter the discourse community of applied linguistics and wanted to demonstrate my command of the dissertation topic. Therefore, in the process of writing, I tried to get access to and present all the key theories and studies related to my topic on the acquisition of academic literacy. Following my training in course work, I tried to present information as completely as possible. For example, I came across two major models of teaching and learning academic literacy: the cognitive apprenticeship and enculturation models. Although it seemed to me that only the enculturation model might be related to my dissertation study, I presented the two models side by side for the purpose of presenting a complete discussion of the topic. I was worried that not including the other model would leave readers with incomplete information on the topic of teaching and learning academic literacy.

When I was constructing the theoretical framework of my dissertation study, I made efforts to target a few of the theories that could work together to constitute a strong theoretical basis for the study. Besides the theory of academic literacy that was an appropriate theory for this study and was built in naturally in the section on discourse community, genre and academic literacy, I came across sociocognitive and sociocultural theory, which was applied by many researchers as the guiding theory in research on academic literacy mainly back in the '80s or earlier. Guided by the thinking that comprehensive theories would improve the value of the study and the assumption that current theories would strengthen the theoretical framework, I included the sociocultural theory into my theoretical framework. I was satisfied with such an inclusion. First of all, although sociocultural theory was developed by Vygotsky (1962, 1978) long ago, it has regained its vitality in recent years. I realized that it was a "hot topic" and widely adopted as the foundation for all types of studies in second language acquisition (e.g., Lantolf, 2000). I believed my study would be greatly improved if I explained the acquisition of genre knowledge from the sociocultural theory perspective. Second, I felt that the quality of the proposed study was improved with theories supporting each other and thus forming a powerful theoretical framework for my study. After the theoretical section was completed, I felt the foundation of the literature review was solid and its merit was increased. The inclusion of the sociocultural theory made my research look complete and current.

When I was writing the dissertation literature review, two roles I was trying to perform were those of objective information-organizer and critical thinker. However, I always found myself in a situation where I struggled between the eagerness to show my critical thinking skills and the need to perform my role as an information organizer to present studies objectively. My training taught me that being critical meant to identify weaknesses and problems in the existing research rather than wholly accepting it. At the same time, an information organizer has the responsibility to present the information to the audience without her own biases. I did not know how to enact the two roles simultaneously, so I developed a strategy of borrowing other people's voices to announce my own doubts about the existing literature. For example, when I read and cited the studies of "Nate" by Berkenkotter, Huckin, and Ackerman (1988, 1991) in my literature review as key studies, I had some doubts about whether Nate could be regarded as a novice writer since he had been an experienced composition teacher. However, I was not comfortable about pointing that out because I wanted to present this study objectively. To project objectivity, I cited Schilb's (1988) critique of the research, which raised the same question that I had. In this way, I reached the goal of being simultaneously critical and objective by borrowing Schilb's authoritative voice to announce my questions of the existing research.

Theory in Practice: Reading the First Draft (Wei)

Rui's dissertation study adopted a qualitative case study design and aimed at examining the role of computer-mediated communication in non-native English-speaking students' development of academic literacy. Rui submitted the first complete draft of the literature review as part of the first draft of her dissertation proposal. The literature review was divided into four major sections, with each section subsequently divided into subsections. The first section was devoted to a discussion of the concept of discourse community, the role of genre in discourse communities, and models on the development of academic literacy. The second major section presented the theoretical framework comprised of sociocultural and sociocognitive theories, and the third section provided a synthesis of research on computer-mediated communication and second language learning and writing. The last major section offered a review of key studies on disciplinary writing in both L1 and L2 contexts.

When I read Rui's first draft of the dissertation literature review, I was impressed by the overall organization of the review, by the scope of the research covered, by Rui's consideration of the audience (e.g., Rui had included an end-of-section summary for each section), and by her efforts to present a balanced review of the research literature. Rui clearly demonstrated a familiarity with the theory and research related to her chosen topic, and she clearly established the need for her study at the end of the literature review by pointing out a gap in the existing literature. At the same time, I was drawn to three features of Rui's literature review concerning the overall approach to the literature review, the theoretical framework, and the author's voice and presence in the literature review.

From my point of view as a reader, the approach to Rui's first draft of the dissertation literature review seemed to be largely topic/information-oriented, with the goal to provide a comprehensive overview of information relevant to the research topic. This topic-oriented approach was partly reflected in the juxtaposition of information whereby different views, models, theories, and studies were presented side by side to provide an overview of the topic. This was particularly evident in the first two sections of the draft literature review in which different theories, models, and views on academic literacy were summarized and presented. For example, in the first major section of the draft literature review, two different models of academic literacy development—cognitive apprenticeship and enculturation—were discussed. Concepts and tenets related to each model were presented, and different emphases of the two models were clearly pointed out. However, I was not quite sure about the implications of the two models for Rui's study. With my understanding that the primary purpose of the dissertation literature review would be to advance an argument for the specific dissertation *study* and the expectation that information reviewed would be relevant to the *study* rather than the general *topic* (i.e., the development of academic literacy), I had hoped to see discussions indicating in what ways these models would be relevant to Rui's study. Although Rui tried to establish the relevance of these models to the general topic area, stating that "genre knowledge can be acquired from the combination of both channels," I had expected Rui to evaluate how these models would contribute to an argument in support of the proposed study.

An important section of Rui's literature review was devoted to the theoretical framework of the dissertation study. In this section, sociocultural and sociocognitive theories were each presented in a subsection. The propositions and constructs of these theories were described, and their relevance to the development of academic literacy discussed. With my understanding that the theoretical framework is a part of the research design and guides data collection and analysis, I had several questions while reading this part of the review. For example, how did the theories influence the conceptualization of the proposed study? What concepts and constructs from the sociocognitive and sociocultural theories were crucial to the proposed study, and how could they be integrated into a coherent framework to guide the study in terms of the research focus, data collection, and data analysis? Although the two theories were described and discussed, how they might be integrated and how the integrated framework might guide the study were not very clear in the draft dissertation proposal. Although I was pleased with Rui's knowledge of the different theories, I was hoping to see more connection between the theoretical framework and the proposed dissertation study.

In the draft literature review, Rui came across as an objective and knowledgeable presenter of the information on the research topic. Sometimes, however, it appeared that the author's voice was muffled by those of the scholars whose work was being cited. In several places of the literature review, Rui was careful to include critiques of the research studies she was reviewing. In these sections, Rui would first summarize and present the studies under discussion and then follow her summaries of the studies with critiques of the studies. An interesting feature was that critiques of research under discussion were often presented in the voices of other scholars, as she did in her critique of Berkenkotter, Huckin, and Ackerman (1988, 1991), mentioned above. I wondered what Rui's own thoughts were on the research studies reviewed and if she agreed or disagreed with the critiques presented. I was puzzled as to why Rui foregrounded the voices of others rather than her own. Expecting the author of a dissertation literature review to be more of an emergent expert who would analyze, critique, and evaluate the research literature presented and who would make her own voice heard, I had hoped to see a stronger "authorial stance" (Ivanič, 1998) and to hear a stronger voice of Rui as a researcher and author.[2]

Reflection and Negotiation

What led us to an initial discussion of Rui's literature review writing experience was Rui's difficulty in addressing some of Wei's suggestions for revision. Rui indicated to Wei that she did not always understand her feedback or was not always sure as to how to address the feedback. We will not detail all the feedback and initial revision issues here since our focus is on the negotiation process, but will simply say that we decided to meet to discuss Rui's difficulties. Little did we know that our first meeting would mark the beginning of a process in which we would explore, discuss, and ponder issues related to the dissertation literature review and to the interaction between the major professor and the student during the dissertation writing process.

As part of our negotiations, we had a number of face-to-face sessions as well as numerous email exchanges. In the early sessions, we discussed Rui's difficulties with Wei's feedback on the relevance of some of the information presented in the literature review as well as the theoretical framework. In order to better understand Rui's difficulties and the rationale for her decisions about the dissertation literature review, Wei conducted "discourse-based interviews" (Odell, Goswami, & Herrington,

---

[2] A stronger authorial presence and voice emerged toward the end of the last section of the literature review.

1983) with Rui based on her draft literature review. Wei asked Rui about certain rhetorical strategies adopted in the literature review (e.g., why Rui attributed critical analysis of research to other scholars), about the role of the theoretical framework and her approach to the dissertation literature review (e.g., how the theories included in the theoretical framework were connected to the study), and about Rui's views of the theory and research covered in the literature review (e.g., what Rui's assessment was of the significance and relevance of the theory/research reviewed to her proposed study). In response to Wei's initial questions, Rui clarified the nature of her difficulties and shared her rationale for making decisions about her literature review. These discussions suggested that we might have had different understandings of some aspects of the dissertation literature review, which prompted Wei to ask further questions in the face-to-face sessions as well as through email exchanges. For example, Wei asked Rui what she believed to be the main characteristics of a successful literature review, what she learned through writing the dissertation literature review, and what roles she assumed in writing the literature review. These questions elicited Rui's articulations of her understandings and assumptions about the dissertation literature review as well as explanations about the factors that influenced the development of Rui's understandings. Rui's responses and articulations prompted Wei to reflect on her own understandings and assumptions about the dissertation literature review. Our understandings and assumptions were then shared, compared, and negotiated.

Our discussion and reflection helped us realize that we were bringing different personal theories about the dissertation literature review to the dissertation process. We also began to understand how our personal theories were developed and how they influenced our approaches to and expectations of the dissertation literature review. Our discussion and reflection led to not only articulation, but also negotiation of our personal theories of the dissertation literature review. We shared our personal theories and examined our assumptions and beliefs. We asked each other questions to clarify thoughts and to scaffold thinking about our theories. We explored the nature of the contexts and task environments in which our theories were developed and discussed the extent to which those contexts and environments were similar to that of the dissertation study. Through this comparison, we began to see that writing the dissertation literature review is a different task from writing other kinds of reviews, and that personal theories developed in contexts such as some course work that emphasize completeness and knowledge display are not entirely applicable to the dissertation literature review. We thus clarified our thinking about knowledge display in the context of the dissertation literature review, and came to agree that what needs to be displayed is the doctoral student's ability to use existing theory and research to inform the design and conceptualization of the dissertation study rather than to display knowledge of the research topic per se.

Reflection and negotiation of our personal theories deepened our understanding of the dissertation literature review. For instance, at the beginning of Rui's dissertation process, Wei felt that the dissertation literature review was somewhat different from other literature reviews but was not consciously aware of the extent and precise nature of the differences, such as the centrality of using literature to construct an argument as opposed to using it for a summary-style overview. For her part, Rui initially believed that the dissertation literature review, although more difficult and complicated, was similar to other literature reviews, and that criteria such as completeness and currency would apply to all literature reviews. We now agree that the literature review does not represent a single and monolithic genre—literature reviews serve different purposes in different contexts and require different approaches for the different purposes served.[3] Rui in particular has come to see the dissertation literature review in a new light, and her personal theories have shifted toward Wei's. She still thinks that knowledge display is important for the dissertation literature review; however, she accepts Wei's view that the purpose for knowledge display is to advance an argument aligned with research questions, data collection, and data analysis. The display of knowledge should facilitate the development of the argument. Rui has also realized that in her initial draft, she missed one of the most important factors of a successful dissertation literature review—that is, relevance. Compared with completeness, relevance seems more important to help the writer select appropriate information to present. It now seems to Rui that it may be extremely difficult for a writer to provide a thorough report on the dissertation topic due to the large amount of existing literature. Focusing on the development of an argument in support of the proposed dissertation study through analysis, synthesis, and evaluation may be a better route to achieve unity and coherence.

---

[3] We found some support for our understanding in an article we read while revising our paper. Maxwell (2006) distinguishes between "literature review articles for publication" and literature reviews for dissertation and considers the latter "primarily reviews *for*, rather than of, research" (p. 28, italics original).

Rui's perception of the role of the theoretical framework has also changed. She has begun to see theory as playing a fundamental role in the conceptualization of the whole study; that is, it is more than just a necessary part—it holds the whole study together. No matter how comprehensive and popular a particular theory is, it should not be included if it does not address the research question raised for the dissertation study and connect with research questions, data collection, and data analysis. She has also developed a better understanding of the role of the author in the dissertation literature review and of the relationship between being a critical thinker and objective information-organizer. Rui's modified view is that being an information organizer does not necessarily prevent the writer from analyzing, synthesizing, and evaluating the information. She no longer sees these two roles as contradictory, and is pleased she is free to have her own voice heard in the literature review.

Rui's modified personal theory about the dissertation literature review led to several revisions. First, to the extent possible, Rui made a great effort to relate the information presented to the proposed dissertation study. For example, she modified her presentation of the two models of learning and teaching academic literacy, presenting in detail only the one that was appropriate for the study. As for the other model, she gave up her goal of being complete, and instead mentioned the model briefly for the purpose of contrasting it with the appropriate model to give the reader a clear idea of the influence of the model on the study. Thus, Rui was no longer just presenting the information, but presenting the information in the context of her own study.

In another aspect of her revision, when Rui reconsidered the theoretical framework, she realized it was not necessary for her to apply sociocultural theory as a whole. Her study was only closely related to two constructs of sociocultural theory: scaffolding and mediation. These two concepts offer valuable theoretical lenses to examine the development of academic literacy. Therefore, she deleted sociocognitive theory from the theoretical framework. In the revised theoretical framework of her dissertation study, she integrated concepts from academic literacy theory such as learning discourse conventions, gaining access to discourse community, and understanding and performing genres with constructs of scaffolding and mediation from sociocultural theory.

Rui also demonstrated her critical thinker role much more extensively than in the initial draft and showed her confidence as an emergent expert. Coming back to the example of "Nate," Rui raised the doubt that Nate might not be considered as a novice writer based on the fact that he was an experienced composition teacher. Rui did not totally disregard similar voices from other experts. However, she presented them in a way that other voices would support and strengthen her own voice.

In sum, through our reflection and negotiation, we began to understand how important it is for the professor and student to share and examine personal theories about the dissertation literature review specifically and about the dissertation in general. Our experience has helped us realize that the professor and the student need to go beyond the text itself to address issues underlying their understandings of the dissertation literature review and the dissertation study. Personal theories about the dissertation literature review and the dissertation need to be made explicit and negotiated early in the dissertation process. This realization helped Wei refine her understanding of the role of a major professor; that is, in addition to the many roles that the major professor typically plays, she or he is also a facilitator in the reflection and negotiation of personal theories about the dissertation. Our negotiations eventually helped Rui successfully revise her literature review.

Conclusion

In this chapter, we examined our experience working on Rui's dissertation literature review from the perspective of personal theories. We brought different personal theories about the dissertation literature review to the dissertation writing/reading process, and our theories influenced our approaches to the dissertation literature review as writer and reader, respectively. Developed through our experiences with an array of academic writing tasks as members of the larger and local educational communities, our personal theories reflect different views and conceptions of the dissertation literature review. Rui's personal theory reflects what Maxwell (2006) refers to as "the traditional view" of the dissertation literature review, which sees the purpose of the dissertation literature review as the provision of a "thorough review of the research literature in the area of the dissertation" (p. 29). Wei's understanding of the dissertation literature review, on the other hand, aligns more closely with the conception of the dissertation literature review as "a selective review of the literature that relates directly to what the student plans to do, showing these works' implications for the proposed study" (Maxwell, 2006, p. 29). These different views, however, do not necessarily reflect differences between correct and incorrect views of the dissertation literature review, nor do they necessarily represent differences between faculty and student views. Rather, these views probably reflect what Maxwell (2006) refers to as "a division within the educational research community as a whole over the proper form and goal of literature reviews that are part of dissertations and dissertation proposals" (p. 29).

As indicated in recent debates about the dissertation literature review in educational research (e.g., Boote & Belie, 2005, 2006; Maxwell, 2006), there is no clear consensus regarding the goal of the dissertation literature review or the specific criteria measuring successful reviews. As we learned through our reflection and readings when we were revising this chapter (e.g., Maxwell, 2006), the literature review does not necessarily represent a single and monolithic genre. Literature reviews serving different purposes and situated in different contexts may require different forms, strategies, and criteria for assessing their success. Given these, it is not surprising that doctoral students and their major professors may bring very different personal theories about the dissertation literature review to the dissertation process. This does raise questions, however, concerning how the major professor and the doctoral student should deal with personal theories and how effective training on literature reviews can be provided for the doctoral students. Rather than discussing features of literature reviews in general, faculty members may wish to discuss features of successful literature reviews in relation to the specific contexts surrounding the literature reviews. This approach may help foster an understanding in the students that conceptions of successful literature reviews developed in some contexts may need to be reexamined when/if they are applied to literature reviews in other contexts. Our experiences indicated that personal theories need to be made explicit, reflected on, and negotiated, and that reflection on and negotiation of personal theories can afford valuable opportunities to both students and professors for a deepened understanding of the literature review.

WEI ZHU, UNIVERSITY OF SOUTH FLORIDA

I did not really know what to expect when I started my doctoral studies. I remember that when I saw a dissertation for the first time, I was in awe and asked myself how I could ever finish such a daunting task. I completed my dissertation four years after that encounter, and during those four years I learned a tremendous amount about the dissertation as a product and a process through interactions with my mentors. I see opportunities to interact with the faculty as a key to success for doctoral students and now, in my role as a mentor, try to provide those opportunities for my own students.

RUI CHENG, UNIVERSITY OF SOUTH FLORIDA

It was one of the biggest decisions in my life to join a Ph.D. program not only because I would have to devote the "best of my years" to research and study, but also because I had to come across the ocean to a new country. Now six years have passed, and I just got my degree. Looking back, I am really glad I made such a decision. Although I am still a young scholar struggling to find the best fit for me, I believe the training I received in these years, and the degree that resulted, are very beneficial for my future career.

REFERENCES

Anfara, V. A., & Mertz, N. T. (2006). Introduction. In V. A. Anfara & N. T. Mertz (Eds.), *Theoretical frameworks in qualitative research* (pp. xiii–xxxii). Thousand Oaks, CA: Sage.

Belcher, D. (1994). The apprenticeship approach to advanced academic literacy: Graduate students and their mentors. *English for Specific Purposes, 13*, 23–34.

Berkenkotter, C., Huckin, T. N., & Ackerman, J. (1988). Conventions, conversations, and the writer: Case study of a student in a rhetoric Ph. D. program. *Research in the Teaching of English, 22*(1), 9–44.

———. (1991). Social contexts and socially constructed texts: The initiation of a graduate student into a writing research community. In C. Bazerman & J. Paradis (Eds.), *Textual dynamics of the professions: Historical and contemporary studies of writing in academic and other professional communities* (pp. 191–215). Madison: University of Wisconsin Press.

Boote, D. N., & Belie, P. (2005). Scholars before researchers: On the centrality of the dissertation literature review in research preparation. *Educational Researcher, 34*(6), 3–15.

———. (2006). On "Literature reviews of, and for, educational research": A response to the critique by Joseph Maxwell. *Educational Researcher, 35*(9), 32–35.

Dong, Y. R. (1998). Non-native graduate students' thesis/dissertation writing in science: Self-reports by students and their advisors from two U.S. institutions. *English for Specific Purposes, 17*, 369–390.

Ivanič, R. (1998). *Writing and identity: The discoursal construction of identity in academic writing.* Amsterdam/Philadelphia: John Benjamins.

Lantolf, J. P. (Ed.). (2000). *Sociocultural theory and second language learning.* Oxford, UK: Oxford University Press.

Maxwell, J. (2005). *Qualitative research design: An interactive approach* (2nd ed.). Thousand Oaks, CA: Sage.

Maxwell, J. A. (2006). Literature reviews of, and for, educational research: A commentary on Boote and Belie's "Scholars before researchers." *Educational Researcher, 35*(9), 28–31.

McCutcheon, G. (1992). Facilitating teacher personal theorizing. In E. W. Ross, J. W. Cornett, & G. McCutcheon (Eds.), *Teacher personal theorizing* (pp. 191–205). Albany: State University of New York Press.

Odell, L., Goswami, D., & Herrington, A. (1983). The discourse-based interview: A procedure for exploring the tacit knowledge of writers in nonacademic settings. In P. Mosenthal (Ed.), *Research on writing* (pp. 221–236). New York: Longman.

Paltridge, B. (2002). Thesis and dissertation writing: An examination of published advice and actual practice. *English for Specific Purposes, 21*, 125–143.

Pape, S. (1992). Personal theorizing of an intern teacher. In E. W. Ross, J. W. Cornett, & G. McCutcheon (Eds.), *Teacher personal theorizing* (pp. 67–81). Albany: State University of New York Press.

Ross, E. W., Cornett, J. W., & McCutcheon, G. (1992). Teacher personal theorizing and research on curriculum and teaching. In E. W. Ross, J. W. Cornett, & G. McCutcheon (Eds.), *Teacher personal theorizing* (pp. 3–18). Albany: State University of New York Press.

Schilb, J. (1988). Ideology and composition scholarship. *Journal of Advanced Composition, 8*, 22–29.

Vygotsky, L. S. (1962). *Thought and language.* Cambridge: MIT Press.

———. (1978). *Mind in society: The development of higher psychological processes* (M. Cole, V. J. Steiner, S. Scribner, & E. Souberman, Eds.). Cambridge, MA: Harvard University Press.

Yin, R. (2003). *Case study research: Design and methods.* Thousand Oaks, CA: Sage.

Negotiating Online Postings and Publications: Identity Construction through Writing

YANBIN LU AND GAYLE NELSON

> *We define who we are by the ways we experience ourselves through participation. . .by where we have been and where we are going. . . .*
> Wenger, 1998, p.149

Yanbin:

My name is Yanbin Lu, and I am a doctoral student in applied linguistics at Georgia State University (GSU). During my first semester of study in the United States, my identity was transformed from that of an outsider to that of a legitimate participant in an online discussion group in one of the courses I was taking. Through participation and practice in online discussions, I changed from a cautious student carrying on a private conversation with the instructor to a more open student carrying on conversations with all the students in my discussion group. Additionally, the online discussions changed the way I conceptualized learning. I used to believe that the professor was the primary source of knowledge, but through the practice of online posting, I realized that my fellow classmates were also sources of knowledge who had ideas to enlighten me. Some of their postings helped me gain a better understanding of the reading materials, and some of their viewpoints presented another perspective that I had never thought of before. I came to realize that I can learn as much from them as from my professors.

My experience seems to embody Casanave's (2002) concept of writing as a "serious game." Novice players, being new to a game, usually do not play very well, and need to observe and imitate experienced players. They then need to participate, practice, and internalize the rules. I started as a new player in the game of "Online Posting" and became more experienced and competent through observation, imitation, participation, and practice. I identify with Canagarajah's (2003) assertion that "it is not formal study of rules but actually practicing the relevant discourse of the community one wishes to join that leads to one's insider professional status" (p. 197). How my identity transformation came about through this kind of practice, and how my professor's identity changed as well, is what our chapter is about. You have read the end of the story. We now go back to the beginning to trace some of the details of the transformation.

Gayle:

Yanbin began her doctoral program in the Department of Applied Linguistics and ESL at GSU in the fall of 2004. Soon after she arrived, she became an informant for a study I was conducting on academic socialization. As a component of the research, Yanbin kept an oral journal in which she recorded her observations as a new doctoral student. She uses the transcripts from her oral journal and her online postings in telling her story in this chapter. I was also her academic adviser and instructor for a course on intercultural communication. One of the requirements for the course was for students to post on WebCT,[1] an online discussion board, at least once a week on the readings for that particular week. The class was divided into two discussion groups, one of 10 students and one of 11. The groupings stayed constant for the course. I hoped that the students in these subgroups would get to know each other and build some trust. On the first day of class I informed students about the posting requirement for the course. Each week I provided a topic or question on which students posted from the readings.

Yanbin:

My first encounter with the word *posting* was in the first class I had with Dr. Nelson. When she was explaining the course syllabus, she told us we would post on the readings in WebCT on a weekly basis. I had no idea what she was talking about because I had never heard of "WebCT,"

---

[1] GSU uses an online course presentation and management system called WebCT, and each university course is automatically connected to the WebCT system. One of the components of WebCT is the option for students to write text and post it for other students and the instructor to read.

"post," or "posting" before. I did not know what kind of writing it was or what expectations the professor had, except for the posting being "about one screen long." She showed us how to log on to WebCT and the discussion board and how to post. The procedure for posting was easy for me to learn, but the composing of postings was another matter. My very first posting took me more than three hours, not including the time for reading the required article.

Since this type of writing, or genre, if it can be recognized as a genre, was totally new to me, I was unsure about the standards or criteria of such writing. I wondered what kind of writing style the professor expected, whether it would be enough to answer the professor's questions with information from the reading, and whether my answer was correct or would be up to the expectations of the professor. I was concerned about the correctness of my answer out of a habit that I formed due to my prior education in China. In my academic community in China, I had been trained to find the correct—usually the only—"standard" answer to a question. So at the beginning of the semester, I would often try to gauge what the professor expected as the correct answer.

The strategy that I took was to model someone else's posting. I believed that other students knew what to do for such assignments because, even though the discussion group for the course was newly formed, the practice of online posting was not new for most of the students in this class due to their prior experience in the broader academic community of American higher education. Later on when I was introduced to sociocultural theories of learning, I realized that this strategy corresponds to Vygotsky's notion of learning from "more capable" or "more experienced members" (Hall, 2002, p. 49). By following the more experienced members, we learn to recognize what is taking place and how to take action and develop a shared base of knowledge about the practice within the community.

The first message posted on WebCT served as the embodiment of the underlying criteria of posting and provided me with a concrete picture of a posting message.[2] The first student who responded answered the prompt question briefly, stated his opinions about some related concepts, and used some quotations. He also asked two questions related to the topic under discussion. Using his message as a model, I tried to compose mine. I was not used to asking questions, so I focused on answering

---

[2] Later on, through more experience with posting in other courses, I learned that the criteria for posting varied considerably, depending on different course instructors' requirements.

the prompt question in detail. In order to show my understanding and to support my argument, I quoted the information from the article. In fact, I quoted the reading six times in my first posting, and I used quotation marks and page numbers to indicate the source of my citations.[3]

Because I was used to writing for teachers in China, the audience for my first posting was Dr. Nelson. When I received the full number of points for my posting, my worries and anxieties were a little relieved, but I received no other feedback except for the points. I was still apprehensive about whether or not I had posted correctly, and I had no idea what the professor thought about it. Even though I understood that it was unrealistic for me to expect detailed feedback from the professor considering the size of the class (21 students), as a newcomer unfamiliar with the practice and with little confidence in myself, I was very concerned about the professor's opinion about my posting and my academic work in general. Such worries and anxieties completely disappeared in the sixth week when the professor sent me a message via the WebCT private email system, commenting on the message I posted that week. She wrote, "This response is beautifully written. I love your comment that. . . ." I learned that the professor was satisfied with my posting, and I was greatly encouraged by this message.

In the second week of posting, the professor instructed us to build our messages on previous postings, and I saw that other group members were responding to the messages of other students. I realized that online postings were designed not only for the presentation of ideas, but also for the discussion of ideas through the interaction of group members. I came to know that online postings were not homework for the professor to read, but a discussion for all the group members to interact with each other.

I wanted to respond to other group members, but it was not easy. I had to read through their postings very carefully to make sure that I understood their points of view. Honestly, sometimes I could not thoroughly understand what they wrote, mostly because I lacked background knowledge. I did not dare to ask questions or comment on their postings, because I was worried that if I asked questions, it would betray my ignorance; or if I commented, it might show my

---

[3] Later I learned that postings do not have to be that formal. But at that time, I had no idea that an online posting was actually a more informal genre with participants talking and discussing as if face-to-face.

misunderstanding. I believed that, relative to other students, I was a newcomer to this community and so was still very self-conscious.

However, in the fifth week I had a breakthrough. I even posted twice to interact with other group members. The first interaction was with a classmate who expressed her wish to move to China due to her longing for the practice of "saving face" or "keeping face" "in order to not disrupt group integrity" (posted by Susan).[4] I felt just the opposite, so I added one short paragraph at the beginning of my posting, replying to her message:

> Susan, if you move to China to settle down, I'm afraid you'll feel it so tiring and complex to deal with "protecting face" and to maintain "guanxi." Even as a product of Chinese culture, I find them difficult. I think it is a lot more easier [sic] to be frank and direct.

My second interaction was a reply to a message posted by a Russian student who expressed her surprise at some of the phenomena that were very much alike in China and Russia. Based on my knowledge of Chinese and world history, I felt I knew the reasons for the similarity, so I replied to her message, offering my explanation of the phenomenon:

> Iryna, you said you were surprised to see how much Chinese and Russian cultures are alike. The fact is. . . .And I agree to what you have said about this system, especially this sentence. . . .

These interactions were made possible because of the topic for that week—China, a topic with which I was familiar and about which I was very excited. When I had the necessary background knowledge, I felt that I was competent and that I was able to contribute something meaningful and useful to the whole group. This topic served as both an entry point and a scaffold for me to participate in the discussion. I was also no longer writing about what the professor might expect, but was stating my own opinions, firmly and directly. I was no longer writing only to the professor, but was considering the whole group as the audience. In

---

4   All the names used here are pseudonyms.

fact, I addressed the whole group that week. At the end of my posting, I wrote: "I'm sorry that my posting ran so long. As a student from China, I'd like very much to share with all of you my perspective."

By the eighth week, I was interacting even more with other members in my group on an individual basis. I mentioned three of my group members in just one paragraph of my posting:

> I was taken aback when I saw the number "38" <u>in John's posting</u>. What a detailed and specific list! <u>As Kate</u>, I went back to the reading and looked for the ones that I missed. I had listed the values mainly according to the subheadings stated by the authors, <u>just as Kate has</u>, (except for the last one), so I'll not repeat the list here. <u>Amy has made a list. . .most of which I agree</u>. And I'm also puzzled by the criteria . . . .What I'd like to point out is the role of the group leader or chairperson:. . .the chair is a facilitator (<u>my understanding seems to be contrary to Amy's</u>). . . .

By then, I was able to put forth my own point of view not only about the course readings but also about other students' reactions to the course readings. Additionally, I was no longer worried about showing my ignorance or inability to understand the article or others' messages. I admitted that I was "puzzled" by the reading. I also showed my disagreement openly (e.g., "my understanding seems to be contrary to Amy's"). I felt more and more comfortable doing online postings and interacting with group members in the virtual world.

Gayle:

Postings were also a relatively new pedagogical practice for me. I had used postings in one course before this one. From conversations with other faculty and from WebCT workshops, I had learned the technological procedures for using WebCT and some pedagogical points such as—a good length for a posting is one computer screen; it's not too much for the reader to read and not too little for the writer to write. My reasons for asking students to post were (a) to connect with the content of the readings by expressing their own points of view, (b) to interact with each other online, (c) to become more familiar with members of their groups for the in-class discussions, (d) to give students who prefer not to speak in class a venue for their ideas and for participating in a scholarly conversation, (e) to think more deeply about the readings, and (f) to demonstrate that students read the articles (they received points for posting). What I told students was that the purposes of postings were to engage personally with the content of the readings and to build community in their groups by interacting with each other online.

I also had assumptions of what I expected from students, although I could not have clearly articulated them at the beginning of the course. Because posting was still a relatively new form of interaction for me, my expectations were still emerging. My expectations became more concrete once students started posting and I recognized postings that included my hidden criteria and those that did not. When I became aware that I valued a particular element in a posting, I mentioned it to the students. For example, when I noted that students were writing stand-alone postings that resembled essays, I asked all the students in the class to refer to each other's postings and to carry on an online discussion of the topic. In retrospect, I am able to make the posting expectations explicit, but at the beginning of the course they were still in the process of development. I expected that students would (a) respond to each other, that there would be back-and-forth discussion, (b) read all of their peers' postings, (c) write in a style that was not too academic but not too conversational either, (d) use first person pronouns, (e) use personal examples (but I would get concerned if the personal examples overshadowed the main points in the reading), (f) refer to each other by name, (g) be kind and polite to their peers, and (h) collectively create a thread of postings linked by references to each other. The points students received, however, were related to their demonstration of having read the articles. At the time I was unaware of the contradiction between the criteria for awarding points and the hidden criteria I had in mind for postings. The disconnect between stated and hidden criteria and Yanbin's desire for personal comments on postings were personal realizations I experienced as a result of writing this chapter.

Expectations I had for myself included writing the weekly prompt, reading the postings, occasionally interacting with students online about the content of their postings, and assigning weekly posting points. As a newcomer to this relatively new educational practice, I was unsure how to structure it. I wanted students to interact with the readings and bring in personal experiences, but I did not want personal experiences to take over the discussion. Also, I was concerned that students might find the practice make-work, work for the sake of work. As a result of my uncertainties, I put a great deal of effort into writing prompts, using Bloom's taxonomy (1984) to help me develop topics or questions that asked students to use critical thinking in their postings. Whether or not my struggle with verb choice and question type, choosing verbs such as *analyze* over *discuss*, resulted in more thoughtful postings, I do not know (but it quieted my doubting self). Since then, I have been involved in discussions with colleagues who have commented that they believe that graduate students write more thoughtful postings if they have a sense of ownership over the topic and write about issues of interest to themselves. My current practice is to negotiate authorship of the posting prompt with my classes with possibilities ranging from students' making a posting with no prompt, to students' creating the prompt, to my creating the prompt. In Yanbin's class, however, I held the reins of the prompt.

I often checked WebCT at least twice a day to read any new postings. Being able to see how students learned from and interacted with each other and how they processed the information in the course (e.g., applied it to their lives, their teaching, and their definitions of selves) was a dimension of their learning that I might not have been privy to if it had not been for the postings. Then the night before the next class, I made a cup of tea, lined up some Hershey kisses, and settled in for a relaxed reading of the complete thread. What students probably did not know was how much I reflected on their words and ideas. I had intended to engage in one-on-one written dialogue with students, but my inner editing voice prevented me from making many types of comments, such as *I enjoyed reading what you wrote* or *an insightful point of view*. Because I knew that these kinds of responses appeared generic and that by making them I was evaluating the posting instead of interacting with the content, I tended to say nothing. I was also hesitant to respond because I was in a power position and my comments would not be those of a co-learner. The task of engaging individually with 21 students each week about their ideas proved to be impossible for me. Not only was it time consuming, but my concerns about the effects of teacher comments held me back much of the time. Upon reflection, my concerns and resulting silence may have been my friends. My responding to students would have taken away from one of the purposes of the postings: for students to learn from each other.

On the other hand, as Yanbin has revealed, although the numerical points awarded reduced her anxiety somewhat, a personal response from the instructor amplified her sense of having correctly negotiated the posting practice. After working with her on this chapter, I again am asking myself whether or not I ought to respond to students individually. Another conundrum relates to numerical points. In my ideal learning community, students would post for the joy of writing, thinking, reading, and learning. I try to create that learning community by rewarding students with points, but as I noted earlier, in Yanbin's class, my point system did not match my hidden criteria for posting. The criterion for distributing points continues to be elusive. I attempt to reward students for thinking critically about the ideas we are reading about and other students have discussed, and give a holistic score that I hope covers the criteria listed in this chapter and given in the syllabus. However, I often wonder if I am giving points for their having completed the posting assignment (full points) or not having completed it (no points).

Yanbin:

As Wenger (1998) points out, when one moves from one community of practice to another, there will be significant challenges and possibly an identity shift for the learner. I was not conscious of an identity transformation until I began analyzing data for this chapter. As I was learning to post, I believed I was simply learning a new practice. I was not aware of the connection between practice, participation, and identity, that developing a practice means negotiating "ways of being a person in that context" and involves a negotiation of identities (Wenger, p. 149).

In the process of analyzing my postings for the course, I began to notice a change in my use of pronouns. Hawkins (2004) demonstrates that an analysis of pronouns can reveal how students speak from "voices" specific to the identities they feel they can legitimately claim in a given context. At the beginning of the semester, I was conscious of my national identity as a Chinese and of being a newcomer in a new community. As I wrote in my first posting,

I'm very much concerned about developing my communication skills with <u>people from a culture other than my own</u>, and try to understand their words and behavior from their perspective. . . .In the <u>Chinese culture</u>, <u>we</u> believe in. . .and <u>we</u> value. . . .(August 29, 2004).

Here I was contrasting "the Chinese culture" and cultures "other than my own." I regarded myself as a member of the former, whereas people from another culture were members of a group "other than my own." By the fifth week I had started to interact with other members in the group, but I still assumed a Chinese identity:

> . . .as students in Chinese culture, <u>we</u> tend to show <u>our</u> respect for <u>our</u> teacher by offering help whenever possible. <u>We</u> would often carry books or bags for <u>our</u> teacher when <u>we</u> are walking together with him/her, even if the teacher is only a few years older than <u>we</u> are.

It seems that I was still talking and writing as a student in Chinese culture, even though I had graduated a decade before. I positioned myself in alliance with Chinese students, indicating my group identity that I felt subconsciously at that time. In contrast, I referred to Americans as people from another group:

> With the value of individualism, <u>Americans</u> are brought up to be independent and to show that <u>they</u> are capable, so <u>they</u> won't ask for help unless necessary.

I put Americans into a group other than my own, whose characteristics were not shared by me. I felt that I was a total outsider to American culture. Even though I had started interacting with other classmates, a practice in which I could be regarded as a peripheral participant of this community, subconsciously I was classifying myself and my American classmates in national cultural terms: Chinese and American. As Wenger points out, we all belong to many communities of practice and the construction of an identity—the nexus of multimembership—requires reconciliation and integration of our various forms of membership. For learners moving from one community of practice to another, this work of reconciliation is a significant challenge. At that time, I had many newly acquired memberships—as a doctoral student in the U.S., a graduate research assistant, a student in a particular course, and a participant in an online discussion group, but I had not reconciled these memberships into my identity. For approximately two months after arriving in the United States, my old longstanding Chinese identity seemed to prevail over all these new memberships.

To my surprise, by the ninth week, I was no longer using "we Chinese." I wrote in my posting:

> That is why <u>Chinese students</u> are more willing to listen to the teacher giving lectures rather than to have group discussion. <u>They</u> tend to think <u>their</u> peer classmates don't know enough to be good exemplars.

Am I no longer regarding myself as a Chinese? Surely I am still Chinese, but I no longer regarded myself as a member of the community of students in China or as a member of the Chinese students who have such beliefs. I used to, as most Chinese students do, believe that students learn primarily from teachers' lectures and not from class discussions. However, I have come to realize the value of group discussions from the courses I was taking, so I no longer share those views. It seems that I have excluded myself from such a group of Chinese students by referring to them as "they." I started to think and write as a member of the community of students in an American university. In the 12th week, I wrote in my posting:

> <u>We</u> can see a number of similarities between Allen's approach and <u>our</u> experience. . .I believe both <u>our</u> class and Allen's approach fit. . .one difference I noticed between <u>our</u> program and Allen's program is. . . .

I was referring to the program at GSU as "our program" and comparing the similarities and differences between "our class" and another group. I must have felt a sense of belonging by then and must have considered myself a member of the new community that I had joined three months before.

I used to consider myself from Chinese culture, viewing culture as a homogenous whole. Now I have come to question the idea of a unified culture, recognizing that within national boundaries, a great deal of variation exists. I still consider myself Chinese, but I have acquired new identities through my active involvement and participation in the practices of the community and through the adjustment of my values and concepts, in Wenger's terms, through "engagement" and "alignment."

This realization of identity change as witnessed in the use of pronouns did not come until later when Dr. Nelson and I were reviewing the data from my postings and my oral journal for analysis. Had I not taken a part in the process of analysis, I might not have come to this conscious awareness of my identity shift.

Gayle:

When Yanbin and I began this project, I was the researcher, the instructor, and the adviser, and she was the participant, the student, and the advisee. Clearly, I was in the position of having more authority and/or more power. During the months of interviewing, I frequently asked Yanbin to *dig deep,* but she did not ask me to dig deep. Even as we began writing this chapter, I continued my authority position, adding authority-as-published-writer to the list of ways in which I played the authority role in her life.

As the work on the chapter continued and the content began to emerge, it became clear that it was Yanbin's story and I struggled to find my place in the chapter, initially providing theoretical comments or an analysis of Yanbin's experiences. Eventually the editors, Christine Pearson Casanave and Xiaoming Li, urged me to dig deeper into my own reactions, behaviors, and feelings. They asked me to reflect on what I had discovered about myself.

For two decades, my discoursal self (Ivanič, 1998) has been that of an academic applied linguistics researcher making claims based on the data generated by studies. This position was relatively comfortable for me. When confronted with opposition, I could fall back on my data with comments such as ". . .but the data support X." I have seldom published a personal and reflective discoursal self in my academic outlets (one exception being Nelson, 2003). It is this reflective, softer, more fluid discoursal self that I thought I could conjure up for this chapter, but she was buried deep. Although I perceive myself as a person who mentors and encourages graduate students, presents with them at conferences, and co-publishes with them; as someone who is careful about ethical boundaries, I was surprised to discover that on reading drafts of the chapter, I was interpreting Yanbin's experiences and continued to play the role of the researcher even after I thought that I had stopped doing so. Similar to Yanbin's analysis of her postings, I was surprised to reexamine drafts of this chapter and discover my identity as "interpreter of co-author's experience." In the process of writing this chapter, the editors encouraged me to engage in a different practice, collaborative *reflective* writing as an equal co-author, a practice emerging in the field (Casanave & Vandrick, 2003).

Writing reflectively was difficult for three reasons. First, I had to figure out how to reflect. What was I supposed to write? What literature could I go to? Was I supposed to just sit and think? What I discovered was that my personal reflection demanded other people; my thoughts needed resistance in order to change. Through conversations, email, and editors' comments, I was able to rethink my role in relation to Yanbin. The second reason writing reflectively was difficult was that it felt self-referential and, perhaps, even self-absorbed. Third, admitting to my peers, as I have done earlier in this chapter, that I use verbs from Bloom's taxonomy in formulating prompts for online postings and that I am unsure about how to respond to students' online postings is slightly face threatening. I define myself as an L2 writing researcher and feel that I should know how to write prompts and respond to students' postings and although I know that "we" (L2 writing researchers) all have doubts now and then about our teaching and writing, I have doubts about baring private faces in public places.

Yanbin and Gayle:

Throughout this chapter we have been using terminology from and referring to communities of practice. We have used the term loosely, referring to a theory of learning, our course and all it included, and our continued involvement with the course.[5] The notion of communities of practice sounds reassuring; it assumes, more or less, that if newcomers participate in the practice and interact with old-timers, then they will become part of the community. As Haneda (2006) notes, "examples of communities that Lave and Wenger described appear to be relatively problem-free" (p. 811). However, Haneda is critical of communities of practice for exactly this reason. The community of practice concept glosses over struggles and tensions that members experience and also does not address issues of power. Similarly, Lea (2005) argues that the concept is simplistic and does not recognize the "contested nature in communities of practice. . .when participants are excluded from full participation. . . ." (p. 184).

We have discussed issues of struggle and power in this chapter in a manner that we feel illustrates how these issues may emerge when a

---

5   Because we have continued to examine the course, we believe that although the course ended in "real" time, it has not ended for us while we are working with the data.

newcomer embarks on the journey of joining a community of practice. In the case of Yanbin, even though she was not technically any more of a newcomer than the other students, she felt that the other students were further along in their understanding of the trajectory that needed to be followed in order to progress from absolute newcomer status to a somewhat-less-of-a-newcomer status. As a result of her beliefs about herself in relation to the other participants—students and teacher—Yanbin felt disempowered during the first weeks of this course while struggling to find her voice in the online discussion group. Her path from absolute newcomer to an increasingly more participatory status (i.e., a new identity) was challenging to the other identities she brought to the experience. In a similar fashion, both Yanbin and Gayle struggled as their identities were called upon to shift yet again in relation to their experiences in writing, rewriting, and responding to editorial suggestions for this chapter. Thus, the notion of learning as identity change through participation in a community of practice implies a process that is inherently challenging as we do not easily lay aside our other identities in favor of the new ones offered to us.

For both of us, the changes that occurred were gradual. This gradualness makes sense when considering the challenges to one's own assumptions and beliefs. Individuals resist. When we participate in a community of practice in which we are full members, we feel competent. We understand what we are doing, why we are doing it, and how to do it. It feels good. Even though this process was at times difficult, we would like to encourage other students and faculty to participate in research with each other and, reflectively, with themselves. Endeavors such as this one are good reminders that teaching and learning are negotiated acts that include the participation of all participants in both acts; we are all teachers and learners.

YANBIN LU, GEORGIA STATE UNIVERSITY

Coming to the United States for my Ph.D. study, leaving behind my six-year-old daughter and my ten years of experience as an EFL teacher in a prestigious university in China, was the most radical decision I've made in my life. I've had moments of doubt about whether my decision was wise or my efforts worthwhile. But the community that I entered (in the Department of Applied Linguistics at Georgia State) proved to be academically nourishing and extremely supportive. I've realized that doing a Ph.D. is a test of one's perseverance. I will keep going and hope my hard work will pay off one day.

GAYLE NELSON, GEORGIA STATE UNIVERSITY

I took a risk in selecting a doctoral program. I had taught EFL/ESL at Kuwait University, West Virginia University, and the American University in Cairo, and my long-term goal was to train English language teachers. At that time, the safe choice would have been a linguistics or education program. The risky choice was following what I was passionate about: culture and intercultural communication. I went to the University of Minnesota, later wondering "What applied linguistics program will hire me with a Ph.D. in Intercultural Communication?" Fortunately, I found a great position at Georgia State University, and I am still passionate about my field.

Acknowledgments

We are grateful to Christine Pearson Casanave and Xiaoming Li for giving us insights into our writing and for exposing some of our hidden assumptions; to Lauren Lukkarila for insightful discussions on communities of practice and for commenting on the manuscript; to Diane Belcher for encouraging us to write this chapter and for providing supportive feedback; and to Dara Suchke for transcribing the data quickly and accurately.

REFERENCES

Bloom, B. S. (1984). *Taxonomy of educational objectives*. Boston: Allyn & Bacon.

Canagarajah, A. S. (2003). A somewhat legitimate and very peripheral participation. In C. P. Casanave & S. Vandrick (Eds.), *Writing for scholarly publication: Behind the scenes in language education* (pp. 197–210). Mahwah, NJ: Lawrence Erlbaum.

Casanave, C. P. (2002). *Writing games: Multicultural case studies of academic literacy practices in higher education*. Mahwah, NJ: Lawrence Erlbaum.

Casanave, C. P., & Vandrick, S. (Eds.). (2003). *Writing for scholarly publication: Behind the scenes in language education*. Mahwah, NJ: Lawrence.

Hall, J. K. (2002). *Teaching and researching language and culture*. London: Pearson Education.

Haneda, M. (2006). Classrooms as communities of practice: A reevaluation. *TESOL Quarterly, 40*, 807–817.

Hawkins, M. (2004). Social apprenticeships through mediated learning in language teacher education. In M. Hawkins (Ed.), *Language learning and teacher education* (pp. 89–109). Clevedon, UK: Multilingual Matters.

Ivanič, R. (1998). *Writing and identity: The discoursal construction of identity in academic writing*. Amsterdam: John Benjamins.

Lea, M. R. (2005). 'Communities of practice' in higher education. In *Beyond communities of practice: Language, power, and social context* (pp. 180–197). Cambridge, UK: Cambridge University Press.

Nelson, G. (2003). A Fulbright adventure: Just do it! In P. Byrd & G. Nelson (Eds.), *Sustaining professionalism: Professional development in language education* (pp. 105–111). Alexandria, VA: TESOL.

Wenger, E. (1998). *Communities of practice: Learning, meaning, and identity*. Cambridge, UK: Cambridge University Press.

It Takes a Community of Scholars to Raise One: Multiple Mentors as Key to My Growth

LU LIU
WITH IRWIN WEISER, TONY SILVA, JANET ALSUP, CINDY SELFE,
AND GAIL HAWISHER

In 2001 I entered the Purdue graduate program in rhetoric and composition with a multidisciplinary background in English, communication, and sociology. Although I held two master's degrees, I had no clear understanding of the process of doing academic research. In addition, the multidisciplinary nature of my research interest made it hard to identify one single advisor. I decided to seek out as many mentors as I needed. That strategy led to the formation of my relationship with my multiple mentors.

Five years later, I grew from a confused graduate student to a fledging scholar. I published one journal article, wrote my dissertation funded by a research grant, and joined Peking University as an assistant professor of English. In retrospect, I attribute my growth to my close work with my multiple mentors, who have provided me with abundant support and guidance. As my chair and co-chair, Irwin ("Bud") Weiser and Tony Silva provided me with guidance in the fundamentals of doing research and getting published. As a mentor whom I sought out on campus, Janet Alsup, one of my dissertation committee members, has enlightened me not only with her expertise, but also with her insightful views of doing research and getting published. Cindy Selfe and Gail Hawisher, who collaborated with me on a research project, taught me by example about the various stages of conducting and composing research. This multi-vocal essay incorporates my own reflection on how my mentors played an important role in my growth as a scholar in graduate school. My mentors respond in turn.

Benefiting Most from Formal Advising: Bud and Tony

Learning to do research is a long and difficult process, which requires regular sharing, talking, and guidance. My growth could not have been possible without formal advising, and looking back, I found it vital to have mentors who were available for regular meetings, conscientious, and willing to share. Bud and Tony were both my formal mentors for two teaching practica. Before I took those courses, I was not clear about what it meant to be a mentee. In both practica, Bud and Tony shared their own teaching materials with the mentees and met regularly to talk about each unit of the course. The sharing and regular meetings set the tone for my relationship with them later as an advisee, which was vital for my growth as a scholar.

Bud gave me a proper introduction to the socialization process in academia, which helped me to start on the right track. As my dissertation chair, he helped me to stay realistic, guard against my perfectionism, and stay focused. In my first semester in the rhetoric and composition program, I took a course with Bud. Bud designed the course so that the students worked on their final papers in the same way scholars work on their conference papers. First, students submitted abstracts as conference paper proposals. Bud reviewed the abstract, and then wrote a letter to each student in the capacity of the program chair for the "2001 Occasional Conference on Writing Across/In/Through the Curriculum at Purdue University." After putting together panels, he sent an invitation letter to the presenters and invited both faculty members and students to attend the presentations. The formality of the process pushed me to think of a significant topic for my own project. That term paper became the first draft of my first manuscript that evolved into a pilot study for my dissertation research and later a published journal article. Taking that course with Bud, I saw how he strived to help students grow as scholars. I knew that Bud had the traits of a mentor I was a looking for.

I then worked with Bud in his practicum on teaching academic writing and research. The mentoring group used a course packet, a precursor of an upcoming textbook authored by Bud. Several things about Bud further impressed me. First, he shared with the mentoring group a hard copy of his textbook proposal. There I spotted the Number 1 quality of a good mentor, the readiness and willingness to share his or her successful work. A second trait of Bud's that impressed me was his responsiveness. While taking a research methods course with Bud, I designed a questionnaire that required a faculty member's sponsorship to get approval from the human subjects committee. Bud readily agreed to be the sponsor, did the paper work, and obtained the permission promptly.

Bud was also willing to admit his unsuccessful experiences when it was helpful for graduate students. I remember that when it was time for us to hear from the Conference on College Composition and Communication (CCCC) about proposal acceptance/rejection, students lamented about rejections. Bud said with his signature smile: "We all have to keep trying." That demythified my misperception that my professors never have their proposals rejected. That comment also prevented me from losing heart when I worked on manuscripts.

Furthermore, Bud accelerated my growth with occasional prods or reminders, especially when my perfectionism led to unproductive behavioral patterns. For example, when I worked on my grant proposal for my dissertation project, as a perfectionist, I automatically wanted to please everyone who read the proposal, including several tutors in the campus writing lab. When I talked to Bud about my frustration, he hit the nail on the head: "You need to satisfy yourself!" That helped me see my propensity to please everyone just for the sake of pleasing others. Similarly, when I could not stop working on my grant proposal although I had revised it several times, Bud told me frankly: "You need to know when to stop revising." Bud's straightforward suggestions brought me face to face with my weaknesses, thus helping me to transcend them and grow. Another pitfall that my perfectionism tends to create is that it causes me to set unrealistic goals. When I wrote in my dissertation prospectus that I hoped to propose a pedagogy based on the findings and implications of my findings, Bud detected the over-ambition and suggested that I discuss the implications only, which turned out to be a much more feasible goal. That reminded me of Bud's advice: "There is always the next project."

All of Bud's timely reminders would not have been possible if he had not been available for regular meetings. Those meetings also kept my dissertation work structured. We met biweekly to discuss my progress, concerns, and my writing. Those meetings provided me with a sense of consolidation. It was extremely helpful when I could not read my own draft for a certain section anymore and hoped to move on. I called my writing a hot potato at such a stage. I was comfortable enough to pass the hot potato on to Bud when I felt it was hot enough. Bud always took over the "hot potatoes" and gave timely feedback. That was critical in my dissertation writing process because I felt that I was not 100 percent alone in the project and I always had an ally.

One might say that Bud's simulation of socialization in the academic community put me on the right track in the beginning of my Ph.D. studies. His reminders kept my feet on the ground, and the regular meetings helped me to keep the momentum of my work. Tony, as the co-chair of my dissertation committee, guided me more in the details of joining the academic community, gaining my own voice, getting published, and networking. I got to know Tony in his class on ESL curriculum and design. For the course project, a classmate and I worked on a course Tony had designed and developed, English 002, Written Communication for International Graduate Students. Tony was easily available for consultation and answered our questions with great patience and care. I liked the way he took his time to think through our questions. Later I became an instructor of English 002, and Tony was my mentor for the teaching practicum. He provided the new instructors with a zip disk with all the course materials, including samples of student writing. I was soon aware of the important trait of Tony as a mentor, a readiness to share.

Because of my interest in second language writing, I continued to seek out Tony for advising regarding my research and manuscript preparation. Tony, as a journal editor himself, has helped me understand the manuscript review and submission process. The first obstacle he helped me to overcome was my diffidence. My first manuscript started out as an article on a comparative analysis of writing instruction in Chinese and American textbooks. When I expressed my sense of insecurity about the literature review section, Tony reminded me: "You know a lot about this topic." I took a course with Tony and did my term paper on the literature on contrastive rhetoric. Tony's comments boosted my confidence.

Another obstacle in my first try at manuscript submission to journals was my fear of rejection. Tony dispelled that with one sentence: "Editors are looking for articles to publish, not to reject." In addition, I was intimidated by critical reviews. Incidentally, the instructional materials Tony provided for a manuscript review assignment or English 002 helped me overcome that fear. For that assignment, Tony provided students with an earlier version of a journal article and three reviews. One of the reviews was harsh, but the other two provided constructive criticism. I learned that that article was eventually published in the journal.

With the two obstacles cleared, when I did work on the manuscript seriously, Tony also helped me to fight against my perfectionist tendencies. For my first manuscript, I was not sure when to send it out. The paper was a substantial revision of a manuscript that I had finished at the end of a fall semester. Tony, who was kind enough to meet me during the winter break to talk to me, gave me the best antidote to my perfectionism in manuscript preparation: "Just send it out to see what happens." That was the push I needed to let go of my fear of rejection of my first manuscript.

As chair of the biannual Symposium on Second Language Writing, Tony also provided me with the chance to network with scholars in second language writing. He invited me and other students to the symposium. Not only was I able to attend some sessions that interested me, but I was also able to attend the final party at Tony's home for scholars and the volunteers. It was at one of the parties where I met Ruyko Kubota, who also works on contrastive rhetoric and who gladly shared her work on writing instruction in Chinese and Japanese secondary textbooks (Kubota & Shi, 2005), a project helpful for my dissertation project.

Like Bud, Tony also shared with me stories of his successes and failures. When one of my manuscripts was rejected after revision, Tony encouraged me: "You are doing much better than I was when I was at your stage." And he talked about how choosing the right journal can make a difference, using the case of a recently published work of his: "Every manuscript can eventually end up being published somewhere." I found these comments from Tony very encouraging. Tony also shared with the class one of his own manuscripts that he had done in collaboration with a colleague and talked about the multiple revisions they did before its publication. Therefore, when I substantially revised the first draft of my first submission, I did not feel alone. Instead, I was able to look at revisions in a positive light. That is, I recognized that the editors and reviewers had seen potential in the project and had offered suggestions to help the project mature and grow. That was my new understanding of the review and revisions process for manuscript submission.

Of course, all the important guidance Tony provided would have been impossible if he had not been generous with his time. He was available even during his sabbatical. I remember vividly that even a few days before Christmas, Tony was willing to meet with me to talk about the revisions of my first manuscript to be resubmitted to a scholarly journal. Because of that timely meeting, I was able to submit the revised version immediately after that winter break.

Bud's Commentary

In my experience, it's rare for mentors to have the opportunity to read about their influence on students. It's also flattering and a bit embarrassing to see oneself praised in print, particularly when one is also asked to comment on what has been written and on the relationship with the student. As I read Lu's description of our work together as mentor/mentee, teacher/student, dissertation advisor/dissertation writer, I thought both about what enabled Lu's and my relationship to be a successful one for her and a rewarding one for me.

Much of the credit of this mentoring relationship and perhaps any successful and satisfying mentoring relationship lies with the student. Lu's work with me was in large part chance—she chose to take a course I taught, she was assigned to be in my practicum section—so our working relationship was not really one that began because of any conscious choice on either of our parts. It worked not simply because Lu is smart—all Ph.D. students are smart—but also because she is very committed to learning and to becoming a successful member of the discipline of rhetoric and composition.

The mentoring relationship, as Lu suggests, is a mutual and collaborative one. It works best when both parties are committed to the larger intellectual project that brings them together. And, from a mentor/faculty member's perspective, it works best when the mentee/student is, like Lu, enthusiastic, focused, and well organized. While Lu refers to sometimes being unprepared for her teaching during the semester she taught Academic Writing and Research, I don't recall that about her. What I recall instead was her eagerness to develop as a teacher and her openness to trying new ideas and materials. Throughout our working together, Lu initiated as much, if not more, of our working pattern than I did. It was Lu who asked to have biweekly meetings, and it was Lu who often came with a particular agenda for those meetings, with specific questions about her reading or her methodology or resources. Sometimes our meetings were very brief, sometimes because Lu didn't have much on her agenda, but on occasion because she'd come in, sit down, and "confess" that she hadn't made any progress. But she kept her appointments, and even those short, confessional meetings gave us an opportunity to discuss what she planned or needed to do to get back on track. As I'm sure anyone who has mentored or served as an advisor knows, Lu's way of working is a major reason for her success. She is proactive as a student, and she understood from the beginning that the Ph.D. program is not a destination; it's a stop on the way to her goal to become a practicing academic.

Working with a student like Lu is an opportunity to learn about being a mentor by paying attention to her characteristics as a student. I don't mean to suggest that one could or should try to persuade every student to follow her example. Rather, I mean that every student we mentor provides us an opportunity to become better at figuring out how we can be helpful and supportive mentors—how we can tailor our mentoring to the variety of styles of working that students provide, how to know when to push, when to be patient, when to set deadlines or goals, and when to give students the time they need to work at paces that are best for them. Higher education has become increasingly interested in what's often referred to as preparing the future professoriate. Lu's discussion of how she discovered and in some cases sought mentors emphasizes the importance graduate faculty mentors play in this most rewarding preparation.

Tony's Commentary

Graduate faculty who have read this far have recognized Lu as the kind of graduate student who makes us look good. She's very bright and knowledgeable, highly motivated, and easy and fun to work with. She's the kind of student you know is going to succeed at whatever she decides to do. All I really did for Lu was to listen, offer encouragement, and introduce her to the second language writing discourse community. She took it from there.

Here's what I got in return: In my graduate course, I got a well prepared student who asked insightful questions, spurred class discussion, and turned in skillfully crafted writing assignments. As her mentor, I got an experienced, talented, and innovative teacher who stimulated her students to produce their best work and contributed much to the curriculum. For the Symposium on Second Language Writing, I got a personable and energetic assistant who helped put attendees and speakers at ease.

As the co-chair of her dissertation committee, I got to read interesting, informative, and polished chapters and to meet on a regular basis to talk and learn about Chinese and American philosophy, rhetoric, and writing instruction. And as the editor of the *Journal of Second Language Writing*, I got a contributor who had the lead article in a recent issue.

All in all, I'd say I got a pretty good deal.

Seeking out Interdisciplinary Help and Additional Mentoring: Janet

In their unique ways, Bud and Tony provided me with the guidance I needed for working on my dissertation, funding the project, and joining the academic community. I was lucky enough to get to know them in the capacity of both a mentee and a student and later to invite them to be my chair/co-chair. The development of my relationship with Janet, however, was initiated totally by me for my dissertation project and evolved into a mentoring relationship.

I did not know Janet before I invited her to be my dissertation committee member. I, however, had heard her ask insightful questions at interdisciplinary lectures sponsored by the rhetoric and composition program at Purdue. I was impressed. When I decided to work on my dissertation project, a comparative study of written argumentation instruction in secondary textbooks in China and the U.S., I needed one committee member from the field of English education. I checked out the Purdue website for its English Education program and found that Janet's interests in rhetoric and composition and English education seemed to fit well.

Janet's first response to my email about my dissertation project and my intention to invite her to be a committee member confirmed my decision. She sent a substantial message, replying to my questions about relevant sources by suggesting that I look at the major publishers of secondary school textbooks who design standardized texts and provide textbooks for states with a textbook adoption system. That helped me to narrow down the sample textbooks for the dissertation project. In the latter stages of the dissertation project, Janet continued to refer me to important references, such as the *Handbook of Research on Teaching the English Language Arts* and an important book on teaching writing in secondary schools.

In my first meeting with Janet, I detected the traits of a mentor I needed. After greeting me, she left her desk chair, took out a notepad, and walked over to the chair set next to the chair I was invited to sit in. During our talk she took careful notes. I was impressed with how engaged she was during our talks and how she thought of sources that could be useful to me and turned to her bookshelves frequently. Her engagement in the discussions also generated fresh perspectives. For example, she was very interested in what Chinese language arts textbooks for secondary schools look like. When I showed her the Chinese textbooks, she marveled at Chinese characters: "They look beautiful!" This reminded me of something I took for granted and forgot for so long: the aesthetic color in Chinese literacy education. The way one writes a character has been connected with how beautiful and balanced the characters should look. This important concept of beauty and balance is an important component of Chinese philosophy, which became an important focal point in my dissertation.

Janet not only provided me with indispensable guidance in a subject area that is not my expertise area, she also offered me new perspectives on being an academic and shared her successful experience. To me, Janet is an inspiration. Within five years after getting her Ph.D., she co-edited a book, published journal articles, wrote a book, had it published, and made tenure. She became my resident consultant regarding being productive. Because I had a research grant for my dissertation myself, I faced a problem with working on the dissertation only, which initially led to a very unproductive pace. She won a grant for her book project and focused on the writing in one semester. She shared her experience of time management: limiting the time spent on her book daily. She worked on the writing every morning from 8:00 to noon and disconnected the phone. That debunked my misperception about the "more time, the merrier" in terms of time spent on writing daily. Janet also told me that after every morning, she just let the project stay at the back of her mind. Later I found books that do advocate that kind of work schedule, working on something in the morning and then stopping, at which point the subconscious can continue working on it. I also limited the time I spent on my writing and found my schedule more effective. The time limit was a great antidote to my perfectionist tendencies, too. As my job search approached, our discussions covered job search strategies. She even shared her tenure materials with me.

One factor that negatively affects the productivity of scholars is the pressure to publish. Janet helped me gain a fresh perspective about getting published and getting tenure. When I talked about the pressure to publish, Janet commented: "It is the other way around." Her words enabled me to see the pressure to publish in a new light: Focused research and writing will naturally lead to publication. After publishing my first manuscript as a journal article, I did find myself wanting to write my second manuscript instead of feeling pressured to write for publication.

Like Bud and Tony, Janet was easily available during her office hours and by appointment and very generous with her time. Her willingness to carry on an open-ended dialogue about my concerns/questions made our meetings extremely productive.

Janet's Commentary

I remember first meeting Lu and being excited when she asked me to join her committee. I found her to be smart, diligent, and energized about her work. She conducted her research methodically and reflected critically on her scholarly results. I remember the hours we spent talking about her questions, her research process, and her writing timeline, which was strategically organized so she could maximize work during productive times of the day, meet other professional obligations, and enjoy at least a little bit of personal time! I believe this development of effective scholarly habits, including time management and setting priorities, is an important part of mentoring—a part that probably most distinguished my mentoring relationship with Lu.

Certainly, our conversations were about Lu's research project comparing and contrasting U.S. and Chinese secondary school composition textbooks and pedagogical approaches; however, our talks also addressed her imminent transition from university student to university professor. For Lu and me, conversations about her dissertation research naturally led to more wide-ranging discussions about her future scholarship and teaching as an assistant professor of English. For example, upon her request, I shared with Lu some of the documents I prepared when going up for tenure and promotion in my department so she could get a sense of the expectations of a research institution. When Lu went on the job market, she would bring in job advertisements and we would discuss their pros and cons as Lu sifted through them, deciding where she would apply. During the time I served on Lu's committee, I was finishing my single-authored book, so we often discussed our mutual writing processes and schedules. Together we pondered how a busy academic finds uninterrupted time to write, whether the text under construction is a book or a dissertation. How does a graduate student or professor structure his or her writing time so that productivity is maximized and other personal and professional responsibilities are also met? While there may not be a definitive answer to this question, there are certainly strategies that can be shared, such as scheduling separate blocks of time to work on scholarly research and meet with students and resisting an overload of committee assignments, especially as an assistant professor.

Questions about university expectations, interviewing for academic positions, and effective time management for assistant professors are often not addressed in graduate programs, even in one-on-one discussions with committee members. Sometimes experienced professors assume that these issues will be dealt with effectively by the student when the time comes and therefore must be learned "on the job," not as part of a graduate program. Or they have been in the system so long they have forgotten the difficulty of making the transition from graduate school to a full-time academic job where publication is a requirement, along with successful teaching and service responsibilities. Informal mentoring is a perfect opportunity for doctoral students to ask questions about such professional concerns, concerns that are related to, yet differ from, feedback about revising a dissertation or evaluations of teaching performance. Such "professionalization" is vital for students as they near the completion of their graduate work and accept their first university position. These conversations can help students such as Lu find academic jobs that are right for them and begin successful careers as scholars, teachers, and, of course, generous mentors to their own students.

Collaborating to Learn: Cindy and Gail

Although not intended, over time, my collaboration with Cindy Selfe and Gail Hawisher on a research project has evolved into an informal mentoring relationship. Different from a formal mentoring relationship, their mentoring was more through example than explicit advising.

I met Cindy and Gail at the 2003 Computers and Writing Conference at Purdue. I was among the audience at their presentation about their study on four women and their literacy experiences in the global context. At the end of the session they called for co-authors who could work with them as both research participants and co-authors on a similar project. I met them in person after the session, expressed my interest, and we exchanged email addresses.

The collaboration enabled me to see the evolution of a research project based on personal narrative and reflections. Soon Cindy and Gail sent me a multiple-page set of questions and a consent form. I was able to see what kinds of questions they generated. After I answered those questions, they sent me follow-up questions. Because the literacy survey is very detailed (about my family and my entire literacy experience), I felt that they had gotten to know me. I kept them updated about the progress of my graduate studies and my achievements. As the project progressed in the fall of 2003, I was able to develop a special bond with Cindy and Gail. Cindy sent a Christmas letter that was refreshing and heartwarming; from that letter I also learned about her love for nature due to her detailed description of that winter in the Upper Peninsula in Michigan and her childlike curiosity that is critical for doing research.

In addition, the collaboration with Cindy and Gail enabled me to watch and learn beyond the data collection stage. By reading the drafts they sent in order to email them my feedback and comments, I saw how they integrated theory with data analysis. At the 2004 CCCC, I also witnessed how they presented their latest findings and dealt with getting feedback. When the draft was submitted for review and sent back for revisions, Cindy and Gail sent me additional reading and invited me to reflect on the draft by incorporating the theoretical insights of the reading. I realized that a lot more writing (especially revising), reading, and thinking were done between the first draft stage and the final publication of one manuscript. In summer 2006, the manuscript based on our collaborative project was published as a journal article. The timeline of publication for our collaborative project confirmed my own experience: Doing research and getting published requires patience, hard work, and stamina.

In the collaboration process, I learned that Cindy and Gail had been working on this topic since 1998. I decided to follow their latest research trajectory and see the project in the big picture of their evolving research agenda. In 2004, I saw their presentation on our project at CCCC. I was able to witness how they presented the research in the form of a conference paper. In 2005, although I was unable to attend CCCC, I was able to search online and read notes online about their presentation on the project in the pre-conference Research Network Forum. At the 2006 CCCC, I attended their presentation again and saw how they had moved on to new projects and integrated visual elements into their research narrative about women and electronic literacy. Viewing their research activities in action both as an insider and outsider, I have gained better understanding of the importance of staying focused, revising, and sharing the research findings with the academic community both through various forms of conference presentations and publication.

During the years, Cindy and Gail turned to me for help as a colleague, which not only boosted my confidence, but also helped me realize the importance of turning to colleagues for help with obtaining information or certain sources for research projects. Soon after our collaboration began, Gail emailed me about a question one of her colleagues had about the concept of race in China. I thought it over and gave a careful response. Cindy also emailed a question about Internet usage in China. I did some research and sent her some important links to authoritative Chinese research websites on the topic. Instead of seeing myself only as a graduate student, I began to view myself as their colleague and collaborator. Therefore, when I worked on my own manuscript on online sources on argumentative writing, I sought out Cindy for sources regarding computer and education and was able to refer to the Pew Internet & and American Life Project and U.S. National Center for Education statistics websites for computer usage rates among American public schools.

In contrast to my other mentoring relationships, I initiated my relationship with Cindy and Gail in the role of a junior colleague and collaborator. When signing up for the project, I did have in mind the intention to collaborate and learn the craftsmanship of doing research. By working with them closely, however, I was able to observe them from the perspective of a mentee. Both Cindy and Gail were very responsive whenever I had questions, whether it was about my own research topic or the collaborative project. Their responsiveness, like that of my other mentors, made the mentoring relationship possible and productive.

Cindy and Gail's Commentary

Formal mentoring relationships are strange phenomena—sometimes, the harder you try, the less successful the results! Formal mentoring programs, for instance—even when they are quite carefully designed—can fail because mentees and mentors are paired according to selective, but not especially critical, characteristics. In such cases, formal mentoring relationships falter not because they lack laudable goals, but rather because they are artificial and, thus, less than robust, less than dimensional or nuanced.

Unlike more informal mentoring pairs that are often established more naturally and in contexts meaningful to the participants, formal mentoring may unintentionally ignore personal preferences, working styles, and self-identified needs that partners factor in as part of their normal interpersonal exchanges. While key to the success of a mentoring relationship, these factors often become evident only over time and through shared experiences. We believe these characteristics explain why mentoring relationships generally take time to mature, why they are so personal in nature, and why they so often self-organize around projects that incorporate mutual interests.

When we began working with Lu Liu, for example, none of us anticipated the prospect of forming a mentoring relationship. Rather, we met under very natural circumstances at a professional conference, attending a paper on digital literacy, a topic in which the three of us already shared an interest. Later, when Lu helped us out on a related scholarly project—completing an extensive questionnaire about her own literacy experiences—we discovered not only more shared interests, but shared intellectual values, as well. As we worked more with Lu—collaborating on a scholarly paper; asking her follow-up questions; exchanging emails in which we talked about the mundane details of the passing seasons, travel, and the cultures in which we each lived—we found that we shared similar working styles, that we all valued the exchange of cultural information, that we could count on each other to accomplish tasks on time. We came to know Lu as an intelligent woman, but also one with a sense of humor and responsibility. We came to value her incisiveness, her willingness to exchange information and to learn, and her ability to focus on a task. We came to know and trust and genuinely like her on multiple dimensions.

Gail and I have worked with many students over the years—and all of them have been smart, insightful, and remarkable in their own way. Many of these students take classes from us and then go their own way to have their own successes. They are good students who focus on the course content, the subject matter of a class, and they commit themselves to learning all they can about it. Other students, however, recognize a curriculum outside of the regular structure of courses, requirements, and exams. Sometimes it feels as if these students are studying *us*—but really, they are much smarter than that. They have an interest in how scholars work and think, how they interact with knowledge, information, and people; how they conduct research and think about data; how they conduct their professional lives; what seems to motivate their actions and curiosity. They are interested in such things, we think, because they are already seeing themselves as scholars and as professionals—even if this vision has just begun to emerge in a recognizable way. These students are often those who establish a different of kind relationship with a faculty member, one that extends beyond the horizon of courses and often involves multiple professional projects, even multiple institutions. These students also realize that mentoring relationships involve reciprocal sharing and risk-taking, as well as regular exchanges that are satisfying to both parties. And these people have a good feel, right from the start, of the generous kind of give-and-take that rests at the heart of professional relationships. We always consider ourselves lucky to encounter such colleagues-in-the-making.

The best informal mentoring relationships we have entered into—like that we have established with Lu Liu—have emerged naturally, informally, and over time. They have allowed all participants to attend to self-identified values and practices that seem to matter on a personal and professional level. These relationships work so well, we think, because they are *mutually* satisfying and intellectually enriching, and because they represent one the very best practices our profession has to offer.

Conclusion

A national survey in the U.S. has found that fewer than a third of Ph.D. students in English said that their programs had prepared them to publish work and although more than 50 percent were interested in participating in interdisciplinary research, only 13 percent felt that they were prepared to do so (Golde & Dore, 2004). The crux of the matter is that some graduate students may expect their programs to prepare them for these important endeavors. Graduate education, however, is an individualized process for each graduate student, and I think every graduate student should shoulder the responsibility of customizing his or her education. Based on their research on Ph.D. education and career preparation of doctoral students in English and chemistry, Golde and Dore (2004) stress the need for doctoral students to "take responsibility for educating themselves about the academic profession and seek out experiences that provide them with mentored learning opportunities" (p. 41). In addition, Golde and Dore (2001) point out that "Students with more than one mentor often benefit from a breadth of perspectives" (p. 37). My work with my mentors is a case in point.

The mentors I actively sought out have accelerated my growth from a graduate student to an interdisciplinary scholar. Bud and Tony have been mentors since the earliest stages. By simulating the process of joining the academic community in his course, Bud cultivated a sense of professionalism in me, hence pushing me to seriously consider the topic of my term paper, which led to my final dissertation project. Focusing early in my research prepared me for the transition from knowledge reception to knowledge production. As I was not sure about my role in knowledge production, it was Tony's demythification of the publication process that helped me to overcome my fear of manuscript submission. Furthermore, by sharing their stories of success and failure, Tony and Bud helped me see the socialization process in academia in a realistic manner.

Janet, Cindy, and Gail are the mentors I sought out at the latter stage of my graduate career. Janet not only guided me in my interdisciplinary research, but also enlightened me on effective work schedules and a positive and productive mentality regarding the pressure to publish—that focusing on burning research questions leads to hard work and efforts to share one's findings lead to publication. Cindy and Gail, by example, have demonstrated for me how to develop one's research interest/questions into multiple projects, conduct research, collaborate, seek help and/or feedback among colleagues through various channels of communication (including presentations, research network forums, and emailing), and finally making revisions for publication.

Looking back, I think it is crucial for a graduate student to identify a research focus, seek out prospective mentors, and ask specific questions. It is up to the student to take the initiative, to communicate with the mentor on a regular basis, develop a sense that they are allies, and to ask, watch, listen, and learn. It is also important for scholars-to-be to gain confidence in their expertise, send out manuscripts, and network with more experienced scholars.

Working closely with multiple mentors has, to a great extent, facilitated my professional development. Seeking out multiple mentors helps, in many ways, to create a supporting network and small academic community with senior scholars. It has not only enabled me to do interdisciplinary research, but also facilitated my socialization in the bigger academic community that had seemed so intimidating. Most importantly, in this process of growth, I have extended my perception of mentorship not only to scholars I know in person, but also to editors of academic journals, editors of books, and anonymous reviewers. Many graduate students may think of senior scholars as gatekeepers who ruthlessly issue criticisms and rejections. In fact, I believe that most of them are actually allies who are willing to help fledging scholars grow, just like formal mentors. The concept of multiple mentors, therefore, can be the key to the growth of a fledging scholar, especially in today's academia where research takes on an increasingly interdisciplinary and competitive nature.

LU LIU, PEKING UNIVERSITY, BEIJING, CHINA

I thought I knew how to do graduate school when I entered the Ph.D. program at Purdue after obtaining a master's in China and London, respectively. Not until I came across the word *mentor* did I begin to see the best thing about being a Ph.D. student—to work closely with my mentors. Working with them kept me motivated, informed, supported. It also helped me to graduate and get published. Now as an assistant professor myself, I not only keep in touch with my old mentors, but also make myself available as a mentor to my own students.

IRWIN WEISER, PURDUE UNIVERSITY

I've been mentoring graduate students for most of my career and have always found that I learn at least as much from the people I mentor as I think I'm able to teach them. Being a mentor has helped me become a better teacher and scholar and has provided me with lasting friendships.

TONY SILVA, PURDUE UNIVERSITY

I never planned to go to grad school. And if I had known what it would involve, I probably would not have gone. But that would have been a shame. In graduate school, I encountered people, places, and ideas that opened up the world for me and made my life richer than I ever thought it could be. I often think about how fortunate I was to stumble onto this path and how uneasy it makes me feel to think about where other, more predictable, paths might have led me.

JANET ALSUP, PURDUE UNIVERSITY

When I entered graduate school at the University of Missouri–Columbia, I never imagined that I would be teaching at Purdue University a mere five years later. I only wanted to become a better teacher. Well, my graduate school experience did that for me—*and* much more. I credit my mentors at Missouri for introducing me to an entirely new intellectual and professional world. Daily, I work to provide my current students with the same kind of guidance, instruction, and support that was so generously offered to me.

CYNTHIA L. SELFE, OHIO STATE UNIVERSITY

I consider it a personal and professional responsibility to work with scholars from other countries to explore ways of sharing information, communicating and acting in more respectful and productive ways, and teaching for peace and for a better world than the one we now inhabit. Working with graduate students and colleagues from other countries, traveling, and learning about their part of the world has taught me a great deal about how to pursue these goals. I am deeply grateful for the thoughtful and generous exchanges of which I have been privileged to be a part, and I am hopeful that we can learn to be better citizens of the world.

GAIL HAWISHER, UNIVERSITY OF ILLINOIS AT URBANA-CHAMPAIGN

After doing lots of graduate work at several universities like the University of Georgia and Ohio State University, I was thrilled to earn my Ph.D. at the University of Illinois. At both Ohio State and Illinois, generous faculty members became my mentors and made all the difference in my own professional life. I have similarly tried to be there for graduate students and have found that—more than anything—I have been the one who has learned from them. I remain grateful for the opportunities they have provided.

REFERENCES

Golde, C. M., & Dore, T. M. (2001). *At cross purposes: What the experiences of doctoral students reveal about doctoral education*. Philadelphia: The Pew Charitable Trusts. Retrieved from *www.phd-survey.org*.

———. (2004). The survey of doctoral education and career preparation: The importance of disciplinary contexts. In A. E. Austin & D. H. Wulff (Eds.), *Paths to the professoriate: Strategies for enriching the preparation of future faculty* (pp. 19–45). San Francisco: Jossey-Bass.

Kubota, R., & Shi, L. (2005). Instruction and reading samples for opinion and argumentative writing in L1 junior high school textbooks in China and Japan. *Journal of Asian Pacific Communication, 15*(1), 97–127.

PART 3

Situated Learning

It's Not in the Orientation Manual: How a First-Year Doctoral Student Learned to Survive in Graduate School

NATSUKO KUWAHARA

Introduction

Throughout the first semester of my doctoral program, I found myself struggling to adjust to the complex culture that defines academic life. I was steadily losing confidence in myself and my intellectual abilities and was drowning in anxiety. Amidst this turmoil, I constantly asked myself, "I don't know why I got accepted here. Why was I accepted?" Worst of all, I felt a deep sense of guilt stemming from the belief that I wasn't meeting the expectations of my professors, of my peers, and of all the people who had worked so hard to give me the opportunity to go to graduate school in the U.S.

Though I'd been accepted into the doctoral program, it wasn't until later that I actually felt like a "real" doctoral student. As a non-native speaker of English and a foreigner, my first year was all about learning the rules of the game and becoming a "real" doctoral student in the U.S. In retrospect, I realize that I hadn't become a doctoral student the day I received my acceptance letter—rather, it took a conscious effort and hard work to uncover and learn the norms, expectations, and values espoused by the academic community before I could identify with it.

Identifying First-Year Challenges

Assuming the admissions process is effective in selecting the most qualified candidates, why do so many doctoral students struggle during their first year of graduate school? Almost without exception, doctoral students say that their first year was their hardest (Golde, 1998). Furthermore, while only half of the doctoral students who enter their programs go on to obtain Ph.D.s, at least a third of those who leave do so during their first year (Bowen & Rudenstine, 1992; Golde; Lovitts, 2001).

This high rate of first-year discontinuation is due to the "intense and influential" transition (Lovitts, p. 41) that students undergo during their first year of graduate school. This process of socialization involves a variety of learning experiences that transform the freshly minted graduate student from an outsider in their new academic community to an insider as time goes by (Weidman, Twale, & Stein, 2001). Thus, students begin at the periphery of the graduate school community, but gradually acquire more privileged roles and the skills needed to become full participants (Lave & Wenger, 1991). In graduate school, failing to accept these changes and norms often results in difficulties that may lead to students leaving school.

While there are many reasons for these difficulties, they tend to arise from three fundamental challenges (see Golde; Lovitts; Taylor, 1975):

1. identity crisis and lowered self-image due to an inability to perform up to standards
2. isolation and discomfort due to a diminished support network
3. lack of clear goals and guidance

Though each of these challenges is distinct, they reinforce each other to make the first year of graduate school especially difficult. Moreover, these struggles are even more of a challenge for non-native speakers of English, who often lack the cultural and linguistic capital of their native speaker peers. A strong command of the language, highly developed verbal skills, and good political sense are the basis of communicating in an academic environment. Thus, in addition to the typical socialization that occurs at the graduate school level, non-native students have the added burden of developing their linguistic skills and cultural awareness when adapting to their new environment.

In the first portion of this chapter, I explore these challenges by examining where they come from, what they mean, and how they affected my own first year of graduate school. Later, I discuss how first-year graduate students can negotiate these challenges to make their first year of graduate school a more manageable experience.

Identity Crisis and Lowered Self-Image Due to an Inability to Perform up to Standards

As a new member of the graduate school community, first-year doctoral students lack the knowledge and skills of their professors and more advanced peers. Therefore, although these students may have inhabited positions of privilege prior to matriculating into graduate school, they enter at the bottom of the hierarchy, in an "apprentice position" (Leonard, 2001, p. 171). This peripheral status and inability to perform to personal standards may result in feelings of anxiety, which are often at their highest during the first phases of the graduate student socialization process (Phillips & Pugh, 1987). These issues of identity are compounded in non-native speakers, where this loss of academic position coincides with a further drop in social standing due to the change in language and culture. Thus, even though students may be eloquent and well regarded in their home language/culture, the change in setting often means a fundamental inability to communicate at the level that is expected of them, which is often felt as a sign of incompetence.

The Language Standard: The Fundamental Challenge

of Communicating in an Academic Environment

Language plays a central role in the graduate school experience. In a place where the highest value is placed on the transmission and negotiation of ideas, any language difficulties are certain to result in lowered standing. Furthermore, as academic writing can sometimes devolve into a mishmash of jargon, made-up words, and incomprehensible phrases, having confidence in one's linguistic abilities is necessary to maintain confidence in oneself.

I entered my doctoral program after several years spent teaching English in Japan, and although I had the advantage of having earned my master's degree in the U.S., the years away meant that I had much to relearn. I was certainly thrilled with being a student again, but the change from being a native speaker in Japan to a non-native speaker in the U.S. was harder than expected. I often found myself frustrated as I felt that I was unable to fully express complex thoughts and often had to put up with people misinterpreting my explanations as simplistic. I was also slower in my responses than my native peers, meaning that I was less able to participate in class. After some time of this, I started to feel inferior to those around me. I remember looking at my professors and peers with awe, how their every word seemed fraught with meaning, confirming their fundamental belonging in the academic community. On the other hand, everything I said was either overly simple or just plain wrong. In this way, I felt that although those around me were able to constantly confirm their belonging, for me, attempts at communication served mainly to mark me as an outsider, unfit to partake in academic life.

Culture: The Challenge of Knowing What to Communicate

Non-native speakers of English from foreign countries also have to acculturate into American academic society. This often requires replacing their old cultural values with the values of their new school and country (Taylor). This cultural transition appears to be especially difficult for students from East Asia (Berry, Kim, Minde, & Mok, 1987; Church, 1982; Cornell University, 2004; Hull, 1978; Sam & Eide, 1991) because of different expectations around classroom participation, writing, and communication patterns (Sun & Chen, 1997).

In my case, the norms and values of the Japanese educational system deeply affected my performance, especially in terms of class participation and academic writing. Many of the rules I had learned while in Japan were no longer valid in the U.S. In Japan, students initiate discussions much less (Shimizu, 2006) and are rarely asked about their own opinions (Ellington, 1992; Wray, 1999). However, in the U.S., speaking during class is considered an essential part of learning. Also, the content of what students say or write differs between Japan and U.S. In the U.S., students are expected to synthesize the ideas and provide commentary on the strengths and weaknesses of various theories, rather than just offer a review of previous studies.

Similarly, the style in which meaning is conveyed differs as Japanese academic writing would be considered rather non-linear and obtuse to Americans. This meant that even though I had a wealth of experience in writing in English, having received my master's degree at a U.S.

institution, I struggled against what I had previously considered "good writing" and needed to learn to find an authoritative voice that could present arguments in linear streams of thought.

In this way, I found myself not only lacking the language of academia, but also the content and style. Therefore, I had to learn not only how to communicate in a new culture, but also what to communicate.

Isolation and Discomfort Due to a Diminished Support Network

The loss of confidence and resultant identity crisis associated with the first year of graduate school occur at a time when students may have difficulties in deriving support from their normal sources. For international students, entering graduate school often entails a geographical move, which can quickly put them out of range and out of mind of their existing support networks. Thus, international students often find themselves trying to adjust to a new culture and language without the friends and family who were so instrumental to their previous successes.

To make a difficult situation even more challenging, long hours of study and work complicate those personal relationships that survive the initial transition. Many first-year graduate students have to engage in long study and work hours until they become used to working at a graduate student level. For non-native speakers, this adjustment often takes longer, which means spending even more time on assignments than do their native-speaker peers. This further decreases the amount of time left for communicating with and/or spending time with friends and family and so strains relationships and support networks.

After countless sleep-deprived nights, there were moments when I felt completely alone in this new country. However much I wanted to hear the familiar voices of home to regain confidence, the 12-hour time difference and seemingly endless assignments made calling Japan extremely difficult. I remember one winter night when I could not stop crying because I was lonely, doubting my ability, and questioning whether I was doing the right thing. The stress became almost unbearable as I was unable to share my insecurities and fears with other graduate students who were also trying to "make it." "I should not complain because I chose to come." "This is something I should solve by myself." "Everyone is managing this, why not me?" These inner voices choked me and I couldn't say that I needed support from others, and so the tears came out that night, overflowing from my frustrations and loneliness.

Lack of Clear Goals and Guidance

Having a successful graduate school experience requires having a clear set of goals and then creating a workable strategy to achieve these goals. Although explicit instructions and goals are necessary to succeed in graduate school, the current system relies largely on the individual doctoral student's ability to decipher the unwritten rules of the game (Casanave, 2002; Wulff, Austin, Nyquist, & Sprague, 2004; Wulff & Austin, 2004). Faculty are often too busy to meet with junior students, and so students must find their way "in the context of the values and emphases of their faculty advisors and disciplinary contexts" (Austin, 2002, p. 106) without explicit guidance from faculty members. Therefore, it is not surprising that many first-year doctoral students have difficulties in grasping the "big picture" and end up in spending much of their time floundering before they are able to find their footing.

I was assigned a temporary advisor upon entering my doctoral program. Since there was no overlap between his research interests and mine and he was very busy, there was little connection between us. I started to distance myself from this professor and other professors since I thought that I was a burden to them. Feeling envious of my other classmates, who seemed to be more relaxed around professors, I struggled to find a niche for myself as a doctoral student. I tried hard to find out what was expected of me by looking at how other American students learn the culture and the rules of conduct in an academic community.

Even though the first year of graduate school is full of challenges, there are many ways to ease the difficulties of the first year in a doctoral program. In the next section, I will share the strategies that I employed in my own first year that helped me grow and become a part of an academic community.

Overcoming First-Year Challenges

During my first year, I employed a number of strategies, both conscious and unconscious, to ease my socialization into graduate school. Of these, I feel that two decisions I made early on were key. The first was to look for and create support networks where I could learn essential academic skills in safer, more nurturing environments. The second was to approach graduate school as an apprenticeship, fully embracing my role as an apprentice. Through these strategies, I was able to make my transition to graduate school far easier than it might have been otherwise. In the following section, I will explore these two approaches, what they mean, and why they were helpful.

1. Building Support Networks

Entering graduate school often means having to leave friends and family behind. This is especially true for non-native speakers of English, where going to graduate school may mean leaving their home country. Having been stripped of my old support network, it was critical that I build a new one within the context of my new graduate school. Forming support networks through study groups and with administrators supported my academic progress and professional development. However, other groups like the Japanese community as well as like-minded advanced doctoral students worked to encourage my efforts and keep my spirits high.

Building an Academic Support Network

At the start of my first semester, I was excited to be back at school and eager to learn new skills. Perhaps not surprisingly, these feelings soon faded under the weight of how much I would have to learn before being able to perform my role as a "real" doctoral student. Fortunately, I had the chance to participate in several smaller, comfortable subcommunities nested within the larger academic community (Tinto, 1993). These subcommunities gave me a nurturing place where I could gain the skills that would allow me to become more competent within the larger academic community. By sequentially moving from smaller, nurturing communities to larger, more challenging ones, I was able to move from the periphery to become a "real" doctoral student. Some examples follow.

Study Groups

During my first semester, I took part in two study groups, one of which included a faculty member. Each of these groups was instrumental in giving me a safe, nurturing community in which to mature as a scholar. Each group, however, provided distinct learning experiences and facilitated my socialization in different ways.

The peer group was formed with two other students from my cohort who were taking the same classes I was. Each week, we met to discuss articles assigned in these classes. By taking turns presenting articles, we were able to practice our presentation and critical thinking skills in an environment where we were forced to present but didn't have to worry about looking bad in front of the faculty. This group also functioned to create a support network of like-minded people who were going through similar experiences. As a non-native speaker, having close contact with other students was especially helpful as I was able to learn things including how my American peers prepared for class, how to speak up within a group, and what to say.

I also joined another study group, which included a faculty member and five students from her class. This professor led semester-long weekly meetings during which we developed our abilities to think like academics. More important, through closer personal contact with a professor, I was able to see my professors as real people and started to feel more comfortable when talking to them. Last, through interactions with the faculty member, I was able to gain greater insight into many of the activities of my future academic life, including critiquing and publishing papers and presenting research ideas.

Administrators

When building a support network, it is important to remember that even the best academics require support from non-academic sources. Having good relations with these groups can greatly ease students' time in graduate school while poor relations can make their life much more difficult. Important resources include the Financial Aid Office, Doctoral Program administrators, the Career Development Office, Student Affairs, and the International Student Office. By going in and making myself known in these departments, I gained insight into topics such as what to keep in mind when applying for scholarships, what an appealing resume looks like, and who to ask for help depending on the need at hand. These people played important roles not only regarding administrative issues, but because their candid advice came from years of experience with numerous students, faculty, and others associated with the doctoral program.

Building an Emotional Support Network

Support from native speakers was influential in assisting my academic progress, enabling me to gain cultural and academic skills and knowledge. However, I also needed emotional support from people who had either experienced or were experiencing similar struggles. In this, I was lucky to be around other international advanced doctoral students and other Japanese students and researchers. While international advanced doctoral students allowed me to see what successful non-native doctoral students look like in my own field, the Japanese academic community provided a place to feel at home and take comfort in my abilities without having to face a communication barrier.

Advanced Non-Native Doctoral Students: Seeing What Success Looks Like

Advanced doctoral students can serve as valuable role models, providing insight into a range of topics including approaching faculty members, choosing an advisor, and narrowing one's research focus. These role models are particularly important for international students. For me, just being able to see successful non-native advanced doctoral students gave me hope and the courage to try harder to overcome the disadvantages of being a non-native speaker of English.

These senior non-native doctoral students also helped in assuaging my feelings of inferiority in the presence of my American peers. One student in particular helped me tremendously, telling me that "being a doctoral student isn't just about writing papers with perfect English, but the ability to think and analyze clearly and logically." I heard similar comments from other international advanced doctoral students, and their words encouraged me not to give up because their words had come from their own experiences and struggles.

Japanese Researchers' Network: Reminding Myself of Who I Am

For me, not being able to fully communicate in English was one of the toughest parts of graduate school. In this respect, I was fortunate that Boston has a Japanese researchers' network and school- and city-wide Japanese graduate students' organizations. Having a group of people who were going through similar language/cultural transitions gave me a place of encouragement and a place to remember my own strengths. Within this group, I was able to create my own support network with visiting scholars whom I could ask for advice on grant applications and research design. Furthermore, by assuming a more active leadership role in these groups, I was able to reconfirm my own value in an academic community.

The Japanese researchers' community was also helpful in giving me the opportunity to listen to and engage in complicated discussions and issues in my own language, refining my academic communication skills without the burden of the language barrier.

2. Approaching Graduate School as an Apprentice

To become full participants in the community, it is crucial for new members to have access to performances of expert knowledge and skills (Lave & Wenger). New students have to understand their roles in this equation and accept their roles as apprentices. For me, this meant acknowledging that I wasn't going to start out with all the answers and that I was going to have to work very hard to become a part of the community. This led me to view my professors and advanced doctoral students as mentors rather than competitors, allowing me to take lessons from them. By framing my early graduate school interactions as an apprentice relationship, I was able to maintain a healthy sense of my own identity and learn from experiences that I'd otherwise find disheartening.

Learning How to Navigate through Graduate School: Leveraging Course Work

Taking the apprentice route to learning how to navigate graduate school meant listening to people for advice on how to excel in my classes, how to refine my research, and how to enter into opportunities to find mentors. Early in my graduate school career, I made my research topic known to teaching fellows and professors through course assignments. By doing this, not only did I place myself and my research topic into the minds of these professors, but I was able to do so in an environment where it was easy to get detailed feedback. In fact, some professors and advanced doctoral students even sought me out to give me references, offer alternative interpretations to my hypothesis, or to point out the limitations of my study. These early courses gave me the opportunity to test my basic ideas and then gain input from multiple expert sources. As confidence in one's research topic is often the best way to gain confidence in oneself, these comments were especially helpful, not only in helping me learn essential skills, but also in giving me the confidence that I belonged in graduate school and that my ideas were valuable.

After having confidence in one's research project, the most important factor in finding a place in graduate school is to find good mentors. These mentors became role models whom I could learn from as they showed me how to navigate through the graduate school and academic worlds both directly and indirectly. Practically, this means that one's mentor should be someone whom one can trust to give criticisms yet still support one's overall progress. Finding the right advisor is often a difficult choice as one must match not only topics and methodologies, but also personalities (Fujioka, this volume).

Taking classes was one of the best ways to see my potential mentors in action on a regular basis without having to impose on their busy schedule. Seeing how faculty members teach class and interact with students was one of the best ways to figure out whether I would want them as mentors. Not only did these classes give me greater insight into their research and how they look at a problem, they also gave an idea as to how they deal with students. Furthermore, as these professors were looking at my proposed research topic, I was able to see what kind of insight they brought to my research and whether they were supportive of my topic and methodology in general. In this way, the feedback I received on my assignments gave me a way of scouting out which professors might help me the most in terms of both the content of my research and my socialization as a scholar into the academic community.

In researching this chapter, I looked back through my old diaries. One day, near the end of my first year in graduate school, I wrote: "As long as at least one professor like my advisor believes in me, I should stay here and strive more." That's how important my advisor was to my ability to stay in graduate school. I was fortunate to have met my advisor who is not only a knowledgeable and impressive scholar, but also very caring and encouraging. Her comments were critical in encouraging me as a novice member of the community who could easily get discouraged by "constructive feedback." At the same time, what she said had enough rigor that I learned what it means to be an academic. During the first year when I was depressed and frustrated by my inability at graduate school, the fact that a professor believed in me was invaluable in allowing me to feel not only that I belonged, but that I could succeed.

Learning How to Speak Like an Academic: Giving Conference Presentations

In addition to learning how to navigate through graduate school, I needed to learn how to speak in a community where most activities pivot around a complex discourse (Casanave). Again, I used a strategy where I could present in smaller, more nurturing groups while feeling safe as an apprentice. One of the first places where I presented my research was at a student research conference at my school at the beginning of the second semester. Speaking in front of many friends and familiar professors was less stressful, since there was a sense that it was a practice run for me as an apprentice academic. At the same time, getting insightful feedback and warm encouragement from professors and classmates was a great confidence builder that prepared me to go to larger conferences. Since then, I have aggressively applied for larger conferences so that I may continue to gain experience speaking like an academic and so that I can get more time to listen to other academics. When I encounter a good presentation, I take notes not only about the presentation itself, but also about what made the presentation so interesting and impressive, with the hope that one day I will be able to give a presentation that is just as good.

Learning How to Conduct a Study: Collaborating with Faculty Members

As an apprentice, it was important not only to learn the basics, but also to work in conjunction with more experienced researchers to learn the intricacies of what happens at the highest levels of academia. To do this, in my second semester, I approached a faculty member and suggested an independent study that would be done under her guidance and supervision. This was a good way not only of getting practical experience, but also of seeing how I worked in the field and how we worked together. Through this project, I learned how studies are actually conducted and discovered that I actually liked doing them. This realization motivated me to stay in the academic community and encouraged me to believe that the goal of becoming an academic was right for me.

Around the same time, I took another step, creating the opportunity to collaborate with a faculty member in the preparation of a couple of research grants. To do this meant finding a topic where I could bring something to the table. I came up with a research project, searched for a collaborator in Japanese universities, and coordinated efforts between both Japanese and U.S. research teams. Since I was not yet ready to actively participate in large-scale class discussions, taking the lead in this small research group gave me the feeling that I was contributing something of value as an academic, while learning intricacies of both grant writing and collaboration.

The Changes from the Beginning and End of the First Year: Identity, Learning, and Investment

Graduate school is a time of intellectual and personal growth for many students. By the end of the first year, I started to feel more comfortable with my role as a doctoral student. I found myself taking the initiative more often, conducting an independent study, choosing my advisor, and applying for grants and fellowships, all of which would have seemed impossible at the start of my first year. I also became more involved in my own work and the supporting network I was establishing inside and outside of school. Taking initiative and becoming more involved required constant investment but were crucial during my first year, giving me the ability to create greater opportunities to assume more mature roles in the community of practice and to become a full participant.

Weidman, Twale, and Stein define the core elements of graduate student socialization as knowledge acquisition, investment, and involvement (p. iv). To facilitate this process, I found two approaches especially important: (1) building support networks, and (2) approaching graduate school as an apprentice. In building a support network, I found that creating supportive "nested communities" (Tinto) is an effective way of gaining skills in a nurturing environment in which I was able to balance both the need to become more assertive and to diminish the fear of being seen negatively. Similarly, by approaching graduate school from the perspective of an apprentice, I was able to put myself in a position where I actively looked for the best mentors and learned from them without feeling a loss of self-esteem.

Graduate school is often described as a lonely journey. Getting through graduate school, however, cannot be accomplished by oneself, especially in the case of non-native speakers. Since the first year in doctoral program is often critical to setting the stage for the rest of the graduate school experience, finding supportive mentors and creating professional support networks beyond the classroom are keys to overcoming non-native and foreigner status. The process is not easy, but with the support from others, it is something accomplishable. It is my hope that international students find their own ways in this enculturation process and that their advisors and peers help guide them through this most difficult year as they move forward toward their future accomplishments.

NATSUKO KUWAHARA, HARVARD GRADUATE SCHOOL OF EDUCATION

When I earned my M.A. in TESOL, I thought, "This is it! I'm done!" I always thought that people who went on to obtain a Ph.D. must have either been geniuses or people who loved to torture themselves with the tremendous pressures that come with graduate school. Four years later though, I found myself entering into a doctoral program with awe. It cost me a job I loved and separated me from family and friends, but it's something I felt driven to do. I am currently still in my doctoral program and look forward with expectation and excitement to what awaits me as I complete my degree.

REFERENCES

Austin, A.E. (2002). Preparing the next generation of faculty: Graduate school as socialization to the academic career. *The Journal of Higher Education, 73*(1), 94–122.

Berry, J. W., Kim, U., Minde, T., & Mok, D. (1987). Comparative studies of acculturative stress. *International Migration Review, 21*(3), 491–511.

Bowen, W. G., & Rudenstine, N. L. (1992). *In pursuit of the Ph.D.* Princeton, NJ: Princeton University Press.

Casanave, C. P. (2002). *Writing games: Multicultural case studies of academic literacy practices in higher education.* Mahwah, NJ: Lawrence Erlbaum.

Church, A. (1982). Sojourner adjustment. *Psychological Bulletin, 91,* 540–572.

Cornell University Asian and Asian American Campus Climate Task Force. (2004, October). *Cornell University Asian and Asian American Campus Climate Task Force Report.* Ithaca, NY.

Ellington, L. (1992). *Education in the Japanese life cycle: Implications for the United States.* Lewiston, NY: Edwin Mellen Press.

Golde, C. M. (1998). Beginning graduate school: Explaining first-year doctoral attrition. *New Directions for Higher Education, 101*, 55–64.

Hull, F. W. (1978). *Foreign students in the United States of America: Coping behavior within the educational environment.* New York: Praeger.

Lave, J. & Wenger, E. (1991). *Situated learning: Legitimate peripheral participation.* Cambridge, UK: Cambridge University Press.

Leonard, D. (2001). *A woman's guide to doctoral studies.* Buckingham, UK: Open University Press.

Lovitts, B. E. (2001). *Leaving the ivory tower: The causes and consequences of departure from doctoral study.* London: Rowman & Littlefield.

Phillips, E. M., & Pugh, D. S. (1987). *How to get a PhD: Managing the peaks and troughs of research.* Buckingham, UK: Open University Press.

Sam, D. L., & Eide, R. (1991). Survey of mental health of foreign students. *Scandinavian Journal of Psychology, 53*, 550–56.

Shimizu, J. (2006). Why are Japanese students reluctant to express their opinions in the classroom? *Hiyoshi English and American Literature University Bulletin, 48*, 33–45.

Sun, W., & Chen , G. (1997) *Dimensions of difficulties mainland Chinese students encounter in the United States.* (ERIC Document Reproduction Service No. ED408635).

Taylor, A. R. (1975). Graduate school experience: Excerpts from essays by graduate students. *Personnel and Guidance Journal, 54*, 34–39.

Tinto, V. (1993) *Leaving college: Rethinking the causes and cures of student attrition* (2nd ed.). Chicago: University of Chicago Press.

Weidman, J. C., Twale, D. J. & Stein, E. L. (2001) *Socialization of graduate and professional students in higher education: A perilous passage?* San Francisco: Jossey-Bass (E.L. ASHE-ERIC Higher Education Report, 28, 3).

Wray, H. (1999). *Japanese and American education: Attitudes and practices.* Westport, CT: Bergin & Garvey.

Wulff, D. H., & Austin, A. E. (2004). Future directions: Strategies to enhance paths to the professoriate. In A. E. Austin & D. H. Wulff (Eds.), *Paths to the professoriate: Strategies for enriching the preparation of future faculty* (pp. 267–292). San Francisco: Jossey-Bass.

Wulff, D. H., Austin, A. E., Nyquist, J. D., & Sprague, J. (2004). The development of graduate students as teaching scholars: A four-year longitudinal study. In A. E. Austin & D. H. Wulff (Eds.), *Paths to the professoriate: Strategies for enriching the preparation of future faculty* (pp. 46–73). San Francisco: Jossey-Bass.

Chapter 13

Positioning Expertise: The Shared Journey of a South Korean and a North American Doctoral Student

MARCIA Z. BUELL AND SO JIN PARK

Marcia's Email to So Jin

It hit me that if you wanted to, I could work with editing your paper, if I could use sessions and discussions as fieldwork. (I would probably need to also interview you as we work and perhaps observe contexts where you work on the dissertation.)

So Jin's Reply to Marcia

It sounds like a great idea! As you know that anthropologists research about other people, but sometimes for them to be the researched would be a good experience.

Progressing through graduate school means developing expertise in a field, which generally means gaining comfort speaking and writing about as well as using advanced theories and research methods and generally becoming "fluent" with academic genres. The development of expertise also includes building and operating through collegial and professional relationships, which shift across contexts, networks, and roles (see Lave and Wenger, 1991, for discussion of such shifts outside academia, and Geisler, 1994, for a discussion of expertise in academic literacy). Our compilation of narratives and dialogues, written at times in our individual voices and at times in a collective voice, explores how over a period of six years, the collegial relationship between So Jin, a

South Korean doctoral student in Anthropology, and Marcia, an American doctoral student in Writing Studies, configured and reconfigured expertise in our academic fields as we engaged with each other's work and research. As we came to understand the interactive nature of graduate learning (Prior, 1998; Casanave, 2002), we actively broke down the binaries supposedly defining native speakers and non-native speakers of English across academic networks.

In 1997, So Jin took an English conversation course that Marcia was teaching. After the course, So Jin enrolled as a doctoral student in Cultural Anthropology. Two years later, Marcia began a doctoral program in Writing Studies at the same university. After completing her ethnographic fieldwork in South Korea in 2003, So Jin brought her young daughter back to the university, which Marcia still attended, in order to begin writing her dissertation. Because we often brought our children together to play, we had opportunities to talk informally. Consequently, we started to draw upon each other's experiences in teaching, collecting, and representing data, and navigating the requirements of our programs. In late 2003, we made an unusual bargain: So Jin would participate in Marcia's ethnographically based study, and Marcia would help edit So Jin's dissertation. Though apparently simple, this arrangement ultimately challenged our understandings of ethnography, academic writing, and dichotomies of native and nonnative speakers as So Jin was analyzing and interpreting her own ethnographic data while Marcia was interviewing her, observing her writing networks, and editing sections of So Jin's dissertation. Because of our agreement and because of our existing friendship, we simultaneously took on roles of researchers, participants, editors, interdisciplinary colleagues, and advanced graduate students.

Learning the Practices and Languages of Each Other's Disciplines

So Jin's Voice: When the Researcher Becomes the Researched

When Marcia asked me to be her research participant and in turn she would edit my dissertation, I had ambivalent feelings, anticipating that it would be a much more complicated deal than it initially looked. In retrospect, such ambivalence came from both my need of help editing my dissertation draft as an international student and from my disciplinary experience as a cultural anthropologist.

On the one hand, I was pleased because, as an international student, I was thinking of finding a professional editor for my dissertation. On the other hand, as an anthropologist, since I well understood the nature and the problems of qualitative/ethnographic research, I also had an uneasy feeling about being the "researched" after having learned to play the role of the researcher.

In the discipline of Cultural Anthropology, since the 1980s, the traditional works of anthropologists and the unequal power relationship between anthropologists and the researched have been on trial (Clifford & Marcus, 1986; Rosaldo, 1993; for a feminist anthropologist perspective, see also Visweswaran, 1994, and Behar & Gordon, 1995; see also Holstein & Gubrium, 1995, for a discussion of "the active interview" beyond anthropology). Within classical anthropology, it had been perceived that anthropologists as detached outsiders and authoritative observers can analyze "other cultures" better than can the researched, who were too familiar with their own culture to see themselves with the eyes of a researcher. However, as now many anthropologists have acknowledged, the relation between the researcher and the researched cannot be free from the broader historical context and political and economic relations among different cultures. Moreover, when a term such as *native anthropologists* (so to speak, meaning anthropologists who study their own culture) emerged, the boundaries between insiders and outsiders became rather ambiguous. When anthropologists began to be aware of this complexity of their research, they no longer assumed that the researcher was a detached outsider and thus stopped giving the sole authority to his or her voice, which is "inherently partial—committed and incomplete" (Clifford, p. 7). With this "reflexive turn," anthropologists began paying more careful attention to the power inequality between the researcher and the researched.

Trained as a cultural anthropologist in this disciplinary context, I anticipated that the experience of being the researched for Marcia's project could be complex in terms of our own different subjectivities and backgrounds and our relationship. Moreover, while being the researched in her research, I myself was writing a dissertation based on my own ethnographic research. I anxiously imagined my ambiguous moving back and forth between the roles of the researcher and the researched. I first understood Marcia's suggestion about our mutual assistance within the ethical concept of "reciprocity" between an ethnographer and her research participant (i.e., her editing of my dissertation is her way of giving back to or reciprocating with her participant) (see also Behar, 1993;

Visweswaran). Since I as an anthropologist always had asked someone to participate in my ethnographic research, I felt obligated to help others' research as well.

I thus agreed, but when I imagined reading what she would write about me later and my giving some feedback to her, I jokingly asked whether she would be comfortable to hear my feedback on her writing about me (see also Willis, 1977, for an example of including the feedback from the researched in an ethnography). My other concern, which also stemmed from being a cultural anthropologist, was whether and how her reciprocal suggestion of editing my writing would affect her qualitative research about the writing and writing resources of students of English as additional language (i.e., her editing affects my writing as well). Coming from a different disciplinary background, Marcia seemed not so worried about this effect, even when I asked directly about it.

Marcia's Voice: Disciplinary Definitions of Qualitative Inquiry

I was delighted that So Jin responded favorably to my proposal to participate in my study in exchange for editing. I did see the agreement as operating on the principal of reciprocity that she had mentioned and wanted to give something back for the data I would be receiving. As So Jin would be sending me text as she worked on it, I saw editing as a good opportunity to collect a corpus of data on her texts in progress. My interests lay in how writers shaped their texts based on responses from readers across a variety of contexts and not with language acquisition concerns, such as changes in grammatical forms over time. Therefore, I did not worry much about possible effects I might have on the texts themselves through editing, as I did not think I would suggest any far-reaching changes to content. My preferred editing style (as discussed below) involves asking about possible changes to see what the writer is trying to say, before inserting those changes.

However, I had not fully anticipated the effects of So Jin's own experience with ethnographic research. Throughout her studies in anthropology, methodology had been a key focus, so she could dually position herself as a researcher even while being researched. Since she was near the end of the dissertation experience, she had more fully internalized approaches to data than I had, given that I was at the beginning of an extended study, so there were times when she would supply data about her writing practices and then suggest ways that I could follow up on the information.

It was not surprising then that So Jin engaged philosophically with the larger research project, especially as she interrogated the roles of the researcher and the researched, a dichotomy embedded in anthropological discussions. Her concerns included the question of consulting with participants about their statements prior to a work's publication. My methodological training in this area comes more through qualitative inquiry in education and in composition studies than through anthropology, and in a broad sense, I always took consulting with participants at various stages as a given (Bogdan & Biklen, 1998; Patton, 1990), but often without the strong concern for power relations that So Jin had worked through in the historical context of anthropological research.

So Jin's Insert: Reapproaching Interdisciplinary
Understanding of Qualitative Research

In retrospect, I felt that my thoughts and understandings about this unusual deal were shaped by my anthropological background. In a sense, the researched, who in this case is an anthropologist, could not help but be an unusual subject of the research. The process of Marcia's research and my participation in it made us both reevaluate our own disciplinary practices. Writing this reflexive piece together, I realized that my initial assumption about the similarity of our ethnographic methods was problematic. My concerns about how Marcia's editing of my dissertation as a reciprocal deal might affect her research stemmed from my vague understanding of Marcia's research project.

As Marcia pointed out above, despite the seemingly similar approach of our ethnographic methods, her methodological approach is not from anthropology, but from a different disciplinary background. Moreover, her research combined the analysis of the context and texts that her research consultants produced, which is a common research practice in Writing Studies (see Prior for detailed discussion of text-based interviews). Because her research, unlike most anthropological research, focused on writing and the writing environments of her main consultants, I did not have a clear idea of how she would analyze the written texts in relation to the contexts surrounding the writing practices of her participants. As a result of our interdisciplinary dialogue, we began to become familiar with the other's disciplinary vocabularies and theories. Sharing our respective expertise facilitated our fluid understanding of qualitative research in a hybrid way that helped us bridge disciplinary boundaries.

Marcia's Insert: A Native Speaker as a Novice in Another's Discipline

In addition to our both needing to reexamine our understanding of methodologies, I also needed to learn how anthropologists communicated with each other. Many of our research and editing interactions were informal, arising during our conversations in shared social activities revolving around our children. However, So Jin also invited me to observe when her work would be discussed in academic meetings. During those times, I took on more formal observer or participant observer roles.

About three weeks after my second daughter was born, So Jin presented her fourth chapter to her dissertation writing group, a group that she had actively organized and that consisted of two other Korean graduate students and two European American students in the Anthropology Department, all of whom were in the writing stages of their dissertations. Surprisingly for me, though So Jin had submitted nearly 30 pages and had asked for specific feedback on the draft in an email to her colleagues, much of the writing group's discussion centered on one section and moved in and out of theoretical articulations, feedback that So Jin later said was highly valuable. In that section, So Jin was seeking to portray cultural perceptions of class as manifested by location, in her case of two neighboring districts in Seoul.

During the discussion about how class is delineated, everyone spoke in English, but her Korean group mates offered their understandings of the relationship between the neighboring locations, which was a complicated distinction for Koreans to explain even among themselves. An idiom Americans might offer on first hearing this discussion might be "the other side of the tracks," but this did not capture at all the nuances of how these Korean communities defined themselves in relation to each other. To give a sense of nuance, the Korean students first had to translate their own idioms and then test them out with non-Koreans who interpreted the class relationship through their own cultural lenses. So Jin carefully attended to how her Korean colleagues represented a cultural construct of class and how her non-Korean colleagues asked about it. She orchestrated the conversation to both address the cultural nuance and to develop a theoretical perspective that she felt she needed. As I observed, I saw how many different influences and voices came through such a cross-cultural text. I also found myself thinking about the language acquisition theories I had learned and accepted in the early 1990s but was coming to question. These theories recommended that learners of English not associate too much with speakers of their native tongue if they wanted to gain fluency in the language. Such theories, now discounted by critical linguists such as Suresh Canagarajah (2002), could not account for the complexity of linguistic interaction in which So Jin and her colleagues engaged when defining cultural perceptions of class.

In the process of defining class through a cultural construct, her group mates also began to link their ideas to scholars such as Bourdieu and Foucault, adding yet another cross-cultural dimension to an already complex discussion. I could latch on a little to configurations of capital that emerged through discussion of Bourdieu, but felt lost during the rest of the exchange, because it assumed a disciplinary understanding of the connection across theories and how they applied to the context that So Jin was examining. Lack of sleep from the new baby could only partially account for my inability to follow the threads of the conversation. Lack of disciplinary and philosophical foundations and the relevant conceptual and linguistic associations accounted for the rest. As anthropologists, her group mates could make references or use shorthand to refer to the concepts, whereas I needed to first have a picture of the concept before understanding its application. Not being able to fully comprehend the discussion caused me to feel an uncomfortable gap in my own language proficiency, in that people who had grown up speaking languages other than English were conversing fluently.

This made me think about how speakers of English as an additional language are conventionally seen as having to count on native English speakers for articulation, and how very misleading that perception could be once students from non-English-dominant countries become encul-turated in their disciplines. When this happens, they develop linguistic as well as content area expertise, and the linguistic expertise merges with the content expertise. All the participants in the writing group drew on their years as anthropologists in training to speak as those in their discipline would speak. By articulating and applying theoretical constructs from scholars who are themselves often read in translation, along with testing and refining cultural metaphors to express nuanced perceptions of the elusive category of class, So Jin also synthesized both theory and perception to create an analysis that could appeal to a Korean and a non-Korean audience. The students in the writing group drew upon language to give shape to abstract ideas and pull diverse world views into communication, which is so much more than the simple communication of needs or basic expression of feelings often attributed to language proficiency.

These are complex practices that are developed through disciplinary engagement and therefore do not just fall into the domain of students who grew up speaking English. My difficulty following the discussion reflected my inexperience with disciplinary practice and ways of knowing. Terms like *native speaker* and *non-native speaker* are inadequate to describe language users in this context, as disciplinary styles of English are not native to anyone. To more appropriately describe language users in this context, we need to think more about a speaker's or writer's developing experience and less about a country of origin. As I read more of So Jin's drafts and heard more group talk about her work, I felt that slowly I was learning some of the language of Anthropology.

Editing and Feedback: Positioning Ourselves in Each Other's Texts

Marcia's Take: Negotiating Unquestioned Authority of Writing When Editing

When So Jin and I talked about editing, neither of us approached it as something that was highly theorized. However, as we reflected upon editing practices as we prepared this chapter, we realized that our perceptions of editing tied directly into our experiences as students and writers, and in my case as a teacher of English. So Jin pointed out that my approaches to editing aligned well with my approaches to teaching in that they both worked in opposition to deficit models of language education. Like my dissertation topic itself, my approaches strived to position English as an Additional Language (EAL) writers as negotiating numerous aspects of identity when they were writing in English. So Jin based this comment on her sense that I did not read only to find errors and did not assume unquestioned authority when suggesting changes to texts. Though I would change some of the minor, single-word grammatical features in So Jin's chapters without explanation, often I tried to offer possible interpretations for the ways sentences were worded, so she could either see the rationale for the change and decide whether or not to change the sentence herself. For example, she had the following sentences in a draft of her second chapter, with the sentence in focus highlighted in italics and underlined:

> Moreover, others, who were more ambivalent toward private after-school education in general and "learning ahead" in particular, often mentioned that children who did not have private after-school education could not help but be disadvantaged or behind because all the other kids study in advance through private after-school education. . . *Although this "learning ahead" problem becomes worse and worse for middle and high school levels, it becomes more and more popular at the elementary school level.*

I had been a little confused about the juxtaposition of something becoming worse at one level but more popular at another and marked the text with this comment:

> Not sure I can see why it becomes worse at the higher levels or even more popular at the lower. Perhaps another sentence or so of explanation or a signaling statement about its economic impact would set up this idea more clearly.

When I could not interpret an idea, I had to evaluate whether it was my own misunderstanding of what I had read or whether the words somehow detracted from the meaning. These judgments entailed more complex interaction than merely my changing a word here or there and assuming that by doing so I was presenting the clearer articulation. My doubts about my own comprehension contrast with the commonly held view that when it comes to English language use, an EAL writer will usually be wrong due to an insufficient grasp of the nuances and complexities of language. In this case, our interpretations of text and audience depended greatly on dialogue and negotiation between ourselves, because sometimes the words that I would choose, based on general language use, did not accurately represent the cultural nuances that So Jin sought to portray.

So Jin's Take: Seeking Good Editors and Understanding Different Audiences

Finding a good editor for international graduate students—especially for their dissertations—seems very difficult because they already have considerable fluency in English and in their areas of expertise. One of my international friends often expressed her disappointment with editors, many of whom just fixed the articles (e.g., adding or changing *a* and *the*) in her dissertation drafts. In fact, I had also had a frustrating experience with a paid editor. After showing the paid editor one of my dissertation chapters, I discontinued my association with her. Along with my international friend, I felt that editing a dissertation requires much more than just the fluency of English writing itself. As Marcia discussed above, the language of the area of expertise can be a "second" language even for educated native speakers of English. Consequently, good editing requires some kind of familiarity with a dissertation's content area—even in the broad sense.

While sharing my friend's frustration, I appreciated Marcia as an editor for my dissertation because she herself was doing qualitative research and was familiar with ethnographic-style writing. Moreover, since she as a friend had generously helped me edit my previous academic writing, I had great trust in Marcia's editing ability and style. In the process of Marcia's editing some of my chapter drafts, she usually asked me what I meant by this or that sentence, and we would also often discuss broader aspects of my writing. While involved in these interactive conversations over the text, I often found myself thinking more about the clarity of the writing itself and not just about small errors in language or usage. I felt that this kind of intimate exchange about editing was very different from the case of a paid professional editor, which is often unidirectional (i.e., authoritative editors correct the text, and writers accept those corrections with little question).

The process of Marcia's editing my dissertation was very interactive and multivocalic. Of course, this active process takes more time than having an editor simply mark a writer's text, but it makes writers think carefully about what they want to convey through texts and learn more how to write for a specific audience. For instance, Marcia brought up one example of her questioning approach to my text in the example mentioned above when she asked for clarification of this sentence: "Although this 'learning ahead' problem becomes worse and worse for middle and high school levels, it becomes more and more popular at the elementary school level." The problems of such a sentence are not only wording but also some presumed ideas—in many senses culturally valued assumptions—in my mind (e.g., "learning ahead" as a problem, rather than as a practice). Thanks to Marcia's comment, I was able to rethink the unstated assumptions in my writing, in particular, those that should be clarified or explained to American or non-Korean audiences. In this interactive process, I clarified my ideas and coherently used the phrase "learning ahead" as a practice—rather than as a problem—to convey the message accurately. As a result, I later changed this sentence as follows:

> "Although the practice of 'learning ahead' in the private after-school education becomes more intense for secondary school levels because of the university entrance examination and the special-purpose high school entrance examination, especially for the high grade students, it has become more and more popular at the elementary school level."

Reflecting on my own experiences, I suggest that international students who seek editing help clarify what they expect from editing and negotiate those expectations overtly with their editors without being intimidated by the native English speaker's presumed linguistic expertise. In our case, because of our shared history, approaches to editing did not have to be overtly negotiated. Of course, such interactive editing in the kind of reciprocal relationship that Marcia and I had is not always available for international students. Still, it is important for international students to recognize that what kinds of editors are appropriate for them may depend on what stage they are in large writing projects such as dissertations or book writing, and to recognize as well that they have agency in making these decisions. Although I appreciated enormously Marcia's interactive editing as I wrote my dissertation, I might on another occasion choose a professional editor who actively marked the changes within a short time for another writing purpose such as for a book publication or journal article. The point is that international students need to be aware of the different choices available to them at different stages in their doctoral work.

Flipping the Advisory Roles with Fellowship Applications

So Jin's Voice: Expertise Developing from Experience

While watching our kids play together as usual, Marcia's and my informal conversations about the latest progress in our work moved to our funding applications. While I was applying for campus fellowship funding, Marcia was also preparing to apply for another campus fellowship. When I heard about her fellowship application, I felt that I might be able to help her or give her some feedback about writing funding proposals because I had considerable experience not only writing funding proposals, but also exchanging feedback about funding proposals in a variety of different group meetings. Then, I found out that I had been awarded a national (and not just campus-funded) grant—the Spencer Dissertation Fellowship for educational research. Since Marcia's research project was also broadly related to educational research, she was interested in applying for the Spencer Fellowship one year after me.

Several months later, Marcia asked me to read her application for the Spencer Fellowship before she submitted it. Although I was not at all an expert in her study area, I felt that I could give her some feedback about her fellowship proposal since I had more experience applying for funding and especially since I had applied twice for the Spencer Fellowship and had recently won it.

My feedback mainly focused on the organization of her proposal, while asking for clarification of her use of certain key terms, like EAL (English as an Additional Language) and for clarification of some sentences. When I gave some feedback or comments on Marcia's proposal, I was aware that the due date for this funding application was coming soon, and, therefore, heeded her need to revise practically within the time limit.

I felt that I did not help much because she did not get the Spencer Fellowship in the end. But I was glad to help her at least minimally, and she did seem to appreciate my help. Given that I also had several times failed my funding proposals in the past, I told her not to take this failure as an indication that her research itself was not interesting or important. That was the consoling advice I heard from my advisor or my colleagues when my applications had failed for funding previously and what I now believed.

Marcia's Voice: Unanticipated Rewards from Seeking

Expert Advice

I was surprised when So Jin wrote that she felt she had not helped much because I did not get the fellowship in the end. I say this because by seeking her advice I had learned so much both in terms of clarifying my dissertation goals and concepts and in terms of seeking feedback from multiple sources on important drafts. I have to admit that I did feel strange when I first sought So Jin's feedback on my campus fellowship application. As she surmised, I was not fully accustomed to seeking peer feedback on my writing, and bringing it to a former student made me somehow feel like I had been an "imposter teacher" when I had taught her ESL class six years before. Even though I had been a conversation class teacher, and even though in six years it is reasonable to assume that we both developed a greater repertoire in writing, I still felt that I had always been her language consultant and was embarrassed to show that I struggled with some of the same writing issues as EAL writers. In reality though, none of my previous TESL training, which like many in the field had stopped with a terminal master's degree, had included writing proposals for funding, generally a doctoral-level genre. Additionally, as So Jin's feedback reflected, I had grown accustomed to talking about my work to people who did similar sorts of work and needed to examine how my construction of ideas could make sense to a different audience. Once I could see that I was showing a draft to an advanced colleague, instead of a former student, it was easier to accept that I was showing myself to be a writer who was still learning about writing in various contexts.

About half a year later, my understanding of what it meant to seek feedback on my writing had shifted dramatically. In addition to So Jin and my dissertation advisor, as is fitting for a topic that addresses response and feedback, I had run drafts of my Spencer proposal by several other people, including another member of my committee, a writing center consultant, and my husband. Everyone gave me different kinds of feedback reflecting their various positions on my project, but So Jin's advice was unique. It reflected the expertise she had developed as a graduate student who had gone through similar application processes, as a Spencer recipient who had local knowledge of ins and outs of the Fellowship, and as a graduate student researcher well versed in ethnographic studies.

Consequently, she could raise questions about how the methodology was positioned within the larger study, and offered insights into how the Spencer Fellowship evaluators might read my application.

Through all these roles, So Jin offered validation for the whole project. After the effort I had put into the application, I felt discouraged when I did not make the first cut, but not for too long. Not receiving the funding ultimately allowed me to go in other directions that I have found productive. More importantly, unlike with my previous rejection from the campus program, I had strong support and validation for the project, including these words that I had from So Jin a few days before I submitted my application:

> I'm so excited to see your project. As an international student in the U.S. and your informant, I truly believe in the importance of your research.

Coda: Shared Voice

Some readers might wonder whether what we have reflected on and narrated here is just an exceptional case. We realize that few graduate students will share such a cross-culturally textured relationship with their colleagues as we have portrayed. However, in envisioning and writing this chapter, we believe that our experience can say something about learning to do graduate school much beyond just showing an exception (see Stake, 2000, and Ellis & Bochner, 2000, for perspectives on the role of commonalities as opposed to generalities). By its very nature, doing graduate school, particularly at the doctoral level, means becoming a researcher, but graduate students may also become the researched. In writing, all of us will be edited, but some of us will edit as well, whether or not we are native speakers. Many will be teachers; all will be taught. By revealing a collegial, peer-mentoring relationship between two graduate students who have very different backgrounds and native languages, we have discussed and reflected upon the complex interactive process of ethnographic research, editing dissertations, and the sharing and shifting of expertise across the disciplinary, linguistic, and national boundaries. Our fields are open to interdisciplinary and cross-cultural inquiry, so our reflections on these topics have helped to deepen our understandings of our own fields and locate them within a wider academic network.

Graduate students who did not grow up speaking English may feel at a disadvantage with the language in English-dominant graduate schools, and indeed some quirks of the English grammar will always cause grief. Furthermore, we cannot ignore the many difficulties and feelings of isolation, which many international students in U.S. universities often face. However, we also feel that gaining comfort with specialized disciplinary language does not come naturally to anyone, because disciplinary language is not native to any of us. People who grow up speaking English may mask difficulties (Casanave, this volume) or not conceptualize them as linguistic challenges. In part, this is because fluency with disciplinary language develops in connection with content area expertise, and sometimes it is impossible to distinguish where one ends and the other begins. Thus, although not always apparent, mother tongue speakers of English may not always have the linguistic advantages that they are believed to have. Even so, monolingual European-American students do not always recognize the deep knowledge that their international classmates bring to academic endeavors or see that being an international student tells only a part of her or his experiences as a graduate student. We hope that our story disrupts some stereotypical images that international graduate students hold about themselves and that others hold about them. We also hope that it promotes dialogues and collaborations between international and non-international students and among graduate students across the disciplinary boundaries. After all, expertise takes many forms and is not just distributed between professor and student, but among students of all language backgrounds as well.

Marcia's Wrap Up: An Ending and a Beginning

The evening before So Jin's defense, we enacted the roles we had played throughout our friendship and research relationship, including teacher to student, language advisor to language learner, but also including So Jin as advanced graduate student and mentor to me as a more novice researcher. As I listened to So Jin practice her defense presentation, we played around with minor edits, but as her listener I mainly suggested that she slow down to emphasize technical words or ones that were easily confused aurally, like *micro* and *macro*. However, some of my comments referred to how she could rephrase responses to the examining committee's hypothetical questions in a way that sounded more confident. But the point for me was not just that she sound confident. It was about ownership of her expertise. I did not want anything to take away from how deeply she had explored the theory and how masterfully she had woven it into the complex narratives of her participants. Regardless of her non-native English speaker status, she was now the expert of record on her topic.

Part way through our defense practice, So Jin's daughter came home and was surprised to see me without my daughter, her playmate. So Jin and I explained that I was helping her with something, and then So Jin asked her what was special about the next day. With coaxing, both in English and Korean, the little girl said that the next day, her mother would become a doctor. These words struck me, crystallizing the realization that the next day, I would be present as my former English student, my research participant, my senior colleague, my mentor, and my friend transitioned from graduate student to Doctor of Philosophy.

MARCIA BUELL, UNIVERSITY OF ILLINOIS AT URBANA-CHAMPAIGN

As with other contributors in this book, my entering a doctoral program resulted not by design, but from circumstance. After a decade of teaching EFL/ESL in Japan, China, Hungary, and the United States, I found myself underemployed in a town that hosted a first-rate university. There I met professors who raised important questions about what I had taken for granted as an ESL professional. Pursuing a graduate degree in Writing Studies afforded me the challenging but fruitful opportunity to learn to incorporate new theories with previous practices and to become a colleague of some of my former language students.

SO JIN PARK, YONSEI UNIVERSITY, SOUTH KOREA

My undergraduate years were ones of dramatic social upheaval and repression in South Korea. At that time, I never imagined myself at a graduate school in the U.S. After short working experiences and obtaining an M.A. degree in sociology, I made a decision to pursue a Ph.D. program in cultural anthropology in the U.S. Despite several barriers, as an international student I had more support and recognition from my mentors and friends in the U.S. than at home. Now back home, I am enjoying teaching undergraduate and graduate students and pursuing my research interests in a more democratized and aggressively globalizing South Korea.

REFERENCES

Behar, R. (1993). *Translated woman: Crossing the border with Esperanza's story.* Boston: Beacon Press.

Behar, R., & Gordon, D. A. (1993). *Women writing culture.* Berkeley: University of California Press.

Bogdan, R. C., & Biklen, S. K. (1998). *Qualitative research in education: An introduction to theory and methods.* Boston: Allyn & Bacon.

Canagarajah, A. S. (2002). *Critical academic writing and multilingual students.* Ann Arbor: University of Michigan Press.

Casanave, C. (2002). *Writing games: Multicultural case studies of academic literacy practices in higher education.* Mahwah, NJ: Lawrence Erlbaum.

Clifford, J., & Marcus G. E. (1986). *Writing culture: The poetics and politics of ethnography.* Berkeley: University of California Press.

Ellis, C., & Bochner, A. P. (2000) Autoethnography, personal narrative, reflexivity: Researcher as subject. In N. K. Denzen & Y. S. Lincoln (Eds.), *Handbook of qualitative research* (2nd ed.) (pp. 733–758). Thousand Oaks, CA: Sage.

Geisler, C. (1994). *Academic literacy and the nature of expertise: Reading, writing, and knowing in academic philosophy.* Hillsdale, NJ: Lawrence Erlbaum.

Holstein, J. A., & Gubrium, J. F. (1995). *The active interview.* Thousand Oaks, CA: Sage.

Lave, J., & Wenger, E. (1991). *Situated learning: Legitimate peripheral participation.* New York: Cambridge University Press.

Patton, M. Q.(1990). *Qualitative evaluation and research methods* (2nd ed.). Newbury Park, CA: Sage.

Prior, P. A. (1998). *Writing/disciplinarity: A sociohistoric account of literate activity in the academy.* Mahwah, NJ: Lawrence Erlbaum.

Rosaldo, R. (1993). *Culture and truth: The remaking of social analysis.* Boston: Beacon Press.

Stake, R. E. (2000). Case studies. In N. K. Denizen & Y. S. Lincoln (Eds.), *Handbook of qualitative research* (2nd ed.) (pp. 435–454). Thousand Oaks, CA: Sage.

Visweswaran, K. (1994). *Fictions of feminist ethnography.* Minneapolis: University of Minnesota Press.

Willis, P. E. (1977). *Learning to labour: How working class kids get working class jobs.* Farnborough, UK: Saxon House.

Chapter 14

Finishing the Dissertation while on Tenure Track: Enlisting Support from Inside and Outside the Academy

JUN OHASHI, HIROKO OHASHI, AND BRIAN PALTRIDGE

This chapter relates the story of the dual struggle of a novice faculty member who was still in the process of finishing his Ph.D. when he took on a tenure track faculty appointment. We hope to show how tenure track requirements can have a profound impact on doctoral students' studies as well as on their life outside of the university. Specifically, it is the story of how a Japanese doctoral student, co-author Jun Ohashi, enlisted multiple sources of support from both his home and academic environments in order to survive the demands of this difficult period in his life. His wife, Hiroko, his dissertation advisor, Brian, and he worked together in mutually supportive ways to help him survive a tense and challenging time, under pressure of a fixed deadline set by the university for ensuring the continuation of his faculty appointment. The challenge was particularly burdensome given that Jun and Hiroko, mother-tongue speakers of Japanese, were trying to establish a new life for themselves and their children in an unfamiliar country while Jun was simultaneously finishing his dissertation and dealing with the politics of a new and unfamiliar academic department.

As we look back on these experiences, we have to say that we cannot recommend that doctoral students accept faculty appointments before finishing their dissertations. It is not always that simple, however. Often the timing of such moves may be out of the student's control. Our story, therefore, is one of survival under difficult circumstances. Caught between a rock and a hard place, Jun, with the help of Hiroko and Brian, managed to both write a dissertation and become a faculty member at the same time. Cross-cultural tensions in Jun's department were endured if not resolved. Jun and Hiroko's marriage survived. And Brian happily saw the results of his many months of advising and extra support. We hope, with our story, to offer hope to doctoral students who find themselves in a similar dilemma, and to expand our understanding of the phenomenon of mentoring and of the very situated and local nature of the graduate experience.

Background

Jun and his wife, Hiroko, both from Japan, had studied previously in the U.K. and moved to Australia where Jun had taken up a tenure track position in one department and was undertaking Ph.D. work in another. Jun had different and often conflicting roles in each of these situations. He also had the tension between the identity of a new faculty member trying to find his place in his new academic department as well as that of a graduate student trying to work out the "rules of the game" in the new and (and sometimes surprisingly) different academic learning environment. Brian was Jun's advisor and only knew him, in the early stages at least, as a graduate student working toward a Ph.D. in his department.

This chapter describes this situation from three perspectives: from that of the student and new faculty member (Jun), the student's partner (Hiroko), and the dissertation advisor (Brian), all co-authors of this chapter. Its focus will be on the ways that each person contributed to Jun's survival in the complexities of several communities of practice (Lave & Wenger, 1991; Wenger, 1998) at the university and in an unfamiliar country. Our message will be that graduate students need to reach out actively to enlist and accept support from those in the academic departments that they may be associated with as well as from partners and family members in the home environment. We will discuss key issues Jun faced in this experience, from starting out on the Ph.D. in a new school where he was also a faculty member, through the circumstances under which he wrote his Ph.D., to how he dealt with (and survived) them.

Getting Started

Jun:
I was an academic staff member in a university in the U.K. and a part-time Ph.D. student for several years before I came to Australia. When I took up my tenure track position in Australia, I soon found that I had no choice but to restart the Ph.D. because my advisor in the U.K. retired. Even if my original advisor had not retired, I would have had to meet the requirements set by the new university for admission and progression in my Ph.D. My academic tenure was subject to a term of probation of three years. One of the conditions of this probation was "substantial progress towards the completion of the Ph.D." I met Brian at a research seminar in the School of Languages for the first time, and we met several times in subsequent postgraduate seminars in the Linguistics and Applied Linguistics Department. I found him very knowledgeable in my research field and very supportive of postgraduate students. I approached him and after a couple of meetings he provisionally agreed to be my dissertation advisor. He asked me to submit a 4,000-word dissertation outline before seeing him as my advisor. I handed the manuscript in, and the following week I was asked to come to his office. He said clearly, "If you include an investigation of naturally occurring data, I can be your advisor." My Ph.D. was on Japanese and English cross-cultural pragmatics. I had intended to base my Ph.D. on native speaker accounts of what they do with language (rather than looking at what they actually do). I agreed, but I did not know how important his advice was at that time. It turned out that the analysis of the naturally occurring data became my most significant contribution to the field of study.

The New and Different Work and Study Context

Jun:
My work environment in Australia was very different from that in the U.K. where I had been used to debating issues in meetings in the department, which was made up of four British and two Japanese faculty members. Having a different point of view did not lead to conflict there. I found, however, that debate was not an acceptable way of participating in the new department I had joined. In the new department, I realized very soon that meetings were run very differently from meetings at my

previous university. There was no agenda available prior to the meetings. A senior faculty member who led a section in the department dominated the section meetings—often reporting whatever had been discussed in executive meetings. I suggested that a list of items to be discussed could be useful and that it should be circulated before the meeting or at least presented at the meeting. I was made to realize that I should not have suggested this. My proactive behaviors on other occasions, including my suggestion about redeveloping a new placement test to replace the old unpopular one, and my suggestion about more economical and effective teaching arrangements were not welcomed by the senior member of staff. I wished to discuss these issues openly in the meeting. However, I found that no one was willing to make any comments openly at these meetings. Consequently, I had to face a very harsh reality. One day I was urgently called to a meeting with a professor, the acting head of department and the senior staff member. At the meeting, I was told that I had failed to follow the instruction of the senior member, who had been delegated powers for the supervision of staff in the section. The professor advised that I would be removed from my role as coordinator of the program I was responsible for and would teach 14 hours a week instead. I was not allowed to express my views on those decisions. The professor told me that the expression of views on a subject was of secondary importance to accepting advice or instruction from a supervisor. This caused me immense psychological pain and anger.

At that time, the section also had a culture that was hostile to research. Coming from a university in the U.K. where the Research Assessment Exercise (RAE) was employed in determining government funding to individual departments, I was outspoken about the need for research activities to ensure that individual staff members would survive, in the belief that salaries might depend on similar funding arrangements. I saw that many language teachers stayed until late developing and preparing language materials and tasks for students. I respected their attitudes toward their students and their genuine enthusiasm for their teaching. I was puzzled, however, by all this, especially when a different message was coming from outside the department. At a faculty meeting, the Dean emphasized the importance of research activities and active participation in external competitive grant applications. When I asked for the senior member's signature, which was a requirement for the submission of a research application, I was told that teaching was more important than research and that I should concentrate on my teaching. Research, however, was very important for me. Indeed if I had not completed the research for my Ph.D., I would not have gained academic tenure. I, thus, had many contradictions and unexpected tensions to deal with in my new academic position. I experienced extraordinary stress because of this and because of the staff member who exercised gatekeeping power over my academic career in the new university.

Brian:

When he arrived to take up his position at the university, Jun had to find out who in the university had expertise in his area of research, and establish a relationship with that person so he felt able to ask the person to supervise his Ph.D. When Jun had completed his Ph.D., I asked him a question I have never asked any of my Ph.D. students: "Why did you want me to supervise your dissertation?" Jun told me a story that until that moment I had forgotten. He said, "On one occasion, when I was looking for an advisor, I asked if you could look at a grant proposal I had written. You said you were leaving the next day for the U.S., but if I gave you a stamped addressed envelope, you would read it on the plane, and send it to me from the next airport." I did that, and on my return he asked if I could supervise his Ph.D., I guess, on the basis of my quick turn-around of his work.

The tenure track conditions Jun had on his appointment at the university required him to write a complete first draft of his Ph.D. dissertation at the end of his second year of enrolment, as a part-time student. In Australia, the Ph.D. is a dissertation-only degree and normally takes, at a minimum, three years of full-time study. Most full-time students would not write a first complete draft of their dissertation until the middle, or the end, of their third year of full-time study. Jun was therefore being asked to do what no normal full-time student would do: write a first draft of his Ph.D. at the end of (the part-time equivalent of) his first year of enrolment.

Hiroko:

When we came to Australia, we assumed that this was another English-speaking country, similar to the one we had known in the U.K. We did not expect much of a cultural difference between the two countries. However, I came to learn that Jun had to deal with life in a very different country and a very different academic community. A new faculty member on probation is very vulnerable. He could not remain unaffected by the way he was being treated by the senior staff member. It was very hard for me to imagine that Jun had to be approved of by his immediate senior staff member, a person who was also unwelcoming to him. I thought to myself, How many hurdles does he have to jump? I was very concerned about Jun's situation.

Having found Jun's work environment and the expectations placed on him were not going to be as we had imagined, I decided to become a full-time housewife so that Jun could concentrate fully on his new job and his Ph.D. In the U.K. I had been Jun's colleague and co-researcher and was able to understand his work. Given that after I had become a full-time housewife I had no association with his work environment, it was difficult for me at first to imagine and understand the problems Jun was dealing with.

Brian:

I did not know a lot about Jun's personal circumstances while I was supervising him. I knew that he was married and that he had a family, but I did not know about the sacrifices Hiroko had made for him to get his Ph.D., and the role she took in helping him get there. I remember a striking conversation I had with Hiroko after Jun's dissertation had been passed and he had been awarded his degree. This conversation took place one night in their home, when they had invited me over for dinner. I never met Hiroko while I was supervising Jun. When we met, she said to me, "We would have liked to invite you to our house sooner, but the stakes were too high." I guess by this she meant there may have been times when I might have had to make a tough call on Jun, and she didn't want a personal relationship with his family to get in the way of my having to do this. I never in fact had to do this, but had I needed to, I can see how a personal relationship with Jun and his family could have made it harder for me to do difficult and honest critiques.

Writing the Dissertation and Surviving the Experience

Jun:

Writing a Ph.D. dissertation in English is an enormous task for non-native speakers of English. I used the research support services unit that was available at the university for non-native speakers of English at an early stage of my Ph.D. I was given five tickets with which I was entitled to use the service throughout my candidacy. Each ticket gave me one 30-minute appointment. This was useful not only for improving my writing, but also for clarifying my conceptual confusions, as I had to explain my research intentions to someone outside my field. The data collection process also took a significant amount of time. My ethics clearance for my research was approved only a few days prior to my departure for Japan to collect my data. I was fortunate, however, that I was able to use some of the data I had collected in the U.K. from my previous Ph.D. registration.

The key to the completion of my Ph.D., however, was Brian's supervisory expertise. He helped me frame my dissertation at a very early stage of my candidacy. For example, he explained about the common make-up of a Ph.D. dissertation. My abstract image of a Ph.D. dissertation suddenly took shape. I remember, as soon as I got back to my computer I created a file designated for each chapter. He also said, "At the end of the day, only two examiners who have a good grasp of what your dissertation is about will assess your dissertation." His comment told me nothing new, but helped me realize the importance of shaping the dissertation to their expectations, rather than simply aiming the research results at the wider post-dissertation audience.

Hiroko:
As Jun's wife, I wanted to make sure of Jun's physical and psychological well-being. I often found myself trying hard not to miss any signs that might have shown what kind of day Jun had had at work the moment he came home. Knowing that I had a busy day as a mother and housekeeper, Jun would not say that his day was a bad one, just so he would not worry me. Tone of voice, the look in his eyes, the way he responded to my questions, and the way he smiled at the children were some of the clues. When to comfort him, when to encourage him, when to be his critic, when to talk about personal and family issues all depended on my day-to-day observations of his new life. I also wanted my children to understand that their father was very tired when he came back, and they were constantly reminded that they must not disturb him, even if they had waited for him to be home all day long.

As a former colleague, I also wanted to be useful and thus sometimes became a tough critic of his Ph.D. work. When I learnt that Jun had to complete his Ph.D. within a very short period time, I said to him, "It's good that you can finish it earlier, and you can move on." I tried to help him interpret his uncomfortable, high-pressure situation positively, in spite of his own uncertainty about whether he could succeed in time to secure his job. Although I might have been a little too harsh with him at times, I knew Jun needed to change his mindset. I read whatever was added to his manuscript each day, and thus had a good grasp of his progress.

Although my decision to become his supporter was certain, I wasn't aware until we were well into the dissertation writing process that I was also going to be tested in many ways, both psychologically and physically. Having hoped to start a Ph.D. myself, giving up my academic career and being isolated from the academic community was a difficult situation for me to accept, especially when I was offered a full-time position as a research assistant of a prominent scholar from whom I could have learnt a great deal in order to complete a Ph.D. In our new environment, I couldn't help feeling myself left behind and lonely, remaining at home as "a mere supporter," locking myself up to look after a three-year-old and a newborn baby. Although I was tired and wanted some help, living in a foreign country where there are no relatives means no assistance from family and no friends at first. From time to time, I wondered about my career that was on hold, especially when Jun was not sure whether he himself was on the right track. It is the hardest thing in a long journey if the person you have decided to follow doesn't know where he is and which direction he should take. My anxiety for my own career and my disappointment was put aside, when I told myself that Jun had higher hurdles than mine.

Jun:
My mind was in such turmoil, and a fear of losing my job kept revisiting me. A sense of guilt for Hiroko, who gave up her academic career for me, was growing. She never overtly consoled or pitied me, but said "even if you lose your job, you won't lose your Ph.D." or "I have a wander lust, and I feel like moving again." That was her way of making me feel better. She always sent me a positive aura. Regular meetings with Brian gave me a sense of shelter. He showed he had faith in me, and I always wished to reciprocate it, and thus I worked hard. Teaching 14 hours a week was also tough but it was my self-esteem booster because I knew the students enjoyed my teaching and I could make a difference to their learning.

Gradually I learnt to isolate the conflict with the senior staff and to set it aside from my list of more urgent matters. In other words, I learnt not to react emotionally to the conflict but to focus on what I should be doing to ensure that my tenure-track appointment at the university would be confirmed.

Mentoring and Being Mentored

Brian:

I saw my main role as helping Jun set research and writing goals that would enable him to meet his tenure track conditions, knowing how high (and unreasonable) these goals were. I had, in fact, written a first complete draft of my Ph.D. after two years of part-time study while at the same time working as a full-time academic. The conditions in which I did this were, however, quite different from those of Jun. I was in an academic environment I was familiar with, and my advisor was also my department chair. She was able to give me periods of time off teaching to work on my Ph.D., and I had no tenure track requirements hanging over me.

Supervising non-English-speaking background Ph.D. students is even more complex than supervising local English-speaking background students. I understood, to some extent, how Jun, as a student, might relate to me. I understood, for example, that when Jun said, "I will do my best," he was expressing a typically Japanese cultural deference toward his work and toward his superior. I equally knew, from the university's point of view, "doing his best" was not going to get Jun his tenure. When Jun said this to me, I replied, "No you won't, you'll do it." We joke about this now, but it was, really, no joking matter. Too much hung on Jun's Ph.D., and I had to be sure he got there.

A number of years ago I carried out a study with a colleague at the University of Hong Kong (Paltridge & Lewkowicz, 2000) where, among other things, we asked advisors about their relationship with their students. What was interesting about this particular situation was that not all of the advisors were from an English-speaking background, nor were all of their students. The differences between the native and non-native speaker advisors' responses to this question were quite marked. The non-native speaker advisors' (in this case, Chinese) stressed the importance of a personal dimension to their supervisory relationships. One of the Chinese advisors explained their Chinese students' point of view thus:

> Chinese students tend to expect Chinese teachers to care for them apart from caring about their studies. . . . There is the Chinese cultural view that the teacher must care about the student, apart from caring about their studies.

This view was supported by the Chinese students that we interviewed. They believed much more strongly than the native speaker students, and most of the native speaker advisors, that a close personal relationship with their advisor is essential for successful supervision. One of the Chinese students put her view this way:

> Personal doesn't mean that you get involved, or fall in love, with your supervisor. However, I think that a personal relationship means you deal with each other on a more familiar basis. If you hardly know your supervisor, or your supervisor hardly knows you, it's very difficult to work together.

Jun:
Mentoring makes a lot of difference to students. Apart from Brian's moral support, what I benefited from most for the completion (on time) of my dissertation was his clear guidance and speedy feedback. Meetings were arranged not long after my submitting work to him that I had produced. Advice was given in each meeting, and it was typically specific instructions, very much to the point. For example, "When you analyze these data you should also refer back to the data in the previous chapter because they have significant relevance. You can strengthen your argument by showing this preferred pattern emerging from two different sets of data." Chapter drafts were returned within a week with thorough feedback. Any other queries that I had were responded to on the same day. Brian understood my situation from the beginning and supported me with interest and commitment. I responded with my hard work, and it was not difficult to work hard for someone who clearly cared about my success.

Hiroko:
Despite all the things working against Jun, I still think that he was very fortunate. Brian made him work hard, and he himself worked very hard to help Jun achieve his goal. I now see Jun working as a dissertation advisor who was trained through his own experiences with Brian. I believe he will pass on what he received from Brian to his own students. Jun often repeated some words that kept me going and those were, "It's your turn next, Hiroko," exactly the same words spoken by Brian when Jun completed his dissertation. Although I had not had the occasion to meet Brian until then, I realized that I was also supported and rewarded by him in this process.

Conclusions

The stories we have told in this chapter remind us that there are often important cultural differences that non-English-speaking background students, especially, may not expect they will have to deal with. We cannot always know what these differences will be, but we do need to expect that there will be differences of these kinds and keep our minds open to how we respond to them. No two Ph.D. students' situations are the same. This is even more the case when the student has come from another country to carry out his or her Ph.D.

One of the messages of this chapter is that in order to survive a situation like the one that Jun found himself in it is important to have people around who understand the complex cultural and academic demands of the new situation. It is also important for the students to ask for help with non-academic, as well as academic, issues from their advisor when this is needed. This is something many international students, in particular, may be reluctant to do. There are times, however, when the advisor can "go to bat" for the student and deal with things in a way that the student is simply not able to. This is especially the case when the demands being placed on the student are as high as the ones described in this chapter. On the home front, as well, it is important to have a partner who can share in and help alleviate the stresses of the kind that Jun was going through. Both Brian and Hiroko were sympathetic to his situation and understood his needs. Brian gave him support and advice, and Hiroko supported and encouraged him in all the ways that she could. All of this helped Jun gain a sense of security, and in turn, confidence in his ability to complete his Ph.D. Jun's psychological well being, and the maintenance of this well-being, were extremely important to his success. No one can survive an experience like this by himself or herself. Mentoring, it seems, comes in many forms. Recognizing them, seeking them, and providing them help ensure success.

JUN OHASHI, UNIVERSITY OF MELBOURNE

I can hardly believe what we went through while I was doing my Ph.D. Fortunately, everything has now changed in my work environment, and I now enjoy the academic community I am a member of. My Ph.D. was not just about pursuing my academic interests. It was also a process through which I grew as a human being. My experience, as difficult as it was, lead me to a special relationship with my advisor. It also lead to a stronger family life. As hard as it was, I do not regret the journey my Ph.D. took me on.

HIROKO OHASHI, RMIT UNIVERSITY

When I read academic books, I used to like to read the acknowledgment pages and imagine what life was like behind the publication of these books. During Jun's Ph.D., I often read those pages to remind myself of how people support each other to accomplish their goals. Even great scholars needed support. So did Jun. My name is proudly printed in the acknowledgment page of his Ph.D. I can now see how supporters are also supported.

BRIAN PALTRIDGE, UNIVERSITY OF SYDNEY

What I have learnt from writing this article with Jun and Hiroko is how little we often know about our research students. I often say to my students if I sense they have a problem that is making their progress difficult: "You don't have to tell me what's happening in your life—that's your business and not mine—but you do have to tell me there's a problem. If I don't know, I can't help you." Jun told me enough for me to be able to help him.

REFERENCES

Lave, J., & Wenger, E. (1991). *Situated learning: Legitimate peripheral participation.* Cambridge, UK: Cambridge University Press.

Paltridge, B., & Lewkowicz, J. (2000). *An examination of students' and their supervisors' expectations when writing a master's thesis in English at the University of Hong Kong.* Australian Research Council Grant Project.

Wenger, E. (1998). *Communities of practice: Learning, meaning and identity.* Cambridge, UK: Cambridge University Press.

Chapter 15

The Lived Experience of Graduate Work and Writing: From Chronotopic Laminations to Everyday Lamentations

PAUL A. PRIOR AND YOUNG-KYUNG MIN

In this chapter we reflect on the lived experience of doing graduate school from two distinct perspectives. One of us (Prior) grew up in the U.S. as a native speaker of English, pursued his Ph.D. between 1988 and 1992, took a faculty position at the University of Illinois (UIUC) in 1992, and now experiences graduate school from the position of teacher, mentor, and active participant in a set of complexly interacting disciplinary spaces. The second of us (Min) grew up in Korea as a native speaker of Korean and now experiences graduate school from the position of a student (having begun her doctoral work in 2002 in a cross-disciplinary area of specialization), mentee, teacher, tutor, and emerging researcher (moving from course papers to conference papers and professional writing). However, we also share significant common ground. We both participate in the local graduate and undergraduate programs associated with writing studies at UIUC. Both of us have also experienced the joys and challenges of positioning ourselves in cross-disciplinary spaces at the interfaces of language education, English as a second language, and writing studies. Finally, both of us have developed (beginning in our graduate studies) a strong sense that sociocultural, practice theories of communication, learning, and activity offer valuable ways to understand how people acquire and use discourse.

The sociocultural notion of *chronotopic laminations*[1] is a key intersection between our daily experience of academic life and our theoretical work. The idea that time (*chronos*) and space (*topos*) are laminated (lay-

---

[1] For more information on chronotopic lamination, see Prior (1998) and Prior and Shipka (2003).

ered) captures for us the feel of doing graduate school—the way that the diverse times, places, people, texts, and interactions of our lives get woven together in multiple layers to form the fabric of our experience. It names our sense that academic life is more than a cognitive, intellectual process, that it also involves the social relationships we form, our embodied experiences throughout the day, and subtle linkages of affect, motivation, and identity that have made us who we are. The weave of our experience may be backed by the joys and motives we find in our work. However, *everyday lamentations* are also threaded through that weave: the stress of juggling competing expectations and demands, of trying to attain some balance in our scholarship and our lives. These lamentations, these everyday struggles, are sites of tension, sites where change might happen or perhaps needs to happen.

We write this chapter in three voices. In the introduction and conclusion, we write in a joint voice as we set up the frameworks and issues of our experience. In the body of the text, we write individually, each narrating and reflecting on our own experiences. Our narratives center on the ways that academic writing and work have become woven into our identities and our lives, the way they have transformed us as persons. We do not write about each other, though each of us may appear in some capacity in the other's tale. Our goal here is simply to juxtapose our journeys from a relatively shared perspective and to reflect together on what those journeys say about learning to do graduate school. We agree, for example, that the time you spend engaging in disciplinary and academic work does not turn you into a cookie cut-out. Instead, our experience suggests that who you have been trails along with what you do and how you do it, that academic life itself is complex, contingent, and very much a matter of your position. In other words, each person is forged through a particular trajectory of experiences in the world, through a journey that, like all such journeys, is lived moment by moment and often filled with the unexpected.

Paul: A Graduate Mentor's Tale

As I sat down one morning, cup of coffee steaming next to the notebook where I began drafting notes for this chapter, I considered writing about my days as a graduate student. I had completed an M.A. in Applied Linguistics at Indiana University in 1979 and then did a Ph.D. in Curriculum and Instruction at the University of Minnesota between 1988 and

1992. I also considered writing about my research (e.g., Prior, 1991, 1998) on graduate seminars, on how writing, talk, response, and disciplines intersect. Both options were attractive because I knew how to tell those stories, because both would focus on graduate study from a student's perspective, and, I realized, because both would be safer, distancing me from the tales I told. After all, it had been 14 years since I completed my Ph.D., so whatever I revealed about that person would be old news, cold embers of a long past fire. The other alternative would be to focus on my current position as a professor, as someone who meets almost daily with graduate students, who reads and writes responses to their papers. I was less clear how to tell that story, but it would not be old news. I began to think about examining the chronotopic laminations of my own work—the times, places, and people I engage with in my daily life. I might be able to demystify this professorial position to some extent and let Young-Kyung, who is in the throes of graduate work, articulate the experience of her position. Perhaps I could offer a glimpse into a cycle of my response to the written work of a graduate student, to illustrate how, under what conditions, with what motives and emotions, such responses happen. However, I also began to see practical challenges. I don't have data, *per se*, on my own work. I have to respect the privacy of the students I work with and my own role as instructor. For that reason, I decided to turn to fiction, specifically to structure my contribution here around a fictionalized narrative of a cycle of response to a fictionalized student I have named Kara. It is not a story of Young-Kyung, or of any specific student; however, it is fiction deeply rooted in my lived experience of responding to students.

Scene 1: Texts Arrive in the Night

The house is quiet now as my wife (Julie) and my daughter (Anna) have gone to sleep. I go downstairs. It is midnight. I do the dishes in the kitchen, listening to the BBC news on my local public radio station. It is early morning in London. Then I go into our small study, heavily cluttered with books and papers, and sit down at the computer to get online. I read the homepage of my browser, CommonDreams, for a few minutes and am depressed by the latest political outrage of the day, a kind of constant drumbeat of darkness that has intensified for me since the 2000 election. Then I check my email. Twelve new messages since I last checked about four hours earlier. Several are from institutional lists; I glance at them and move on. The fifth, however, is a note from an advanced graduate student, Kara, thanking me for agreeing to read the manuscript she is preparing for submission to a journal (an earlier version of which she had written for one of my seminars two semesters ago). I open the attached document (to make sure I can), print it out, and reply to Kara that I am snowed in with work at the moment but look forward to reading her manuscript in the next few weeks. I look up. The printer stops printing midway through, so I get up, move the light around, and check the ink supply. The black ink is empty. I change it. The printing complete, I put a binder clip on the paper and move it to a pile on our cluttered dining room table. It doesn't make it into my backpack yet because I know I will have no time in the next week to read it. It is 2:30. I need to take Anna to school at 7:00, so it's time to go to sleep.

In a wired, electronic age, texts arrive in the night, and it's always night somewhere. I probably check my email 20 to 30 times in a typical day—at the office, at home, at a coffee shop. Many of those emails come from current and former graduate students. The email may be about a class assignment, the need to schedule a meeting or exam, a request for assistance, an update on a project, or a suggestion for collaboration on an article or conference paper. Many of the emails have attachments: grant narratives, forms for human subjects research review, informed consent documents, informal seminar response papers, long formal seminar papers, course portfolios, letters of application, dissertation chapters, drafts of articles or book chapters, special field examination lists of readings, course syllabi, and so on. Attachments typically are requests to read, review, approve, respond. Much of my work is in this fuzzy space of responding to graduate students and former graduate students' writing, much of it not connected to a course. These texts—responses to them, discussions of them—flow through my life now.

Scene 2: The Weight of Response

Kara's paper, which I received three weeks ago, is beginning to weigh on me. Literally. For the last six days its 30 pages have been added to my backpack. Psychologically, I'm feeling the need to respond, both because of the timeline I had suggested and because I need to clean my plate so that I can get a couple days of focused writing on a book chapter that was due a week ago. Today is Tuesday. I pick up Anna at middle school at 2:55, so that she can get to her cello lesson at 3:15. We drive the five minutes to her lesson and sit in the car. I brought a can of water and some pretzels for her; she eats, drinks, and tells me a bit about her day. As she heads off to her lesson, I pull Kara's text and a pencil out of my backpack, roll the window down some, and turn on the CD. Garbage's 'Bleed Like Me' begins playing; I start reading. Half a page in, I'm confused by the way she has begun framing the piece. I start flipping through the pages to see where she is going in this draft and look for the references section to see who she is citing. I frown when I see that the references are not included in this draft. I start reading again. On page 2, I turn the paper over and begin writing on the back, a combination of a note and some possible language I'd suggest for how to make the argument clearer. Anna turns the corner, and I put the paper back in my backpack as she gets her cello stored away. We start talking again as we head across town for her Chinese language group. 'Bleed Like Me' is still playing, and Anna tells me about the girl in her class who has stopped cutting herself, though she's still bulimic. I drop Anna off and drive to a natural foods café nearby. I buy a coffee and a vegan chocolate chip cookie and sit at a table near the window. It's 4:15 and I don't have to pick Anna up till 5:30. I start reading Kara's paper and making notes again. On page 19, Kara cites Ben Rampton on speech communities. I'm not familiar with Rampton, so I pull out the computer, get online (the café has wifi), google him, and find a website with a number of working papers on it, including one on speech communities. I click several to download and then check my email. Six new messages. I make a quick reply to one about a problem at work, not expressing my frustration (I hope). I skim Rampton's paper, then look up. It's 5:25, time to pick up Anna.

As my research with Jody Shipka has begun to document,[2] writers write in worlds filled with food, furniture, drinks, music, people, pets, and so on. Reading and writing responses to graduate students also happens in such worlds. I am never reading in some pure world of the intellect. I often break up reading (especially of long documents). I am often not the expert on at least some of the things I am reading, in part because graduate students read, take classes in other departments with other professors, pursue topics and authors I haven't read or sometimes even heard of. On the one hand, it makes reading a challenge. On the other hand, this steady rain of new information, leads to follow, ideas to explore, texts to read, is one of the things that makes working with graduate students so valuable. It is an engine that constantly destabilizes my knowledge, that pushes me to keep up, to expand my horizons, to drink another cup of coffee.

Scene 3: Reading to Write, Talk, and Revise; or Coffee and Herbie Hancock

It's almost 11:00 PM, about six hours since I was reading Kara's paper at the cafe. I have just brewed a couple cups of French Roast (caffeinated) coffee. I sit in the living room chair and begin reading and writing notes again, interrupted over the next two hours only by the dog asking to go out, one of the cats trying to dig our TV cable out from behind the cabinet, and a couple of trips to the kitchen for coffee and dark chocolate. I read a bit more of Rampton in the process. It's 1:00 AM. I get up and go to the bathroom. Then I go

---

2 Prior and Shipka (2003) includes data from interviews with undergraduate and graduate students and professors in which they drew images of the contexts and processes of their writing. They found that writers at all levels were making choices about the environments in which they worked on their writing (choices about time, place, music/silence, food, furniture, and so on).

to the dining room table and pull out my computer, so I can listen to music ("Maiden Voyage" by Herbie Hancock, set on repeat) as I write a set of longer notes. I have decided I should meet with Kara to talk over the manuscript because I think it could use a significant revision before it is submitted. Since I'm writing to help scaffold a face-to-face meeting, I just jot down notes that make sense to me. I end up with five points, written in a form that I should be able to translate and that, after the talk, should make sense to Kara as well (if she can read my handwriting). It's 1:45 AM. I go into the study and get online and write a brief note to let Kara know that I have read her manuscript and to see if she might have time Thursday or Friday to meet. I hit send. Before I get offline, I check email. As sometimes happens, Kara was also online and has emailed to ask if we could meet next week on Thursday between 1:00 and 4:00. I check the calendar on my computer, see I have a meeting at 1:00, and suggest 2:30. The paper goes back in my backpack to take to the office.

As I write the first draft of these words, I really am sitting at 1:45 AM at the dining room table, listening to "Maiden Voyage" over and over again (listening to the same music, whether a song or a CD, is a routine part of my writing process). And there is an empty coffee cup near my right hand. A cat and a dog are sleeping in the living room. My back is stiff. Writing is hard work. Reading and responding is hard work. Physically. Mentally. Emotionally. This mix I have described of some written feedback and a face-to-face discussion is typical of my practice.

Scene 4: Family, Intertextuality and Exercise

It is later on the day I emailed Kara about her draft. Julie, Anna, and I take a walk at 8:00 PM to the video store, about 1.5 miles away from our home. The night is cool and clear. Anna talks about school for a while. Then Julie begins talking about the paper she is writing with Melissa. We talk about different strategies for presenting the data for about 15 minutes. One of the issues reminds me of a question I had reading Kara's paper. I begin telling Julie about it, and we start talking about different approaches to transcription. Julie has fewer questions about the approach Kara took than I had and makes a few comments that relate transcription decisions to the motives for representing talk and other action in interaction. At first, I disagree, but then I see her point. As we are returning from the video store, Julie and Anna begin talking about a song Anna is working on and I tune out for a bit, thinking about what I might say to Kara now about the transcription issue: Perhaps clarifying the motive rather than changing the representation would work as well.

Julie and I have been married for 27 years, and interest in language has always been common ground. Over the past ten years, that common ground has intensified as Julie first completed her Ph.D., studying the discourse of people with aphasia and their communication partners, and then became an assistant professor in Speech and Hearing Sciences. We talk constantly about theories, people, methodologies, texts, and the ways of academic institutions. We have co-authored conference papers and recently an article. Julie studied me playing with the girls when they were young, and I have written about her research in my own texts because what she found had a profound effect on the way I understand discourse and interaction. Intertextuality is a term that is used to refer to how texts (oral, written, thought) draw on and respond to other texts so that utterances never stand alone.[3] Mikhail Bakhtin articulated the key insight of this notion when he said that we do not get words out of dictionaries, but out of other people's mouths, that language is fundamentally historical. Julie and I have a long intertextual trail of discussions, and many have happened on walks. We often recycle interactions with graduate students like Kara, talk through ideas, insights, and problems we see in a theory, method, or text. And we exercise.

Scene 5: Talking about Writing about Writing

It is Thursday, eight days since I finished reading Kara's manuscript. Kara knocks on the door at 2:30. Matt, another graduate student, is still here. We've been talking about Bakhtin's theory of genre and how it might apply to online communication forums for the last 45 minutes. I ask Kara to give me a minute. Matt leaves. I tell Kara to come in and I'll be right back. I walk down the hall, go to the bathroom (having a brief conversation there with a colleague about a change in the college administration), and get a drink of water. I had planned to have 15 to 20 minutes at least to refresh my memory of the paper. Now I don't have that time. I get back to the office and pull out Kara's paper. I go to the last page where my handwritten summary appears, but first we chat for ten minutes about our lives. Then we turn to the paper. Over the next hour and 20 minutes we work through the five points I had written and several that Kara raises, as she has just reread the manuscript after letting it sit for four weeks. It's 4:00. I'm supposed to pick Anna up at the library by 4:30. I hand Kara the paper and tell her I've written a few other comments, some of which might well be superseded by our discussion and her plans for revision. Kara thanks me for the response and mentions a conference that is coming up where she is presenting another piece. We talk about her conference presentation as I pack up and begin walking to my car. We part at the corner, and I call Julie to see if she wants me to pick up some chicken tikka for dinner.

---

[3] See Bazerman (2004) for a nice account of the various types of intertextuality.

Each response happens in the midst of multiple, historical trajectories. This narrative of being a graduate mentor is much more fractured than the narrative I would have written about being a graduate student (though that narrative too would be full of family and other activities) because the fictional Kara is one of perhaps 20 current and former graduate student who I'm interacting with this year with varying degrees of regularity.

Young-Kyung: An International Graduate Student's Experiences

I received a B.A. in English Language and Literature from Chonnam National University in Korea and an M.A. in TESL (Teaching English as a Second Language) from the University of Birmingham in England. I took the M.A. courses while I worked for a small community college in Korea. I taught TOEFL® (Test of English as a Foreign Language), TOEIC® (Test of English for International Communication), and ESL grammar courses at the community college more than five years. I decided to come to the U.S. for graduate study to acquire advanced knowledge about effective ESL teaching methodologies. My ultimate goal at that time was to become an effective TESL educator in my home country, Korea. When I applied to a U.S. graduate school, my idea of being "effective" was directly related to the improvement of students' scores on English examinations. My original interest in acquiring advanced knowledge of effective ESL teaching methodology has greatly changed because of my teaching assignment in my first semester at graduate school. The past four and a half years of my graduate work have become an important benchmark in my life. Here I narrate some true stories from my graduate studies, and I reflect on the difficulties, rewarding experiences, and identity transformations that I have experienced as an international student in a U.S. graduate school.

Scene 1: "You are the instructor?"

It is the first day of my teaching at the university. I am so nervous now. As part of my teaching assistantship this semester, I am assigned to teach ESL 501, a graduate writing class. I have never taught a writing class before. I really don't know why I am assigned to teach a graduate writing class in my very first semester. I will meet the students in about 30 minutes. I feel my whole body is shaking now. I keep saying to myself, "Don't be so nervous. They would not have hired you if they thought you could not do it. Everything will be fine. Just don't let the students notice your nervousness." I take a deep breath and leave the Foreign Languages Building. Now I have to find Gregory Hall where the class meets. According to the map, it is west of the auditorium, but I cannot find it. Where is Gregory Hall? I've lost my sense of direction now. I am getting more nervous. It is already 5:55 and the class is supposed to begin at 6:00. I see an Asian girl passing by and decide to ask her where the building is located. She says, "I am also going there. Just follow me." I am so relieved. On the way, we have a brief conversation. Her name is YangFang, and she is from China. She is a fourth-year doctoral student in Microbiology, and she is writing her dissertation. I tell her that I arrived in Champaign last week, so I am not familiar with the campus. When we enter the building, she asks what classroom I have to be in. I say, "Room 221." She asks, "Are you also taking the ESL writing class?" I reply in a halting voice, "No, I am. . .the instructor." She replies with a very surprised look on her face "You are the instructor?"

It was very difficult for a non-native speaker of English who had just begun her graduate study to teach the graduate writing class. I still vividly remember the terror I had on the first day of the class when I saw some students who were far more advanced in their studies than I. Like YangFang, some students do not fulfill their university writing requirement until the end of their study. The next day, I talked about the first class with the Program Director and the Coordinator and I directly asked them, "Do you *really* think I can do it?" Both of them replied without any hesitation, "Yes, *you* can do it." It turned out to be a very important moment in my life as well as in my graduate school. I ended up teaching the class for three semesters. As time went by, my fear subsided, and I slowly gained confidence as an ESL writing teacher. I spent so much time preparing for class and learned a great deal about the activity of writing as well as the complex nature of second language writing. The experience completely changed the direction of my graduate study. I became very interested in writing and curious about the writing studies program offered by the English Department. Eventually it led me to pursue an interdisciplinary specialization in writing studies.

Scene 2: Shifting Motives and Directions in Graduate School

I am sitting in Room 275 in the English Building now. I am the only international student in this class. The class is the most advanced writing studies class offered by the English department. The American students in the class never talk to me: They make me feel I am not welcomed in this class. I feel like they are saying to me, "You would not be able to understand all the theoretical and metaphysical concepts we discuss in the class.

They are difficult even for advanced American doctoral students like us." The students ask the professor all kinds of weird questions. Jody, in particular, who always looks very serious and never smiles at people, asks incredibly difficult, philosophical questions. I say to myself, "What's wrong with her? She thinks she is a real philosopher or what?" I cannot understand most of the class discussions about dialogicality and heterogeneity of voices, intertextuality, mediated action, mediated authorship, and discourse identity. It all sounds so philosophical and metaphysical that I cannot make sense of it at all. I really don't know how the theoretical and philosophical discussions would help my teaching or improve my knowledge of effective teaching methodologies in the second language writing classroom.

I had never heard of the discipline of writing studies before I came to the U.S. My initial expectation of the field was that I would learn more about the various aspects of U.S. academic writing. In my first writing studies class, I realized that writing studies was heavily theoretical, integrating theories of social practices, learning, language, community, and context. The Bakhtinian and Vygotskian perspectives on mind, mediated action, and language and literacy practices, which we discussed in that class, seemed so metaphysical and philosophical that I could not make sense of them. I had never heard of Vygotsky or Bakhtin before I came to the U.S. Most days, I left the class with a cloudy, dizzy head filled with a myriad of questions.

However, as time went by, I found myself more and more interested and deeply immersed in the theories, asking myself all kinds of philosophical and ontological questions. I started to feel that the sociocultural and practice theories of human communication, human activity, and human mind quenched the thirst I had when I worked as a TOEFL® and TOEIC® instructor in Korea. Working in that capacity, I often felt so thirsty for some broader social view of language learning and teaching. At that time, my view of language learning and teaching privileged grammatical correctness at the sentence level. Most of the time, I left the school feeling so empty in my heart as if my heart were dying. The conceptual frameworks of sociocultural theory and theories of practice and activity, which emphasize the essential relationship between human mental processes and their sociocultural, historical, ideological, and institutional contexts, helped me clarify some important issues percolating in my mind. They made me seriously think about the relationships between micro and macro, text and context, process and structure, situation and society, and cognition and affect. I became fascinated by the sociocultural and practice theories of human communication, learning, activity, and culture, and I began to read extensively the literatures across such varied domains as education, writing studies, sociology, anthropology, cultural studies, qualitative research methodology, and ethnography. My internal library rapidly grew. Taking a walk, running on the treadmill, waiting for friends in a coffee shop, cooking in the kitchen, listening to music, driving my car, swimming, and even during my meditation, I constantly found myself engrossed in theoretical concepts and trying to figure out the relationships between myself and the metaphysical ideas I read.

Scene 3: Graduate Student as Theory Girl

It is the second day of the Bridge Transition Program. I work as a composition tutor for the Program. There are 13 students (8 African American and 5 Hispanic). They just graduated from high school, and I tutor them in basic academic writing skills. Maisha, an African American student, asks me the meaning of the quote in a scholarly article the students are assigned to read in class, which says "texts themselves are in a conversation with previously published texts." Patricia, Katrina, and Donnesha, who are sitting at the same table as Maisha, raise their hands and tell me that they also need some explanation about the passage. I find myself trying to explain the passage immediately by invoking the notion of intertextuality, which I learned in my writing studies class: "I know most of you have never heard of the term. This is basically what the idea of intertextuality is about. It is a very important concept when it comes to academic reading and writing. Let me explain what intertextuality means further. . . ." Shalonda, the reading component tutor, who is in the same room with me because the Bridge Transition reading and composition tutors work together in a team, says to me: "People can always spot you as a doctoral student. You really sound like a big scholar!" With Shalonda's reaction, my mind is immediately thinking: "A-ha! This is an excellent example of the notion of 'chronotopic lamination.' Academic literate activity is not confined to our school work but permeates our entire life: It is not confined to our desks or computers but carries into other personal and social spaces. The particular literate activity gets laminated across time and space, chronotopically, and the identity of the person is constructed through the particular literate activity."

To borrow Bakhtin's notion of dialogism, I started to author the world and myself through the theoretical concepts and ideas I study. When I hear people's conversations that involve the soft drink names such as Dr. Pepper® or 2%, my mind is immediately thinking: "Oh! This is a good example of the concept of a mediated discourse. The discourse involving the soft drinks requires that the participants, both the speaker and the listener, know that Dr. Pepper is the name of a soft drink in the U.S. and 2% is the name of a popular soft drink in Korea. The discourse between the speaker and the listener is mediated through the participants' knowledge of the soft drinks. So, it is a mediated discourse." The moment that I thought I finally understood Bourdieu's notion of *habitus*, almost two years after my exposure to the concept, as a way of "escaping from the choice between a structuralism without a subject and the philosophy of the subject" (Flyvbjerg, 2001, p. 138) made me happier than the moment I received a competitive award in the College of Education. The "A-ha" moments or epiphanies make me feel *alive*. I feel that the theoretical concepts and metaphysical ideas I have spent so much time trying to understand are walking out of the books, coming into my world, and finally *talking* to me. These little moments make me feel like I have started to develop "the eye." (I used to say to people I met in graduate school, "I don't have *the eye*. I just can't *see* what is happening now. I don't know how long it will take for me to *see* things.")

Not only has my academic work been taken up with these theories, which people often call highly valued professional commodities in academia, but they have greatly impacted the way I understand the world and the way I interact with people in various settings. I have often found myself wanting to discuss theories I read and think about in an interdisciplinary research group that I have actively participated in for the past two and a half years. Some of the group members appreciated my theoretical input, but others did not, desiring to leave theoretical issues aside. Though my English is quite fluent, as the only non-native speaker of English in the group, I have found it difficult to participate in the discussions. Their comments often seem deeply grounded in American culture, and as a foreigner, I cannot completely understand the examples they bring up and the subtle nuances of their speech. Because their social realities are different from mine, I feel that theory is perhaps a way for me to get the floor and to participate in the discussions. Theory has also impacted the way I tutor at the campus writing center, where I have worked as a consultant for the past seven semesters. Being a non-native speaker of English, I sometimes face institutional racism at the writing center: Some students request at the front desk that they work with a consultant who is a native speaker of English. I feel that my theoretical knowledge has increased my confidence as a writing consultant. I find myself able to pay greater attention to the coherence and logic of the students' arguments. Working with advanced graduate students, I can often help them to articulate the relationship of their arguments to their methodological and theoretical frameworks, and I sometimes recommend scholarly books or articles related to their work.

Scene 4: Crossing the Interdisciplinary Spaces

Cicily, one of my best American friends, asks me to see a movie and to go to the bar, Murphy's, with the people she met at the Cosmopolitan night event. But I tell her, "I will join you next time. I have to finish the readings for the Speech Communication class, and I need to write a weekly reaction paper after the readings. The readings are 177 pages and the paper is due on Monday morning, but I am just half-way through the readings." She responds immediately "It's a Friday night! Girl, you should go out and hang out with people." The TA office is so quiet now. Most of the students are already gone. I feel like going home too. I leave the TA office in the Foreign Languages Building, and I slowly walk to Sherman Hall, my dormitory building. There is so much reading I have to do for Speech Communication 529 (Theories of Communication in Context) class, but I really like the class. Walking to my dormitory, I think of the assignment for Communications 580 (Advanced Interpretive Methods). As soon as I get to my room, I check my calendar on the wall. I see that the assignment is due this coming Tuesday. Oh, my goodness. I thought the Com 580 assignment was due the week after next week. The class is one of the recommended courses for my Qualitative Inquiry Methodology specialization in my department. I feel dizzy. I sit on my bed for a few minutes and then start to pack up my swimming gear. I need the swimming synergy now. Swimming refreshes and energizes my mind and body. Often, insightful ideas come to my mind on the way home after swimming or on the way to the pool or sometimes during swimming. And, it keeps me sane in my hectic graduate school life.

My interest in sociocultural and practice theories of mind, in socio-anthropological understandings of human communication, activity, and culture, has led me to take classes in cross-disciplinary spaces such as in the College of Communications and the Department of Speech Communications while fulfilling my course requirements in my home department in the College of Education as well as in the English Department for my specialization in writing studies. The heavy readings for each week (often more than 400 pages of dense text) and the extra coursework have made my life in graduate school more difficult. Interacting with multiple literatures and negotiating different disciplinary and institutional practices across the campus, I have struggled. I've found it very difficult to attain some balance between school and life. To finish the readings, to think through some important ideas of the readings, and to complete the course assignments, I've had to sacrifice the time that I would have spent otherwise with my friends for social gatherings and movies. As the title of this chapter suggests, I experience everyday lamentations in my cross-disciplinary graduate work.

All the challenging interdisciplinary work in my graduate school has been driven by my pure love and passion for learning. Looking back, however, I feel that my passion and love for learning was a deeply cognitively oriented view of learning. For a long time, I associated learning with the mental processes of knowledge acquisition and articulation. Trying to enter pre-existing structures as a *peripheral participant*[4] in my cross-institutional as well as cross-disciplinary graduate work and trying to socialize with other participants, I learned deep in my heart the importance of developing interactional skills. As is often the case with ESL students, I have found it difficult to use the mental representation of my knowledge skillfully. My experience has taught me that learning for cross-cultural contexts involves more than linguistic competence; it requires interactive (or cultural) competence. In other words, it involves *doing* the practices of culturally embedded, tacit norms and expectations in interactive settings.

Reflections on My Living, My Loving, and My Learning

Writing this chapter, I realized that my mind is already deeply enculturated in meta-discourse analysis: I might have greater difficulty in writing this kind of personal essay if my mind were still operating under the applied linguistics domains such as syntax or semantics. Writing this book chapter, I have reflected on the paths of my identity formation: as an EFL (English as a Foreign Language) student, TOEFL®/TOEIC® instructor, graduate student in TESOL, ESL writing instructor, graduate student in writing studies, writing tutor, and writing studies scholar. I strongly feel that the confluence of the practices of theoretical writing that I have been engaged in during graduate school has also transformed my identity. As I have participated in writing instruction, writing tutoring, and various genres of scholarly writing activities in graduate school, I have finally become more confident in saying that I am a *writer*. I always liked to express things in writing since I was very young. I used to win awards in poetry contests and essay contests. Writing this reflective essay,

---

[4] Lave and Wenger (1991) argue that we all learn by being peripheral participants in a social practice, by taking up and engaging in the pieces of the practice within our reach at any point. In this sense, even the most expert and senior participants in a practice are still understood to be peripheral in relation to the full history and range of the practice.

I also wonder when one becomes a scientist, linguist, anthropologist, or engineer. I believe that I am in the process of *becoming* a writing studies scholar, and I am standing at the threshold of a very important chapter in my life.

I read Leo Buscaglia's book, *Living, Loving, and Learning* (1982) when I was in high school in Korea. I don't remember what the book is about anymore, but for some reason the title has always stayed in my mind. The first time I saw the title of the book in a bookstore, something deep inside my mind said, "This is it. . . ." I guess I was thinking back then that I wanted a life filled with the three concepts of living, loving, and learning, which includes all three but privileges none, that I wanted a *balanced* life. I want to get married one day, have children, and continue my scholarly work while raising my own children. Perhaps, when I experience motherhood, my perception of the world and my view of academia may be quite different from my perception of the world and academia now. After all, this is all human work. It is all for our humanity. Perhaps a good reason I have become so fascinated by practice theory's understanding of human action, human mind, and human communication is that deep inside my mind I have recognized the gap between my theory and my practice in life, and I have been saying to *myself*, "Put it into action." For my living, my loving, and my learning, and most importantly, for the coexistence of the three, now I have to *practice* it. And, I *will* practice it.

Conclusion

Learning a discipline is often associated solely with mental processes of knowledge acquisition and articulation. It is often conceived as simple transmission, as though graduate students should simply download data from professors, books, and articles. Our experience suggests that learning to do graduate school involves more than one's linguistic competence or one's knowledge; it involves *doing* culturally embedded, tacit practices in the midst of fleeting day-to-day interactions. Lave and Wenger's theory of learning as situated social practice highlights precisely the ways we engage *in* our real social worlds rather than simply study *about* those social worlds. Critically, their notion of learning as situated practice also highlights that we carry all our practices, all the identities we have already forged, into new situations and that, because of that, we begin to alter those norms and expectations of the new community. Our stories and reflections here point away from an abstract focus on knowledge acquisition. They suggest that learning is a very human journey, composed of a history of interactions (often face-to-face) with others; that it is full of joy and despair, relief and frustration, fear and confidence; that it remakes not only what we know but who we are; and that ultimately it changes how we live across the diverse domains of our lives, not only what we think in classroom or professional settings. We have each found that our academic lives have taken unexpected turns because of an event, interaction, or text. We have each found that our academic studies have reshaped how we see the world and how we live in it. And we have both found these processes often overwhelming, making balance a constant struggle. We hope our stories and reflections will help some readers navigate their own graduate work and writing more smoothly, that some will be better prepared for the unexpected turns, the emotional highs and lows, and the changing identities that, for us, have defined the lived experience of graduate work and writing.

PAUL PRIOR, UNIVERSITY OF ILLINOIS AT URBANA–CHAMPAIGN

When I returned to graduate school for my Ph.D., I basically expected that I would get a credential that would allow me to take up more permanent positions in the academy than the one I had at the time (as a non–tenure track ESL instructor at the University of Wisconsin-Madison). Other than that, I didn't really expect graduate school to change me much, to alter my values or my sense of myself. It did.

YOUNG-KYUNG MIN, UNIVERSITY OF ILLINOIS AT URBANA–CHAMPAIGN

It was karma that I decided to get a Ph.D. I had never seriously thought about becoming a professor before I started teaching ESL at a community college in Mokpo, my hometown in Korea. My students ignited my passion for teaching and led me to decide to study in the U.S. to learn more about effective ESL teaching. Almost five years into my graduate study here, I don't exactly know where I am in terms of becoming an effective TESL educator, but I know for sure that my journey of going to graduate school in the U.S. has opened a very important door in my life, a door whose existence I had previously not even imagined.

REFERENCES

Bakhtin, M. (1981). *The dialogic imagination: Four essays by M. M. Bakhtin.* (C. Emerson & M. Holquist, Trans.; M. Holquist, Ed.). Austin: University of Texas Press.

Bazerman, C. (2004). Intertextuality: How texts tell stories. In C. Bazerman & P. Prior (Eds.), *What writing does and how it does it: An introduction to analysis of texts and textual practices* (pp. 83–96). Mahwah, NJ: Lawrence Erlbaum.

Buscaglia, L. (1982). *Living, loving, and learning.* Thorofare, NJ: C. B. Slack.

Flyvbjerg, B. (2001). *Making social science matter: Why social inquiry fails and how it can succeed again.* Cambridge, UK: Cambridge University Press.

Lave, J., & Wenger, E. (1991). *Situated learning: Legitimate peripheral participation.* Cambridge, UK: Cambridge University Press.

Prior, P. (1991). Contextualizing writing and response in a graduate seminar. *Written Communication, 8*, 267–310.

———. *Writing/disciplinarity: A sociohistoric account of literate activity in the academy.* Mahwah, NJ: Lawrence Erlbaum.

Prior, P., & Shipka, J. (2003). Chronotopic lamination: Tracing the contours of literate activity. In C. Bazerman & D. Russell (Eds.), *Writing selves, Writing societies: Research from activity perspectives* (pp. 180–238). Fort Collins, CO: The WAC Clearinghouse and Mind, Culture, and Activity. Retrieved October 28, 2006, from <http://wac.colostate.edu/books/selves_societies/>

Rampton, B. (2000). *Speech community.* Working Papers in Urban Linguistics: Paper #15. Retrieved September 12, 2006, from <http://www.kcl.ac.uk/content/1/c6/01/42/29/paper15.pdf>

Chapter 16

Learning to Do Graduate School: Learning to Do Life

HANAKO OKADA

Reflecting

I entered the school campus for the first time since leaving due to crumbling health. Almost four years had passed since I was here the last time. I wouldn't have stepped in if I hadn't been driving a friend whose son was attending a summer camp that took place at the school. I didn't even think about the fact that I was entering. This was hard to believe when I think of how uncomfortable I felt simply driving past the school or meeting faculty members at nearby restaurants or stores. It got to the point that I lamented living so close to the school. I felt guilty, irresponsible, and ashamed for not being able to teach.

The school lends the campus every year to an English school for their summer camp. Although the students were different, the campus looked the same, smelled the same, and the way voices echoed through the building sounded the same. I walked up the gently sloping ramp leading to the gym, a walk that once seemed like climbing a high mountain at the peak of my illness. It almost felt like I was living in a dream—I couldn't imagine being there after all that had happened. Revisiting the environment started triggering vivid emotional recall, but children walking by gently distracted me from drifting entirely into the past.

Some of the faculty members of the school were working at the camp. Many of them seemed surprised to see me, but they greeted me pleasantly with a smile and asked me how I was doing. I said three things: I am better; I am studying, but I am not well enough to work yet. I then went on asking how they were in order to shift the focus off me. I felt rather uneasy with the attention I was getting.

Almost four years have passed since I abruptly left this school where I last taught. It was my second time leaving the same school due to health reasons—the school that has been so good to me and special in many ways. Why was I able to step onto the school campus this time? Why was I feeling surprisingly calm despite the emotional recall that was taking place? Did time ease the guilt and discomfort away? Was it because I could now somehow identify myself as a student and a novice academic and not a teacher? Or had I just simply gotten used to living life as a chronically ill person who's unable to work?

In this chapter, I first narrate my experiences of encountering and battling chronic illnesses, having to leave my full-time teaching job, and how I became involved in the graduate school life. I then discuss the shift in my identity that occurred at two levels: From a teacher to an academic, and from a receiver of knowledge to a processor of knowledge. Finally, I discuss the notions of identity-in-flux and of narratives as a way to conceptualize oneself.

Farewell to the Tracks

When I began teaching, I was bright-eyed, confident, ambitious, and optimistic—perhaps typical of a young, passionate teacher straight out of school. I thought everything that I desired as a teacher would eventually be achieved if I tried hard. After three years of teaching at international pre-schools in Japan, I was hired at a top-ranking international school where I longed to work. It was a big step for me. I felt important. It felt like my dream had come true. I imagined the future—I will be a veteran, master teacher at this school. I envisioned long shiny tracks set ahead of me. However, within a few months, I started to grow increasingly tired.

Of course I was tired—I was working hard, very hard. I came in early and I stayed late. I taught energetic young children, which was a physically demanding job. I put passion into my teaching. I already knew that the first year or two at a new work place would be tough. But eventually I felt that something was seriously wrong. I was dragging my body when I walked. I would sigh and look up at the staircase, which seemed like an impossibly steep cliff. When I knew that no one was around, I would get down on all fours to go up the stairs. I was often dizzy and occasionally fell. I couldn't lift my body up in the morning, and I had to call in sick more often. Of course, I went to see different doctors. Tests all proved negative. The doctors didn't seem to know what was exactly wrong with me. With the help of American medical books, I self-diagnosed myself as having chronic fatigue syndrome (CFS),[1] but the doctors did not agree with my diagnosis. Besides, CFS was hardly known in Japan at that time. Not getting a proper diagnosis was rough for me. I wasn't sure if I was really sick or if I was just being spoiled, over-sensitive, and lazy. These thoughts made me have doubts about myself as a professional.

After pushing myself for more than a year, I realized that whether sick or not, I just didn't have the strength to teach. Well, it wasn't really I who decided—it was my body. And I left the school. Having pushed myself too hard, I was bed-ridden with extreme hypotension (low blood pressure), low energy level, topped with depression. After an entire year of bed rest, I very slowly started to regain my strength, and I started teaching English part-time. It did not completely satisfy my deep-seated desire to teach, but it was teaching and I enjoyed being with my young students. As I started working, I eventually started envisioning a future when I would be working full-time again. That was when I enrolled in an M.A. TESOL program at an American university here in Japan. I didn't want to go back to full-time teaching in the same state I was in when I left the school. I wanted to go back "upgraded." I wanted to go back with something that I didn't have before—a master's degree in Education. A degree was what I wanted.

The two years I was enrolled in the M.A. program treated me well. I continued teaching part-time at a very moderate level, I went to classes, and I gained strength by the day. I even took up swimming. I felt that I had become a healthy person. Then something important happened to me in the last semester of the M.A. program. I took an SLA/Applied Linguistics class that helped me connect and make sense of all the other classes I took in the program. It answered many of the questions that I had of the field. It helped me develop my philosophy of second language acquisition. I was provided with a new pair of glasses. They made me

---

[1] Although there are numerous sources defining the illness, I have selected the following definition which is short, yet comprehensive enough: Chronic fatigue syndrome, or CFS, is a debilitating and complex disorder characterized by profound fatigue that is not improved by bed rest and that may be worsened by physical or mental activity. Persons with CFS most often function at a substantially lower level of activity than they were capable of before the onset of illness. In addition to these key defining characteristics, patients report various nonspecific symptoms, including weakness, muscle pain, impaired memory and/or mental concentration, insomnia, and post-exertional fatigue lasting more than 24 hours. (*Centers for Disease Contol and Prevention*, 2006)

see a clearer and better picture of the field while simultaneously telling me that what I was seeing was only the very tip of the iceberg. This class was a turning point in my very early academic career. Of course, I cared about getting a degree, and I wanted the degree, but it was no longer of sole importance. The class taught me the joy of learning. I wanted to learn more. I wanted to know more. I wanted to see more. *What's beneath the tip of the iceberg? I might even become a better teacher if I seek further!* I decided to apply for the doctoral program, which was to begin after six months. If I missed my chance, I would have to wait for another two-and-a-half-years, when the next doctoral cohort would begin.

With my shining new degree and even more brightly shining confidence in health, I went back with my head up to the school where I used to work. I couldn't think of any other job but teaching. I couldn't think of anywhere better to work than that school, and I really didn't want to work anywhere else. I saw my future in the school. The school meant a lot to me. I loved being a teacher there. Given that I was planning to study at the doctoral level, I asked for a part-time job. I was asked whether I could teach full-time for four months until the school would hire a full-time teacher, and then I could work part-time. I took the offer. I had four months until the doctoral program began. The school was asking for my help. I owed this school. *I should do it. I can do it. I am now strong enough.*

I was naïve and over-confident. Within a month, I literally fell back into my worst condition. My health regressed like a stone rolling downhill. The thought of being depressed, utterly weak, and bed-ridden haunted me, but I knew I couldn't just leave. But then I couldn't go up the stairs again. I couldn't lift the books. I could only eat finger-food at home because I couldn't stay seated—I was so exhausted, I had to lie down. I knew I had to stop when I started feeling dizzy and fell frequently. I could have asked for a leave of absence, but at that time, I felt that I knew. I knew that I wasn't physically capable of full-time teaching. I knew that I wasn't fit enough to teach young children. Although I felt extremely irresponsible, I thought it would be best for me to leave early on in the school year than cause problems throughout the school year. I was also petrified of becoming bed-ridden for a long time again. I resigned with regrets, sadness, and feelings of guilt. The administrators responded with kindness. The school was run by kind people. Their kindness made me feel guilty. I felt like I was a fool. I hated my lack of strength. I hated my stupidity for over-estimating my health.

I spent the next few months lamenting over my foolish decision and my weakness. I was sick, angry, sad, and depressed. I realized that I could no longer go back to the school that meant so much to me. I also realized at that point that I was doing so well over the last two years because I had such a light workload. I didn't really become stronger. I just had been taking it easy. I had to part once again with the beautiful future that I had painted. There were no more shiny tracks that led toward a bright and stable future. I felt like I had lost it all—my job, my health, my identity as a teacher, my self esteem, my dignity, and any faith I had in myself. What I was left with was meaninglessness.

I spent my days in bed feeling weak and depressed. A couple of months later, I received notification from the university congratulating me on my acceptance into the doctoral cohort. It was something positive—something that I hadn't had for a while. It was welcoming me when I felt that I did not belong anywhere. The letter informed me that classes were to begin in two months. I don't know why, but the words in the letter sparkled like gold. The letter seemed so provocative. I carefully placed it back into the envelope as though it were something precious but a little bit dangerous, and put it away in a folder. I didn't know what to do. I wasn't sure of anything. *How could I be sure of anything when I had lost faith in myself?*

I continued to spend the next few months in bed feeling sick and weak. I did one thing—I would occasionally take out that letter of acceptance and stare at it. I gradually started to think that the university was the only place that was welcoming me. *I want to study. I want to learn. But can I do it? Will my health hold up? Am I asking for crumbling health again? I don't want to do something which I can't fulfill. I don't have to do this. But I want to. But can I?* At the height of my weakness, even the letter was too heavy for me to hold up. I was worn out just by asking these questions to myself, and I would put the letter away. I repeated this for a period of time, and soon it was a month before classes were to begin. I ordered the text books. *Even if I don't enroll, they must be good books to own anyway.*

With the mark of the new year, classes were about to begin. By that time, I felt well enough to go out. Without certainty, I packed my books and went to school. There was excitement, nervousness, and tension in the classroom. With the help of a few friendly faces from the M.A. program, I was calm and relaxed. I wasn't sure if I belonged in the classroom though. A good friend told me he wasn't sure if he would pursue the degree, but he was there to see what it was like and how things would go.

His comment eased my concern. *I don't have to decide.* Unlike a teaching job, I just had to be responsible for myself and not for the students and the school. *I think I'll see how things go too....* Then the professor came in the classroom. The classroom became quiet, and I felt a slight tension in the air. It was the same professor who had taught the M.A. class that had triggered my desire to learn. When the class began, despite my uncertainty in life, I knew I was sure of one thing: I wanted to learn.

I enjoyed the classes. I thrived on them. They kept me focused. They were tough, and at times I felt physically on-edge, but it felt so good to be learning. I felt as if all of the learning that was going on was making my fragmented self more complete. I was fatigued, but I managed two semesters without collapsing. *Maybe I could keep on.*

During summer break that year, I noticed that my body began to hurt. One morning, the entire left side of my body was in severe pain. My body was screaming. From that day onward, I couldn't sit on anything that wasn't very well cushioned. I had to layer towels in order to sit in the bathtub. Any slight touch made me jump in pain. The wind blew, and the gusts would hurt me. Even loud sounds made me cringe. I didn't know what was going on. Shortly after that, I was finally referred to a doctor who specialized in CFS. Ten years had already passed since my self-diagnosis. I thought there must be a specialist by now—even in Japan, which seemed so behind regarding these illnesses. On the first day of the fall semester, I had an appointment with the specialist. After going through tests and other medical examinations, I finally got my diagnosis—something that I had longed for for ten years. I finally had a name for a real illness. I had a fairly bad case of CFS and also fibromyalgia.[2] The doctor told me I must have had CFS for all these years. *Yes, I had predicted that. But fibromyalgia!?* I was familiar with the term because a good friend had the illness. However, little did I expect to have it too. *So that was where all the pain came from....* On top of the two "invisible" illnesses, I had a severe case of hypotension (low blood pressure), which caused dizziness, weakness, and falling. I didn't know whether to celebrate or lament. However, I felt a big sense of relief. With a proper diagnosis, I was finally certain that my condition wasn't a figment of my imagination. I hadn't left work because I was spoiled and lazy. I felt

---

[2] Fibromyalgia is a clinical syndrome defined by chronic widespread muscular pain, fatigue, and tenderness. Many people with fibromyalgia also experience additional symptoms such as fatigue, headaches, irritable bowel syndrome, irritable bladder, cognitive and memory problems (often called "fibro fog"), temporomandibular joint disorder, pelvic pain, restless leg syndrome, sensitivity to noise and temperature, and anxiety and depression. (Clauw & Taylor-Moon, 2006)

as if my past was justified. I now had names to tell myself and others who asked what was wrong with me. I also felt like I was doomed with two chronic illnesses with no known cures. I felt subjected as a "sick person." With the rush of different emotions pouring into me, I wasn't exactly sure why, but all I could do at that time was sit on a bench in the courtyard of the hospital and cry.

After the Diagnosis

Eventually, the diagnosis marked a shift within me—an identity shift. I used to feel lost, insecure, and miserable because I strongly identified myself as a teacher, but this teacher identity was at stake, if not completely lost already. The diagnosis helped me justify my not teaching—I didn't leave my job because of my inefficiency. Although I do not disagree entirely with the view that regards disabilities as a cultural construct (McDermott & Varenne, 1995, p. 9), the diagnosis allowed me to consider the illnesses as a part of me, which was very important at the time. I was a person in doubt of herself for ten years, but I finally gained agency as a diagnosed patient. Through this shift, I was able to (temporarily) let go of my teacher identity in a gentle manner. Until then, I felt like I was clinging on to what had already been stolen from me. I felt that teaching was the only option I had in life. I couldn't imagine working anywhere else but the school I had left. I realized that no matter how much I loved teaching young children and no matter how good I was at it, I wasn't physically capable of doing the job. I wasn't imagining my weaknesses—they were real. As hard as it was to accept, I felt that I was able eventually to let go of my teacher identity because I found a place where I felt I belonged—the graduate school.[3]

I often got remarks from people such as, "Why go to the trouble?"; "You don't need a doctoral degree"; "How do you do it?" My physician also advised me to leave school so that I would get more rest. True, I don't have to have a doctoral degree. I did wear myself out on occasion through studying, writing papers, and preparing for presentations. My inability to focus and memory problems due to my conditions made such tasks even more challenging. I had a difficulty focusing and con-

---

[3]   I do realize that I am a privileged individual who is able to attend graduate school without having to work. I am indebted and incredibly grateful to those who allow me to do this by supporting me in many ways.

centrating, and often had a hard time comprehending or recalling what I had just read or heard. I felt as if there were five or six radios and TVs constantly blasting in my head. Readings often overwhelmed me. I had to read sentences over and over again to comprehend them. I had to take extensive notes because I would forget what I had just read. Given that the illnesses were "invisible," I sometimes wondered if people understood any of these problems I was going through—I generally look well and I do make an effort to put on a strong public face. *What did they think when I was experiencing the "brain-fogs"? Did they think I was stupid?* I felt I had to work harder to compensate for my problems. Sometimes I pushed myself too hard and had to pay the price. I often went through push-crash cycles. *Sure, getting rest by staying in bed may improve my health, but do I want to live that way? I've already been through that.*[4] I knew I was sick but I didn't want that identity to dominate me.

While I felt like I was only losing (against my poor health, and also life in general), the graduate school gave me a feeling of growth and dignity. The experiences at the graduate school allowed me to feel as if I was gaining a sense of purpose through the joy of being exposed to a wealth of ideas through classes, texts, faculty, and peers, and others from the community. For example, I felt energized when I engaged in discussion over controversial issues with my peers. Although very slowly, I felt a sense of growth when I was able to read and understand a difficult concept or an article, or when I wrote something that I was satisfied with, or when I felt I was able to integrate different ideas and theories. I appreciated comments (and even criticisms) that I got from my professors and peers on my written work and presentations, because I thrived on challenge and the opportunity to improve. Some of my classmates, teachers, and post-doctoral students became precious and valuable friends beyond the realm of academics.

Even if temporarily, the graduate school experience has helped me leave my difficulties behind and permitted me to transform the learning experience into a reflexive experience. Ellis (1997) mentioned how she found research and scholarly writing to be healing (p. 128). Like her, I too was emotionally involved with what I was studying, and I found that to be healing. Through engaging in the doctoral program, particularly through the classes that heavily influenced my perspectives such as qualitative research, introduction to postmodernism, and narrative

---

[4]   There are times when bed rest is a must. I am not suggesting that one should always push herself or himself hard. I have experienced severe crashes due to pushing myself too hard.

inquiry, once again, I felt I was provided with a new vision—different and multiple ways to look at the world and at what was happening out there. To me, engaging in academic work became a way of reflecting on larger issues in life. I felt that I was better able to see and negotiate meaning out of what was going on in my life—many aspects of which might otherwise have seemed absurd. Although I might not have the answers, I felt I was now better able to engage in the ongoing questions: "What's going on here?"; "What's happening?"; "What am I doing?"; "Who am I, and who do I want to become?"

During the course of my studies, the distinction between the academic world and the rest of the world began to blur. One of the many ways academics and life merged was through reading personal narratives written by scholars in the field. I had opportunities where I was encouraged by such narratives (e.g., Casanave & Schecter, 1997; Casanave & Vandrick, 2003; Watson-Gegeo, 2005) when I felt that life was becoming just too rough and tough. When I read Watson-Gegeo's narrative of how she came to terms with her severe chronic health problems, I was grateful that I was in the field for two reasons: One, I was able to encounter the article, and two, I was able to understand the depth and the beauty of the article.[5] These narratives were unexpected gifts that I received through the course of my studies.

Academics and life seemed not only to have found each other, but these worlds gradually became intertwined and enmeshed, creating a wider, larger, and more complex (however yet incomplete) whole. I seem to have adopted a more ecological view of learning (e.g., Atkinson, 2002; Atkinson, Churchill, Nishino, & Okada, 2007; Gibson, 1977, 1986; van Lier, 2000).[6] The loss of boundary, I suspect, was a shift in identity as well. I believe the shift occurred at two levels. First of all, I was able to shift my vision of myself from that of a teacher to that of an academic, and to shift how I might be able to contribute to education from a different dimension. Although I may not be able to go back to teaching young children

---

[5] I am grateful to Andrea Simon-Maeda, who sent me this article along with a lovely basket of flowers when I needed it the most—when I was hospitalized, on edge, and wondered whether I had the strength to continue with life, let alone graduate school.

[6] Interestingly, I have developed a more ecological, or holistic, approach to medicine. I have found oriental medicine and other alternative treatments that consider the body as a whole (including the mind-body connection, and also the body-environment connection), and do not regard symptoms as componential to be more attractive and helpful for me. I am by no means disregarding Western medicine, but the holistic approach of oriental medicine seem to work well with me given that there are no known cures for my two illnesses in Western medicine, and that I suffered greatly from side-effects of the Western medications that were prescribed to me.

on a full-time basis like I used to, the graduate school has allowed me to connect to the world of teaching from a different and perhaps broader, more holistic perspective. I no longer have the shiny train tracks laid out in front of me, but I feel as if I have been provided with a firm ground to walk on—with my own feet. And second, although not entirely separate from the first level, I feel that a transformation of my identity as a mere receiver of knowledge to a processor of knowledge has also taken place. Through incorporating what I have been learning in the classroom and books into my everyday life, I have better processed the textual knowledge into more deeply contextualized, "embodied" knowledge.

I believe these identity transformations have occurred because I have found my place in graduate school, or to put it differently, I have found a place for the graduate school in my life. As I look back, I realize that the transformations did not occur within me as an autonomous agent. As Tierney (2000) mentions, "Individual lives are constant constructs embedded in societal and cultural forces. . . ." (p. 541).[7] The illnesses, the circumstances due to them, the graduate school and all that goes around it—they all have taken part in altering my identities, and constructing who I am. We aren't autonomous agents upon constructing ourselves. Identities are fluid, and the ongoing changes I faced in life showed me this. We aren't predetermined. We aren't absolute. We are an "alchemy of multiple identities" (Sakui & Gaies, 2002, p. 9). Societal, cultural, and natural forces may not treat us the way we desire. However, all is not gloom and doom. The postmodern notion of identity is a notion of hope for me. It has taught me that one's identity isn't fixed, predetermined, but partial, contested, multi-layered, and even contradictory (Tierney). This has been incredibly liberating for someone who felt as if her identity was permanently restricted by and bonded to her health constraints. Although somewhat contradictory, such constraints led me to find more diverse identities, and not just the rather rigid, self-essentialized teacher identity that I had created years ago.

Further Reflections on Graduate School and Identity

I may be a somewhat peripheral graduate student due to ongoing life constraints. In fact, I seem to be finishing my course work much more

---

[7] Having gone through various circumstances due to poor health, I would add "natural" to Tierney's list of "forces."

slowly than my peers. I cannot work the way I desire to. My body often doesn't allow me to stay on schedule. I often feel that some of the cognitive symptoms such as inability to focus and memory problems get in the way of my academic work. However, it may well be such constraints that have made graduate school so meaningful for me. As demanding as it is, I have found solace in academic work. Bauman (2007) says, for some students, "college is a life raft in a sea of desolation and destruction" (p. B5). I agree. It has picked me up and saved me from drifting and drowning. The graduate school experience has been a demanding and challenging one, but I can say without a doubt that it has also been a safe one. It has been a safe one in the sense that it allowed me to have a focus in life. It has permitted me to be who I am while simultaneously providing me with opportunities and challenges that acted as a source of hope and inspiration for me to "build" who I am.[8] It has provided me with vision—different visions—to interact with and to negotiate meaning out of life and the world around me. Of course, I am not provided with easy solutions, but I believe that what I have learned in graduate school has permitted me to make better sense out of my life. However indirectly, ranging from classroom learning to learning the ropes of being a novice academic, the graduate school has taught me how to "do life."

I may be all wrong. I am only partly through the doctoral program. My feelings toward graduate school may all be due to the fact that it provides a focus in my life, and my desire to believe that when one has a focus, things tend to fall in place around it. But as I reflect, the graduate school has been, and continues to be a safe haven for me—nurturing me, allowing me to grow. Some people might argue that a graduate school is a competitive and threatening place, far from a safe haven. But to me, viewing the graduate school as a safe haven seems like common sense. I wouldn't call it paradise, but it is safe. In her memoir as a student and a teacher, Jane Tompkins (1996) describes what kind of a place school should be:

> [S]chool should be a safe place, the way home is supposed to be. A place where you belong, where you can grow and express yourself freely, where you know and care for other people and are known and cared for by them, a place where people come before information and ideas. (p. 127)

---

[8] I find it interesting to see the traces of influences from the different classes that I took in this piece of writing. Through my narrative, I see that "I am what I learn." This may well be the kind of growth and nurturing that graduate school provides.

She's got it right. I seem to have the privilege to be in the kind of school she's describing. I have never felt threatened or felt as if my confidence was undermined by school. Dealing with everyday life might be easier without all the work that the graduate school demands, but it is like an anchor holding me in place, which I may well be lost without. At least, this is how I feel as I am writing.

Being a fairly private person, I found much hesitation in writing about myself—my uncovered self, my privileged self, my idiosyncratic self. I was further troubled by the fact that each time I worked on this draft, what I wanted to put on paper differed. Not only about my ongoing experiences, but the way I wanted to tell my retrospective accounts varied. I saw the most marked difference when I compared the two different abstracts I wrote in preparation for this chapter. I wrote the first one at home in a relatively good condition with my computer and with all of my books and articles—I had all the environmental and physical affordances (Greeno, 1994) I needed to write the abstract. A few months later, I was hospitalized, and I wrote the second abstract in the hospital. The only affordances I had to write were a pen and the weekly menu of the hospital food, which I wrote on the back of. The limited affordances I had weren't cooperating—the pen seemed too heavy for me to lift at that time, and the menu was too small to fit the entire abstract. After having spent several weeks in the hospital, I felt isolated and detached from the rest of the world, as well as from my work, and I tried hard to connect with the academic world through writing my abstract. Interestingly, my second abstract was more poetic and dramatic than the first. I believe I was attempting to create hope out of my fairly depressing situation. Perhaps I was encouraging myself more than anything. I was trying to make sense out of my own experience. However different, what I wrote were both parts of who I am—a subjective human being in flux. Structuring the narratives allowed me to make sense out of my experience (Polkinghorne, 1991) and to conceptualize the partial and heterogeneous me. Now, as I am writing my manuscript, I realize that my interpretation of my situation is ongoing and I will have a different story to tell tomorrow. I can't talk about everything—too much has happened. But such is the nature of narratives, and this is my story I need to tell today with all the affordances and constraints at my disposal:

> [Narrative] like life, is a continual unfolding where the narrative insights of today are the chronological events of tomorrow…. narrative is unfinished and stories will be retold and lives relived…. (Connelly & Clandinin, 1990, p. 9)

Through these "unfinished stories" we move forward. As Ellis and Bochner (2000) mention, narratives can be a "source of empowerment and a form of resistance to counter the domination of authority of canonical discourses" (p. 749). Constructing my own narrative brought forth more awareness of how I perceive my life, and also allowed me to be (at least partially) liberated from the daunting negative self-image I had of myself as a chronically ill person who isn't teaching. As Richardson (1997) says, "New narratives offer patterns of new lives" (p. 33). My narrative has empowered me by giving me a voice (Bochner, 2001; Ellis & Bochner; Reed-Danahay, 2001), a voice that permits me to actively participate in my community—the graduate school—however physically constrained I am.

Moving Ahead

This is where my story was supposed to end. However, after I submitted my first draft to the editors, a concern that I had in the back of my head started to grow steadily. *Will publicizing my health conditions stand in the way of my getting a job in the future? Am I shutting off future opportunities?* I started to worry. *Should I put more emphasis on the fact that my health has improved over the last year? Maybe I should add the following: The alternative treatments such as acupuncture I am receiving seem to help. I am starting to do moderate exercise, as recommended for CFS and fibromyalgia patients. I can walk longer distances than before. I have heard from physicians that my two illnesses sometimes wax and wane. I do my best not to let the illnesses get in the way of my career as a student. I hardly miss classes. I do all my work. I attend social functions. I attend and present at overseas conferences. I used to sit while I presented—I couldn't remain standing for the entire allotted presentation time. But this year, I stood! I do what I have to do. Yes, I have illnesses, but I am capable of many things. I need some lifestyle adjustments, but don't we all?*

Upon consultation, co-editor Chris Casanave mentioned that I can *possibly* write this up as an experience of the past, as my concern was a serious issue that could affect my future. Basically, what I would do depended on "how courageous" I was. While I strongly hope that the story of my illnesses will indeed be an "experience of the past" in the not-so-distant future, as much as I am faced with a dilemma, I cannot alter my story. As I have written earlier, this is the story I need to tell now. While I understand the possible risks involved in publishing it, I want to be up front about my experience. I don't want to twist the "narrative truth" (Bruner, 1996; Polkinghorne, 1988, 1991) of my story. *What is the purpose of sharing my story if I can't tell it compellingly and honestly?* Possible circumstances in the future might make me feel differently. But this is the choice that I make today. I may be naïve and optimistic, but I want to be courageous. I want to be courageous for myself, for any graduate students who might find consolation in my story, and for the value of honesty.

In *Writing for Scholarly Publication*, Sasaki (2003) reflected on her experience as a "periphery scholar"—in her case, a scholar who teaches full time, a mother of two children, a wife, and a non-native speaker of English. As a "periphery student," I was touched and encouraged by her narrative. I would like to close this chapter by echoing Sasaki in the hope that however peripheral, I might someday be a distinguished scholar like her:

> As Laotsu recommends, I would like to stand firmly on my own feet, and walk slowly, but I hope to travel a long way, believing that the world I live in has its own value. (p. 220)

I will continue to thrive on learning—this is how I have come to manage life. I believe that in one way or another, we all undergo identity transformations as we go through graduate school. Although my experiences are particular—limited to my own circumstances and issues—I hope that this chapter will be meaningful to other graduate students who are managing identity transformations under constraints that might otherwise be unbearable.

HANAKO OKADA, TEMPLE UNIVERSITY, JAPAN CAMPUS

A biostatement shows how you choose to portray yourself at the moment you are writing it. How do *I* want to portray myself? Honestly, I am not too sure at this point in time. Currently enrolled in a doctoral program, I am busy trying to construct my identity as a novice scholar and a player of the academic game. The more I engage in serious learning, the more I realize that *I am what I learn*. Knowing that I will never cease learning, I enjoy imagining what my future biostatements might look like and how they might transform/evolve in time.

REFERENCES

Atkinson, D. (2002). Towards a sociocognitive approach to second language acquisition. *The Modern Language Journal, 86*(4), 525–545.

Atkinson, D., Churchill, E., Nishino, T., & Okada, H. (2007). Alignment and interaction in a sociocognitive approach to second language acquisition. *The Modern Language Journal, 9*(2), 169–188.

Bauman, M. G. (2007, March 2). If God breake my bones. *The Chronicle of Higher Education*, B5.

Bochner, A. (2001). Narrative's virtues. *Qualitative Inquiry, 7*(2), 131–157.

Bruner, J. (1996). *The culture of education*. Cambridge, MA: Harvard University Press.

Casanave, C. P., & Schecter, S. R. (Eds.). (1997). *On becoming a language educator: Personal essays on professional development*. Mahwah, NJ: Lawrence Erlbaum.

Casanave, C. P., & Vandrick, S. (Eds.). (2003). *Writing for scholarly publication: Behind the scenes in language education*. Mahwah, NJ: Lawrence Erlbaum.

Centers for Disease Contol and Prevention. (2006). Retrieved August 20, 2006, from http://www.cdc.gov/cfs/.

Clauw, D. J., & Taylor-Moon, D. (2006). *What fibromyalgia is*. Retrieved August 20, 2006, from http://www.rheumatology.org/public/factsheets/fibromya_new.asp?#1

Connelly, F. M., & Clandinin, D. J. (1990). Stories of experience and narrative inquiry. *Educational Researcher, 19*(5), 2–14.

Ellis, C. (1997). Evocative autoethnography: Writing emotionally about our lives. In W. G. Tierney & Y. S. Lincoln (Eds.), *Representation and the text: Re-framing the narrative voice* (pp. 115–139). Albany: State University of New York Press.

Ellis, C., & Bochner, A. (2000). Autoethnography, personal narrative, reflexivity: Researcher as subject. In N. K. Denzin & Y. S. Lincoln (Eds.), *Handbook of qualitative research* (2nd ed.) (pp. 733–768). Thousand Oaks, CA: Sage.

Gibson, J. J. (1977). The theory of affordances. In R. E. Shaw & J. Bransford (Eds.), *Perceiving, acting, and knowing; Toward an ecological psychology* (pp. 67–82). Hillsdale, NJ: Lawrence Erlbaum.

Gibson, J. J. (1986). *The ecological approach to visual perception*. Hillsdale, NJ: Lawrence Erlbaum.

Greeno, J. G. (1994). Gibson's affordances. *Psychological Review, 101*(2), 336–342.

McDermott, R., & Varenne, H. (1995). Culture *as* disability. *Anthropology and Education Quarterly, 26*(3), 324–348.

Polkinghorne, D. E. (1988). *Narrative knowing and the human sciences*. Albany: State University of New York Press.

Polkinghorne, D. E. (1991). Narrative and self concept. *Journal of Narrative and Life History, 1*(2 & 3), 135–153.

Reed-Danahay, D. (2001). Autobiography, intimacy and ethnography. In P. Atkinson, A. Coffey, S. Delamont, J. Lofland, & L. Lofland (Eds.), *Handbook of ethnography* (pp. 407–425). London: Sage.

Richardson, L. (1997). *Fields of play: Constructing an academic life.* New Brunswick, NJ: Rutgers University Press.

Sakui, K., & Gaies, S. J. (2002). Beliefs and professional identity: A case study of a Japanese teacher of EFL writing. *The Language Teacher, 26*(6), 7–11.

Sasaki, M. (2003). A scholar on the periphery: Standing firm, walking slowly. In C. P. Casanave & S. Vandrick (Eds.), *Writing for scholarly publication: Behind the scenes in language education* (pp. 211–221). Mahwah, NJ: Lawrence Erlbaum.

Tierney, W. G. (2000). Undaunted courage: Life history and the postmodern challenge. In N. K. Denzin & Y. S. Lincoln (Eds.), *Handbook of qualitative research* (2nd ed.) (pp. 537–554). Thousand Oaks, CA: Sage.

Tompkins, J. (1996). *Life in school: What the teacher learned.* New York: Basic Books.

van Lier, L. (2000). From input to affordance: Social-interactive learning from an ecological perspective. In J. P. Lantolf (Ed.), *Sociocultural theory and second language learning* (pp. 245–260). Oxford, UK: Oxford University Press.

Watson-Gegeo, K. A. (2005). Journey to the 'new normal' and beyond: Reflections on learning in a community of practice. *International Journal of Qualitative Studies in Education, 18*(4), 425–444.

SUBJECT INDEX

AUTHOR INDEX